BASEBALL ITALIAN STYLE

GREAT STORIES TOLD BY ITALIAN AMERICAN MAJOR LEAGUERS FROM CROSETTI TO PIAZZA

Lawrence Baldassaro

SPORTS
PUBLISHING

Sports Publishing books may be purchased in bulk at special discounts for sales promotion, corporate gifts, fund-raising, or educational purposes. Special editions can also be created to specifications. For details, contact the Special Sales Department, Sports Publishing, 307 West 36th Street, 11th Floor, New York, NY 10018 or sportspubbooks@skyhorsepublishing.com.

Sports Publishing® is a registered trademark of Skyhorse Publishing, Inc.®, a Delaware corporation.

Visit our website at www.sportspubbooks.com.

10 9 8 7 6 5 4 3 2 1

Library of Congress Cataloging-in-Publication Data is available on file.

Cover design by Tom Lau
Cover photos credit: Associated Press

ISBN: 978-1-68358-111-6
Ebook ISBN: 978-1-68358-112-3

Printed in the United States of America

To the memory of my brother,
Gerald A. Baldassaro Jr.

CONTENTS

Note: Individuals are listed according to the decade they began their major-league career.

PREFACE

On June 12, 1993, I sat in the visitors' radio booth at County Stadium in Milwaukee, mesmerized by the delightful recollections of Phil Rizzuto. It had been thirty-seven years since the seventy-six-year-old Hall of Fame shortstop known as "The Scooter" had traded his glove for a microphone, but he still retained the boyish enthusiasm and innocence that had endeared him to Yankee fans and teammates. Speaking in his inimitable, rambling style, he reminisced about his family, growing up in Brooklyn, his Navy experiences during World War II, and his career as a Yankee. The interview ended when someone entered the booth with lunch. Rizzuto turned and asked, "Got cannolis there?"

That interview, the first I had conducted with an Italian American major leaguer, motivated me to interview many others, which in turn planted the seed for my previous book, *Beyond DiMaggio: Italian Americans in Baseball*, the first extensive history of the topic. For obvious reasons, *Beyond DiMaggio* contained only snippets of those interviews. Several more have been conducted since its publication in 2011. *Baseball Italian Style* brings all the interviews together in a single volume, enabling readers to "hear" them in their entirety. The goal of this book is twofold: to provide informative and entertaining reading for even casual baseball fans of all backgrounds, and to help preserve the long and distinguished legacy of Italian American participation in major-league baseball.

This collection differs from all other oral histories related to baseball not only in its focus on a single ethnic group but also in its scope of almost a century of major-league history, from the 1930s to the second decade of the twenty-first century. It provides, in microcosm, a chronicle of not only Italian American contributions to the national pastime but also of the evolution of the game itself and the many changes that have occurred on and off the field. The earliest recollections come from men whose careers began in the 1930s and coincided with those of such legendary figures as Babe Ruth, Connie Mack, Jimmie Foxx, Rogers Hornsby, Hank Greenberg, and Ted Williams. The interviews then progress chronologically through the decades, into the eras of racial integration, artificial turf, interleague and divisional play, labor strife, free agency, astronomical salaries, performance-enhancing drugs, and around-the-clock media coverage.

The forty-four narrators comprise a broad representation of Italian American participation in major-league baseball. They include Hall of Famers and Most Valuable Players, as well as stars from each decade and players with less illustrious careers. In addition, you will hear from coaches, managers, front-office executives, and umpires. Their experiences differ, as do the longevity and quality of their careers, and they come from a wide range of geographical, educational, and socioeconomic backgrounds. What they share, in addition to their Italian heritage, are a lifelong passion and respect for the game, vivid memories of their careers, and engaging stories. Their recollections are often astonishingly detailed, no matter how long ago the incidents occurred. Nevertheless, while there is material that will be of interest to historians, this is a book of personal recollections; as such, given the imperfection of human memory, it in no way pretends to provide an infallible historical document.

The inspiration and model for this collection is *The Glory of Their Times: The Story of the Early Days of Baseball Told by the Men Who Played It*, the late Lawrence Ritter's 1966 seminal work which remains the benchmark for any oral history related to baseball. Following the example established by Ritter, I have done minimal editing to the original interviews, primarily eliminating my questions and occasionally rearranging the order to provide continuity and chronological context to the contents of each interview and to make them more readable.

Many people contributed in various ways to the making of *Baseball Italian Style*. My thanks to Emi Battaglia, Michael Bauman, Dan Bonanno, Frank Catalanotto, Larry Freundlich, Frank Gado, Bob Gormley, Dick Johnson, Joe Quagliano, George Randazzo, and Mario Ziino. I'm also grateful to those who helped in securing photos: Robbin Barnes, Bob Cullum, Mary Jo Giuliani, Brendan Hader, Ed Hartig, John Horne, Michael Ivins, Dave Kaplan, Debra Kaufman, Marco Landi, Diane Lodigiani, Suzanna Mitchell, and Mario Salvini.

I'm deeply indebted to my editor, Ken Samelson, for his accessibility and his patient and knowledgeable guidance throughout this project. Thanks also to Ken's Sports Publishing colleagues Marion Schwaner and Sarah Jones as well as proofreader Sean Sabo. And to Gael Garbarino, *la mia cara amica*, special thanks for her wise counsel and invaluable moral support.

As I mentioned earlier, this book is the offspring of Lawrence Ritter's *The Glory of Their Times*. I was fortunate to count Larry among my friends, and

I will always be grateful for his support and inspiration. One of the books I treasure most is my first edition copy of *The Glory of Their Times,* which Larry graciously inscribed to me in June 1999: "For my pal Larry B. With every good wish, Ciao, Larry Ritter."

My greatest debt of gratitude, of course, is owed to the narrators who made this book possible by so generously sharing their memories with me. Meeting all these major leaguers and listening to their stories was a great pleasure and privilege. I hope you find reading their stories as entertaining and informative as I did listening to them.

INTRODUCTION

Baseball has changed in many ways since Yankees shortstop Frank Crosetti, our leadoff narrator, made his big league debut in 1932, a time when games were played only in the daytime, players traveled by train, shared rooms with teammates while on the road, made about as much money as the writers who covered them, and worked in the offseason. But in its most fundamental aspects, the game remains what it was at the turn of the twentieth century.

More than any other American sport, baseball is firmly rooted in history and tradition. The players, and even some teams, come and go, but the action unfolds on the same stage. The game links us to earlier generations, to our own childhood, and to our children. Fans are familiar not only with the heroes of today and their youth but also with the legends of earlier generations. If they shift their minds into reverse, older fans can see their heroes as they remember them. They, in turn, pass their memories on to their children. The players we cheer today are part of a tradition that goes back to the first men to put on a uniform.

The individuals whose voices you hear in these pages helped shape that tradition, and their stories, told in their own words, bring baseball history to life. Statistics that measure players' relative ability have long been a significant part of baseball lore. And the recent surge of sophisticated sabermetric analysis has taken the fascination with data to a whole new level. But while statistics serve to document the history and continuity of baseball quantitatively, they do not capture the human element of the game.

The stories told here by those who made their living in the major leagues reveal the humanity behind the numbers. In these pages, readers will get to know in a more intimate way players who otherwise are known mainly from the data recorded on their baseball cards. At one end of the time spectrum are Frank Crosetti's childhood memories of growing up in the 1920s and playing "one o' cat" with his brother, using corncobs for balls and whittled boards as bats, while at the other end are Barry Zito's zen-like musings on baseball and music. And while there may be no crying in baseball, there is no lack of humor. Dario Lodigiani tells the story of Tony Lazzeri emptying Babe Ruth's bottle of Murine, which Ruth believed helped him see the ball better, and filling it with water. Sal Bando recalls the time Tigers manager Billy Martin, the day after a brawl with the Oakland A's, brought out his lineup card in which he listed Italian fighters Rocky Marciano and Carmen Basilio as his bench players.

Not surprisingly, recollections of Joe DiMaggio, the patron saint of Italian American ballplayers and fans, appear repeatedly. According to Matt Galante, "Not only was he the superstar of that era, he might've been the first where that group of immigrants came to the United States and all of a sudden they've got a superhero." Rico Petrocelli recalls sitting in the center-field bleachers at Yankee Stadium as a kid. "I'll never forget this," he said. "I looked around, and here the pitcher was throwing the ball, but everyone in the bleachers was looking at Joe DiMaggio. No one was even looking at the ball or the hitter. He was such a hero." As Jerry Colangelo points out, DiMaggio's success had a big impact on Italian Americans. "People took pride in Joe DiMaggio's achievements; it gave them hope, in their own families, that if it could happen for Joe, it could happen for any of us."

Whether reliving their days on the diamond or revealing surprisingly personal details of their lives, the speakers in this collection provide a vivid portrayal of life in major league baseball. Some of the issues discussed are familiar to fans: the love of competition and the intense desire to win; the camaraderie within the clubhouse and the animosity between opponents; the unparalleled thrill of winning a World Series. But just to be clear: readers should not expect to find dreamy reveries of the timelessness and sociological significance of baseball. To be sure, there are, on occasion, nostalgic reminiscences of bygone days. But by and large, the narrators provide a dispassionate look into the game as they know it.

Ballplayers readily recall important games lost, the hard work it takes to make it to, and stay in, the big leagues, the frustration of dealing with injuries and enduring the drudgery of rehabilitation, and the hardship of being away from their families. Yet, even while acknowledging the physical and mental challenges of playing the game at its highest level, these athletes leave no doubt that they cherished the opportunity to play on the big stage. Forty-year-old Jason Grilli, in his 15th year in the big leagues in 2017, said, "It's hard to let go of the wheel when you know you've still got something left in the tank." Others express their desire to do it all over again: "I'd give anything," said Dario Lodigiani, "if 1935 could roll around again, and I could play again."

It is fitting that the players in the leadoff spot in our lineup began their careers in the 1930s, the decade in which Italian Americans first appeared in the big leagues in significant numbers. While only twenty-two had ever worn a major-league uniform by 1929, at least fifty-four made their debuts in the 1930s. One player who debuted prior to the 1930s deserves mention here for the prominent role he played. By the 1920s, New York City had a large and growing Italian American population, and the Yankees were looking for an Italian player good enough to appeal to that potential audience. They found him on the West Coast. In 1926, a year after he hit 60 home runs in the Pacific Coast League—a new record in Organized Baseball—San Francisco native Tony Lazzeri became the starting second baseman in the Yankees lineup that would become known as Murderers' Row. The twenty-two-year-old rookie did not disappoint; he finished third in the American League in home runs and fulfilled management's hopes by drawing large numbers of Italian fans. In New York and other AL cities, Italian societies honored the young star with banquets.

In his 12 years with the Yankees, Lazzeri played a key role in their success, hitting .293 and clouting 169 home runs, more than all but six American Leaguers hit over that span. In addition, Lazzeri, who played his entire career as an epileptic, was acknowledged as one of the smartest men in baseball. Overshadowed by legendary teammates Ruth and Gehrig, Lazzeri's greatness was somewhat overlooked until 1991 when he was elected to the Hall of Fame. Nevertheless, at a time when the best-known American of Italian descent was Al Capone, Lazzeri instilled newfound pride in Italian Americans. Moreover, because of his success as a star with the greatest team in America's national pastime and his exemplary conduct on and off the field, it is likely that he did more than anyone before him to enhance the public perception of Italian Americans.

There was quality as well as quantity in the 1930s upsurge of Italian American major leaguers. Ernie Lombardi, Dolph Camilli, and Joe DiMaggio, all San Francisco natives, as well as Chicago native Phil Cavarretta, were the first Italian Americans to win the MVP Award, and Lombardi and DiMaggio are enshrined in the Hall of Fame. Others, such as Gus Mancuso, Tony Cuccinello, and Zeke Bonura, had notable careers.

In 1932, shortstop Frank Crosetti joined fellow San Franciscan Tony Lazzeri to form the Yankees' double-play combo. Four years later, the San Francisco triumvirate was completed with the arrival of Joe DiMaggio, and for the first time, three Italian Americans were in the starting lineup of a major-league team. DiMaggio quickly established himself as the successor to Babe Ruth, leading the Yankees to the first of four consecutive World Series titles. It was an auspicious start to a 13-year Hall of Fame career in which he would win three MVP Awards, nine World Series rings, and receive recognition as the best all-around player of his generation. In the process, he became one of the most famous and admired celebrities of the twentieth century as well as *the*

Frank Crosetti, Joe DiMaggio, and Tony Lazzeri in Fenway Park dugout.
Courtesy of the Boston Public Library, Leslie Jones Collection.

great hero of Italian Americans. Tommy Lasorda summed it up by saying, "He was our hero; he was everything we Italians wanted to be."

The influx of Italian Americans continued in the 1940s, especially between 1943 and 1945, when the absence of major leaguers serving in the war opened the door for players who might otherwise have not made it to the big leagues. But two who made their debut in the early forties achieved stardom: center fielder Dom DiMaggio was a seven-time All-Star, and shortstop Phil Rizzuto made it to the Hall of Fame. Other outstanding players debuted after the war, including future Hall of Famers Yogi Berra and Roy Campanella.

It was in the postwar years that Italian American ballplayers achieved unprecedented prominence. This was most evident in New York, the capital of the baseball world for more than a decade. Between 1947 and 1958, the Yankees won ten pennants and eight World Series, the Dodgers six pennants and one Series, and the Giants two pennants and one Series. Many of the key players on those New York teams were of Italian descent: DiMaggio, Berra,

Rizzuto, Vic Raschi, and Billy Martin with the Yankees; Campanella, Carl Furillo, and Ralph Branca with the Dodgers; Sal Maglie and Johnny Antonelli with the Giants. Between 1947 and 1957, Italian Americans playing for a New York team won eight of the twenty-two MVP Awards, with five second-place finishes. From 1948 to 1951, six Italian Americans were All-Stars each year, and in 1952, there was an all-time high of seven, with five in the starting lineups.

In the economic boom of the postwar fifties and beyond, with greater access to higher education and more opportunities for economic and social advancement, fewer Italian Americans were entering baseball. There was also, in many cases, a diminished sense of ethnic identity in the second half of the twentieth century. Prior to World War II, it was common for both parents of Italian American major leaguers to be immigrants or second-generation Italian Americans who spoke Italian. But third- and fourth-generation players of Italian descent were increasingly likely to be the offspring of mixed marriages and to have little or no familiarity with the Italian language. Yet several of the speakers in this volume who entered the game in the fifties later expressed regret at not having learned the language when they were young.

In the sixties and beyond, there were still many players who had notable careers and were fan favorites, and some achieved greatness. Their collective impact, however, was less evident than that of those in the immediate postwar years when so many stars were playing in New York for the most dominant teams. A few will be mentioned here, though there are several others who deserve more recognition than this brief summary allows.

Since 1971, when Joe Torre won the award, there have been four more MVP Award winners: Ken Caminiti, Jason Giambi, Dustin Pedroia, and Joey Votto. Four pitchers have won the Cy Young Award: Frank Viola, John Smoltz, Barry Zito, and Rick Porcello. Six-time All-Star Rocky Colavito hit 30 or more homers eleven times and in 1959 became the eighth player to hit four home runs in one game. Tony Conigliaro, whose career was cut short when he was hit in the eye by a pitch in 1967, won an AL home run title at the age of twenty and at twenty-two became the second youngest player to hit 100 home runs. In his 21-year career (1984–2005), John Franco recorded the most saves by a left-hander and is fifth on the all-time list. The surest sign that Italian Americans continued to excel is that six of the thirteen enshrined in the Hall of Fame to date were inducted between 2012 and 2016. All four players (Ron Santo, Craig Biggio, John Smoltz, and Mike Piazza) and both managers (Joe Torre and Tony La Russa) began their major-league careers in the sixties or later.

While the number of players of Italian descent declined, increasing numbers of Italian Americans gradually moved into positions of management, both on and off the field. By the last two decades of the twentieth century, Italian managers were numerous and successful. In addition to Lasorda, Torre, and La Russa, other managers have had notable success. Since 1981 those three, together with Joe Altobelli, Terry Francona, Mike Scioscia, Jim Fregosi, Joe Girardi, Bobby Valentine, and Joe Maddon (original family name Maddonini) have taken their teams to a total of twenty-four World Series, winning fifteen of them. Others moved into top executive positions as general managers and owners. In addition, Joe Garagiola Jr. was named Major League Baseball's senior vice president of baseball operations in 2005, and Joe Torre was appointed executive vice president of baseball operations for Major League Baseball in 2011.

The crowning achievement came in 1989 when a third-generation Italian American was chosen as the seventh commissioner of Major League Baseball. A. Bartlett Giamatti, a Yale professor and a scholar of Renaissance literature, also wrote extensively and eloquently about baseball's role in American society. For him, the game was not a diversion but a significant and enduring social institution. "Baseball," he wrote, "is not simply an essential part of this country; it is a living memory of what American Culture at its best wishes to be." In 1978, he became the youngest president of Yale, then chose to leave that prestigious academic position in 1986 to become president of the National League. Three years later he was named commissioner. But he had little chance to apply his talent and passion to the office; five months into his term, he died of a heart attack at the age of fifty-one. Pulitzer-Prize-winning *New York Times* columnist Ira Berkow speculated that Giamatti "might have become the best baseball commissioner we've ever had. He had brains, sinew, and the best wishes of the game."

Giamatti's ascent to the highest position in Major League Baseball represents the culmination of Italian American involvement in the national pastime, from players—at one time, baseball's equivalent of blue-collar workers—to coaches, managers, front-office executives, and owners. In the pages that follow you will hear the stories of those who helped create that history over the past nine decades.

1930—39

Frank Crosetti

A native of San Francisco, as were many of the earliest major leaguers of Italian descent, Frank Crosetti was a star shortstop with the San Francisco Seals of the Pacific Coast League when, in 1930, the New York Yankees purchased his contract for $75,000, a phenomenal sum in the midst of the Depression. Beginning in his rookie year of 1932, Crosetti teamed up with Tony Lazzeri, a fellow San Franciscan then in his seventh year with New York, to form the Yankees double play combination for six years. Crosetti would go on to set the record for wearing a Yankees uniform longer than anyone in franchise history, as a player from 1932 to 1948, and as third-base coach from 1949 to 1968. Over that span the Yankees won seventeen World Series. At a certain point, the team stopped awarding Crosetti the traditional World Series ring, and instead gave the avid hunter engraved shotguns.

A slick-fielding shortstop, "Crow" was known as the holler guy of the Yankees infield. Off the field, however, he was a reserved, private man who shied away from reporters. He was also a master of the hidden-ball trick and led the league in being hit by pitches eight times. Crosetti coached for the Seattle Pilots and the Minnesota Twins before retiring in 1971. He was inducted into the Pacific Coast League Hall of Fame in 2004, two years after his death at the age of ninety-one.

Though surpassed in talent and fame by Lazzeri and DiMaggio, by his very longevity in a New York uniform Crosetti would come to symbolize the long tradition, beginning in 1918 with Ping Bodie (born Francesco Pezzolo), of Italian American ballplayers who wore the Yankee pinstripes. In his letter announcing that he was resigning as a coach, he wrote, "Once a Yankee, always a Yankee."

* * *

My father, who was born in 1877, came to the United States around 1900 from a town near Genoa. My mother was born in California to immigrant parents, also from near Genoa. My father worked as a scavenger, a junk collector. We spoke Italian at home before we spoke English. We learned English when we went to school. I'm an American of Italian descent because I was born in this country. If I were born in Italy, I guess that would be a different story.

I had some childhood illnesses and a doctor told my parents, "If you want a healthy kid, move to the country." So we moved to Los Gatos, south of San

Jose, and my father started a scavenger business there. Baseball came naturally to me. I wanted to play as long as I can remember. My older brother and I would play "one o' cat." We used the big end of the corncob as a ball; for a bat, we'd take a board and shave it down. We'd break a lot of the corncobs, then we'd go get another one. When you threw a corncob it did all kinds of stuff, like a knuckleball.

One o' cat was a kid's game. You've got two people playing. You have home plate, then you mark off fifty, sixty feet for first base. If the pitcher pitches to me and I hit the ball, the pitcher's gotta go get the ball and come back to home plate and I have to run to first base and come back to home. If I beat him back to home plate before he gets there with the ball, that's one run. Now if he beats me to home plate before I get back from first, that's one out. So we played nine innings that way. We played that out in the field somewhere.

I got to playing in different leagues and every chance I got to play I'd play. My mother would have to come and get me. We played all day long. I quit school at sixteen and went to play semipro ball in Butte, Montana, in the Butte Mines League. My mother didn't want me to play ball, but it was okay with my father. In those days the old folks thought you were a bum if you played ball. I remember some friends came over and tried to talk my mother into letting me play. My father was quiet, but finally he stepped in and said, "Let him go." They were paying us $200 a month. We were supposed to play for the Montana Power Company, but we only worked for about two weeks.

That was in 1927. In '28 I started playing with the San Francisco Seals, then the Yankees signed me. My first year with the Seals, Ping Bodie told me, "Go to the butcher shop and get a large meat bone and have your mother boil the meat off and use that to bone your bats." I did that, then when I went to the Yankees, I took the same bone with me. The clubhouse attendant clamped it on a board and that made it easier to use. You take the bat in your hand and rub it over the bone. Before it was clamped to the board you had to put the bat between your legs and bone it that way. Using the bone saved the bat, kept it from "checking." Today they don't care. They break a bat, they get another one. I used that bone for a long time. I should've taken it home with me; I don't know what happened to it.

I met Tony Lazzeri when I was with the Seals. I looked up to him and he was really good to me. He was really a hell of a hitter, but you'd never know it from him. He was a quiet, humble person. He drew a lot of Italian fans to the ballpark. They used to call us the "walloping wops." In those days they were looking for Italian ballplayers. I guess they thought Italians were good players.

There weren't many Italian ballplayers when I was a rookie. Later there was Ernie Lombardi, but of course he played in the National League with the Reds. I knew he couldn't run, but he could hit; he was powerful. A nice fellow, a really nice guy. I think later he went to work for the Giants, up in the press room or something. There were other Italians in the National League: Cookie Lavagetto, and an infielder from the Giants we played in the 1937 World Series, Lou Chiozza.

Babe Ruth used to call me "Dago Bananas," probably because he couldn't remember my name. Babe was a wonderful person. He was great with kids. He did more for the game of baseball than anybody.

In Joe DiMaggio's first year with the Yankees, Tony Lazzeri and I invited him to go with us to spring training. We pooled our money, then I would pay for the gas, food, and hotels. We got to about Florida and Tony and I were doing all the driving. So Tony says, "Let's ask this guy to drive." Joe said, "I don't know how to drive." We didn't say much on the whole drive. The three of us were quiet.

Joe DiMaggio, Tony Lazzeri, and Frank Crosetti about to leave for spring training, 1937. *Courtesy, California Historical Society, image number FN-32203.*

Frank Crosetti
National Baseball Hall of Fame and Museum.

You could tell right away that Joe was going to be something. He was born a natural athlete. He didn't pop off. There were no high fives in those days. We kept our emotions to ourselves. They used to call Tony the "big dago," and I was the "little dago." Then Joe became the "big dago." We didn't mind that name then; it was good-natured ribbing. I'm glad they called me a dago; what's the difference? When they called you that, it was because they liked you. I never felt they were hostile because I was Italian.

Phil Cavarretta

*T*he son of Sicilian immigrants, Phil Cavarretta was seventeen years old when he quit high school in 1934 and began playing professional baseball in the Chicago Cubs organization to help support his family during the Great Depression. At the end of his first and only season in the minor leagues, he made his first start in the big leagues two months after his eighteenth birthday and hit a game-winning homer at Wrigley Field, three miles from his boyhood home and high school. For the next 19 years the left-handed-hitting first baseman-outfielder was a mainstay of the Cubs before finishing his career with the crosstown White Sox. His competitive spirit and relentless hustle made him one of the all-time favorite Cubs players.

Cavarretta was a four-time All-Star, won the National League batting title and Most Valuable Player Award in 1945, and played in three World Series. Over his 22-year career, he compiled a batting average of .293, with 95 home runs and 920 RBIs. For two and a half seasons between 1951 and 1953, he was the Cubs player-manager, becoming, in 1952, the first Italian American to manage a major-league team for a full season. He later managed in the minor leagues and coached for the Detroit Tigers and New York Mets. He passed away in 2010 at the age of ninety-four.

* * *

Mom and Dad, Angela Cavarretta and Joseph Cavarretta, were both born in Palermo, Sicily. They first went to New York, then migrated to Chicago where they had some relatives. They immigrated to America way before I was born. In fact, my brother, Mike, was born in Italy, and I have an older sister, Sarah. She was born here and then I was born here. All we spoke at home was Italian; that was the only language Mom and Dad knew. Naturally, going to school, I learned to speak English. My dad was a laborer and finally got himself a pretty good job in one of our grade schools in Chicago as a janitor. I was proud of my dad. I was born and raised on the north side of Chicago, Cleveland Avenue. The neighborhood was mostly Italian, but there were also Irish and German people. Real good people, family-oriented. If some neighbor needed a hand, they would come over and help you. Later on, when I got married and wasn't living there anymore, it got to be a very tough neighborhood.

I always loved baseball, even when I was a little guy. In grade school they had a big old sandlot and I just took a liking to baseball. I started out by playing softball. I loved it. We would flip a coin and choose up sides. In those days the softball was sixteen inches, and that was a pretty good target to hit. I wish I was hitting that thing when I was playing in the big leagues. Even when I was playing softball, my dad didn't know what the game was all about. A bunch of kids running around chasing a ball. I'd come home with my overalls kind of colored up from sliding and late for supper. If you're late for supper you don't eat. So he said in his Italian way, "Philee, where you been?" I said, "Dad, I was out playing baseball with my friends in the schoolyard." He looked at me with his blue eyes—he was a good-looking man, by the way—and he said, "Base-a-ball, what the hell is base-a-ball? Go to school." That's a true story.

Later on I went to high school at Lane Tech on the north side of Chicago. Then it was an all-boys school and it was noted for its baseball team. The coach we had there was named Percy Moore—may his soul rest in peace—and he was a beautiful Irishman. Not only was he a good person but a good baseball coach; he knew how to teach the kids. The main thing with him was he was fair with everybody. He loved his kids, and that makes you go further and put out a little more.

I was a pitcher. In those days if you threw hard, you were a pitcher. Being left-handed, my control wasn't too good, but my coach got me on the side and showed me a few small things, and finally, I had pretty good control. I threw hard, but actually my best pitch was a curveball. When I wasn't pitching I played first base. That was the position I wanted to play to start out with, but I wanted to play every day, let me put it that way.

Percy Moore was also our coach in American Legion ball. Three years in a row that I played Legion ball we won the championship and went to the regionals. And in 1933 we went to the Little World Series in New Orleans. We beat Trenton, New Jersey, and won the Little World Series. If you won the Little World Series championship you were supposed to go see the real World Series, but for some reason which we never found out, we never did go, which was a sad day.

When I was a kid, Lou Gehrig was my favorite, and when I grew up, he was my favorite. He was such a good person; he would say hello to everybody and give you an autograph, no problem. The first time I saw him was at Wrigley Field, I think in 1931. He hit a home run into the right field bleachers. When we played against the Yankees in the 1938 World Series, Gehrig was the first baseman. He was always very observant. He wouldn't say much, but he was always watching how other people played. I got on base, I think it was the third game of the Series. We got wiped out four in a row, by the way.

Anyway, he's holding me on first, and this was when he was first starting to be ill. You could tell the way he was walking, very slow and wobbly. This was a strong, powerful man. Anyway, I get on first and he's holding me on. I'm kind of looking at him, and I said to myself, "My God, this is my man." He finally in a kind of whispering voice said, "Phil, I've been watching you in all three games we've played and I like the way you play. You're always hustling and that's the way the game should be played. Let me tell you one more thing," and I'll never forget this as long as I live, "Don't change." The rest of my career I always remembered that. I always gave 100 percent; I always hustled regardless of the score. I'll never forget him saying that.

I didn't see that much of Tony Lazzeri as a player, but from his record, he was an outstanding second baseman and a great hitter, a power hitter. I got acquainted with Tony when he came over to the Cubs as a coach in 1938. That's the year we won the pennant. During our meetings we'd go over the Yankees hitters, and he would always stand up and say, "Pitch this guy this way and that guy that way." As I said, we got clocked four in a row. But they had a team, let me tell you. Lou Gehrig at first, a man like Joe DiMaggio playing center field, Dickey catching, Red Ruffing pitching. Good Lord! They were all Hall of Famers.

My senior year of high school it was the Depression, and as a matter of fact, we had a tough time getting anything to eat. My dad couldn't get a job; my brother couldn't get a job. Things were tough. To create some heat in the house you had those potbellied stoves and you'd throw hard coal in there. We didn't even have money to buy coal so I would go down to the railroad yards where the freight trains would come in loaded with coal, and I would pick up the droppings and take them home.

Anyway, my senior year I had to leave school because someone had to go out and earn a dollar. I went to Percy Moore and presented my story, and he's the one who kind of set the needle in the pie to get the Cubs to give me a workout at Wrigley Field. So I went out there and I was seventeen and must've weighed all of 150 pounds. I've got my uniform on and I'm walking around, and all these players are looking at me; they thought I was a batboy. The first guy that came up to me, and may his soul rest in peace, was Pat Malone, and he was a tough guy. He said, "Hey kid, what are you doing out here?" I said, "I'm here for a tryout." He said, "A tryout? You oughta go get something to eat and put some weight on." I was scared to death.

Finally, Charlie Grimm, who was the first baseman and the manager, came up and he was a super guy. He said, "You're here for a tryout?" And I said, "Yes sir." He said, "Well, go get yourself a bat and we'll take a look at ya." In those days everybody used a much heavier bat than they do today. That was heavy lumber for me, and I thought I'd never be able to get around, so I choked up on the bat. To make a long story short, I had a real good batting session and was opening some eyes. One I hit out of the park. So they were saying, "He's whacking that pea pretty good; we'd better sign this kid."

They signed me and sent me to Peoria in the old Three I League. I had a pretty good day in my first game; I hit for the cycle: single, double, triple, home run. But then the league disbanded and they sent me to Reading, Pennsylvania, in the New York–Penn League and that's where I had my first full season in professional baseball. Now the season's over and I'm anxious to get home, and I'm packing my bag when I get a telegram. I thought I was being released. Instead, it said, "Report to the Cubs in Boston, Massachusetts." I thought somebody was pulling my leg. I went up to my teammate, Dom Dallessandro, and asked him if he did it. He said, "Hell, no." I went to Boston and picked up the club there. It was 1934. In 1935, I was in the big leagues at eighteen years old and in the World Series at nineteen.

Once I went to the Cubs, my parents took a little interest because I was bringing in some money. I got paid on the first and fifteenth and I'd bring the check to my mom and dad. Once they got to know a little about the game, they became good fans. They'd sit out there and enjoy themselves. My dad would say, "I'm a Cavarretta fan, not a Cubs fan." Then after I got married, it was a little different. I got married in 1936; it's been sixty-five years, all with one woman. They should present her with a gold star.

I had a big following among the Italian fans in Chicago. In 1935 they honored me with Cavarretta Day at Wrigley Field. They presented me with a nice automobile and a 16-gauge shotgun, which I still have; I thought it was just beautiful. It was organized by the Columbian Club of the Knights of Columbus.

Nineteen forty-five, when I was the MVP, was the kind of year you dream of. Everything has to go your way; your line drives have to drop, the bloop broken-bat hits have to drop. To hit .355, you know, that's a bundle. I was what you'd call a disciplined hitter, a patient hitter; hit the ball to left field, right field, center.

In those days they had a rule, you weren't supposed to fraternize with opposing players. You might say something you're not supposed to. You might go by another Italian player and say, "Hey, how's it going," but that's all. If they caught you it was fifteen hundred bucks, and in those days that was a lot of money.

I enjoyed managing very much, to be honest with you. In those days your players would listen to you. Now they say, "I'm going to do it my way, I'm going to arbitration, I want $52 million," and that kind of stuff. They played the game because they loved it, and they played the game because they wanted to win.

I got fired during spring training in Phoenix, Arizona [in 1954]. Managers go over the club with their coaches; this guy can play first, this guy can play center. We knew the game; we knew the players. I was just trying to be honest with Mr. Wrigley, telling him the truth. I told him, "We need a center fielder and we need a catcher and a first baseman." I was on my way out as a full-time player as a first baseman, and that was it. Before that meeting was over, Mr. Wrigley said, "You know, this is the first time in all the time I've owned the

Phil Cavarretta
AP Photo.

club that a manager has spoken to me on these grounds, and I'm really proud that we sat here and talked." I thought, *Boy, I feel pretty good.*

But I guess my general manager, Wid Matthews, got to Mr. Wrigley and he didn't like what I said. We didn't get along anyway. We went to Dallas to play an exhibition game, and Mr. Matthews wanted to see me at the hotel. I figured we were going to go over the roster and see who we would release. Who are we going to release? He released me! I couldn't believe it. I stayed in the game, still as a manager. I managed Buffalo for three years, managed Lancaster for one year, and then was the hitting coach for the Mets for quite a few years. I also coached for the Detroit Tigers for two and a half years.

Baseball was a game I was proud to be playing and proud to be a part of. I learned so many things from the game itself and the people that were affiliated with the game. It helped me with so many different things in life. I was proud of the game itself, to be honest with you. To be in three World Series, start playing in the big leagues at eighteen years of age while still in high school. I was proud of my teammates. Billy Herman was number one; he was our second baseman and he was a big help to me, playing first base and being inexperienced. He'd say, "Hey, 'Daig,' get closer to the line." I appreciated that and later on he was my roommate. Even the other players might call you "daig," or "wop," but we didn't mind. So what? I was proud to be an Italian. I don't know what I would've done if I didn't play baseball. But if it had come to that point, I was a disciplined person and I think I would've done something pretty good.

Angelo "Tony" Giuliani

*T*he son of Italian immigrants, Angelo Giuliani was born in St. Paul, Minnesota, on November 24, 1912. Following stellar performances with prep school and American Legion teams, the 5-foot-11, 175-pound catcher began his professional career in 1932 with his hometown St. Paul Saints of the American Association, whose ballpark was located only a few blocks from his boyhood home. Selected by the St. Louis Browns in the Rule V draft, he made his major-league debut in 1936. On May 3, he entered the game against the Yankees when the Browns starting catcher was injured. That day a rookie named Joe DiMaggio was making his major-league debut. Giuliani went 0-for-3; DiMaggio 3-for-6.

After two years with the Browns, he spent the 1938 and '39 seasons with the Washington Senators. On July 4, 1939, he and his teammates were on the field at Yankee Stadium as Lou Gehrig made his famous farewell speech. He played for the Dodgers in 1940 and '41, then returned to the American Association with the Minneapolis Millers before completing his major-league career in Washington in 1943. In his seven-year career, mainly as a backup catcher, he appeared in 243 games and compiled a .233 average.

Beginning in 1948, he worked as a scout for the Giants, Tigers, and Senators, who became the Minnesota Twins in 1961. That same year he established the Twins' youth clinics, which became highly successful, ultimately operating in nine states and Canada. He is credited with signing thirty players for the Twins, including Kent Hrbek, one of the franchise's all-time greats.

I spoke with Giuliani in the basement rec room of his home in St. Paul. The room was filled with baseballs, photos, and other memorabilia. On one wall at the end of the room were two photos, one of Babe Ruth and the other of a baby in swaddling clothes. Still spry and spirited at age eighty-eight, Giuliani pointed at the photos and said, "See those pictures? That's me next to the Babe; the two bambinos." He was ninety-four years old when he passed away in 2004.

* * *

My name is Angelo Giovanni Giuliani, but they called me "Tony," which had no connection to my name at all. "Tony" was an Italian type of greeting. I was born in 1912; I'm eighty-eight years old right now, and I'll be hitting the ninety mark shortly. Both of my parents were from the same area in Tuscany, small hill towns near Lucca. That's the olive capital of the world. Italian was the first language I knew. I learned English at St. Luke's School, on Summit Avenue.

My mother had taken me to Italy when I was an infant. Then World War I broke out and we were stuck there. So the war held us there until the armistice. Thankfully, where we were there weren't any armies coming through or firing, so we left unscathed. I'm talking way back in the teens. We came back on a ship that later went to the bottom, so we were lucky.

My dad became a baseball fan in Lexington Park, where the St. Paul Saints played. The Minneapolis Millers were at Nicollet Park. I was born three blocks removed from the center field gate of Lexington Park, at 938 Fuller. When I was eight, nine years old, after a game the Saints players came down Fuller Avenue by my house, and I'd be playing a game, throwing the ball against the steps of the house. Now the Millers, I didn't have that closeness with them as I did for the Saints that came by the house heading to the streets where they rented a room.

As I grew up, I wound up playing baseball for St. Luke's Catholic School, which is on Summit Avenue, and that was the hoity-toity of this city. We played against St. Vincent's, St. Albert's; it was very well organized. We played at Dunning Field; that was *the* park. There were four diamonds there. There were all kinds of scouts in both St. Paul and Minneapolis when you were playing in high school. For example, just recently a kid from St. Luke's got signed. I knew his father. Just a second, I'll think of his name. Mauer, that's it. And he's a home run hitter. I wound up signing with the Saints. Then I went to the major leagues, and the rest is history. I went to the Washington Senators, St. Louis Browns, and the Brooklyn Dodgers.

Zeke Bonura was my roommate with the Washington Senators. Henry "Zeke" Bonura, first baseman. A great big fella. Power beyond anything, like Ruth. He was a natural character; he didn't put on the dog or anything like that. I also played with Dolph Camilli and Cookie Lavagetto with the Dodgers. The players of that era were all good fellas. A few liked to imbibe a little too much, but it's not like they were going to the ballpark drunk or anything.

We used to go to Yankee Stadium on an elevated, and also a subway. Coming back, we got off at 42nd Street and Broadway, which is a song. (Sings) "Give my regards to Broadway, remember me to Herald Square, and

Tony Giuliani
Courtesy of Mary Jo Giuliani.

da-da-dada-da." We stayed at the New Yorker Hotel, which was a class hotel. People that ran the clubs that came into New York liked to stay closer to Yankee Stadium and the Polo Grounds.

Tony Lazzeri was a great infielder and a great ballplayer to the extent of knowing the game. He knew all the odds and ends of the game of baseball. He was an intelligent player. He played very, very well and taught others as well. He played the game very keenly. "Poosh 'em up Tony," they used to call him. He had a great natural talent. He had the home run power too, but not like the Babe. He kind of took a shine to me because I was Italian, but I played against him. So we would speak our native tongue. "Come stai, Antonio?" How are you, Tony? That's the first language I knew. Frank Crosetti was not as verbal as Tony was. A humble individual, he kind of lived in Tony's shadow. I used to needle them a little bit when they were hitting. They'd stop and get out of the box and say, "You dago so-and-so."

A lot of the Italians took on the game of baseball; they didn't have it in Italy. The fans would holler out "dago," "wop," "guinea," to some extent. All that kind of stuff came out when they had people that were not too gracious. That got you a little bit sizzled, and you'd maybe holler back a little, or not at all.

I did some scouting when I was playing with the Millers, and I became a scout right after I stopped playing. Scouting for the Twins, I had five states: Minnesota, Wisconsin, North and South Dakota, and Iowa. I signed a lot of players in that area. It's been some years now that I've been retired. With players that I signed, we won the 1991 World Series. That I'm very proud of.

I recently threw out the first ball at the Metrodome. And I did it from the pitcher's mound. I'm eighty-eight years old, but I've had a great history as far as Babe Ruth and Lou Gehrig. The Babe was the man that made the game popular, and the home run became the big event. He was a great player; there's no two ways about it. It's been quite a life; I've enjoyed it immensely.

Nino Bongiovanni

*A*nthony Thomas "Nino" Bongiovanni's major-league career was brief. Following a two-game cup of espresso early in the 1938 season, he appeared in 66 games for the Cincinnati Reds in 1939. The left-handed outfielder also spent 14 years in the minors between 1933 and 1949, losing three years to military service in World War II. In his first ten minor league seasons, he played in the Pacific Coast and International Leagues, both of which were classified Double A, at that time the highest level in the minors. In 1935, his third year in pro ball, he hit .338 for the Portland Beavers in the PCL and was third in the league in hits, one spot behind twenty-year-old Joe DiMaggio.

After returning from service in the Army Air Corps, he played for three years in the Class C California League and one year in the Class D Far West League. In his final two seasons, he was a player-manager for Oroville in the Far West League (1948) and Stockton in the California League (1949).

While Bongiovanni's major-league career was short-lived, his life on earth spanned ninety-seven years. When we spoke, he was three weeks shy of his ninety-fourth birthday. Nevertheless, he had no trouble calling up memories of his days as a ballplayer. Seventy years after the fact, he was still miffed at the scorekeeper who, he said, robbed him of extending his 43-game hitting streak in 1935 to 56 games. (Other sources indicate that the streak ended after 41 games.) At the end of our discussion, he gladly offered to share the secret of his longevity, after which he laughed heartily.

* * *

I was born in 1911 in Donaldsonville, Louisiana, between New Orleans and Baton Rouge. My parents were both from Sicily, near Palermo. They came here when they were eight and nine years old and met in the United States. They moved to California when I was two years old because my father wasn't making any money picking sugarcane in Louisiana. In California, he was a foreman in a food cannery. I grew up in San Jose. They used to tell us, me and my two younger sisters, to answer them in Italian, but we never did. They used to start a question in Italian and finish it up in English and vice versa.

I never thought I'd play in the major leagues, never even dreamed about it. Baseball just happened to come my way. When I played in the Pacific Coast

League I thought that was going to be it. Then I was drafted. Walter Mails was the baseball manager at Santa Clara, and he was the one that recommended me to Seattle.

My first year in the minors was 1933. I played for Seattle in the Pacific Coast League. They called me Nino or "Bongi"; there wasn't enough room in the newspaper for Bongiovanni. In the middle of '34, I was traded to Portland, and I stayed there until I was sent up to the major leagues with Cincinnati in 1938. I was with them part-time, and then they farmed me out to Syracuse, then called me back in 1939. I enjoyed playing in the Pacific Coast League, but it was a lot slower than in the majors. And the pay was a lot less. I got twice as much when I was signed by Cincinnati.

I didn't like my manager in Cincinnati, Mr. McKechnie. He didn't like me and always called me "Dago," and I didn't care for that. He called Ernie Lombardi by his name, but he always called me "Dago." I was too shy to tell him not to do it. When they sent me my contract for the next year, I asked for a $500 raise, and I was traded to the Kansas City Blues.

Nino Bongiovanni
National Baseball Hall of Fame and Museum.

Lombardi was a great hitter. They used to say he'd hit the ball out of the catcher's glove. The infielders would play him deep because he was so slow. They could throw him out easily if he didn't hit the ball into the outfield. He was a good catcher; he had a good arm. He'd throw to first base to try to pick them off without standing up; he'd just turn sideways. I got along very well with Ernie Lombardi. He was a big, kind-hearted guy. Once in a while he'd throw his arms around me and give me a big bear hug.

I played a lot of ballgames against Joe DiMaggio in the minors and in the World Series in 1939. He was the best ballplayer I ever knew. He could do it all.

I spent three years in the service, the Fourth Air Force, '43, '44, and '45. I was an Air Force dispatcher and I played ball for the base team in Fresno; that's what kept me from going overseas.

What I most remember is opening day in 1936 when I played for Portland. I went 5-for-5, three doubles and two singles. I never slept all night long. I also had a 43-game hitting streak with Portland, but it should have been 56. The scorekeeper took two hits away from me. I hit a hard ground ball to Bobby Doerr, who was playing second base. The ball took a bad hop, hit him on the shoulder, and he couldn't throw me out. That's a hit in anybody's league. In the same game I beat out a bunt, but the pitcher threw the ball into the seats, and the scorekeeper gave him an error and took the hit away from me. I would've hit in 56 straight games because I continued to hit even after that. There were only 12 games left, and I continued to hit until the end of the season. So I would've had hits in 56 straight games. I still remember the scorekeeper's name: "Screwball" Gregory. That's what everybody called him. How can I forget?

I'll be ninety-four years old on December twenty-first. Whenever someone asks me what I attribute my longevity to, I answer, "Four things: one, I never smoked; two, I never took any alcohol; three, I never took any dope; and four, I never had sex until I was ten years old."

Dario Lodigiani

*T*he son of immigrants from northern Italy, Dario Lodigiani was born in the North Beach neighborhood of San Francisco, where their home was located just a few blocks from that of the DiMaggio family. Lodigiani played ball with both Joe and Dom, first at the local playground now named in honor of Joe, and later in junior high and high school. In the major leagues, he played with and against many of the early Italian American ballplayers from the San Francisco area.

A three-sport All-Star at Galileo High School, he turned down a scholarship to St. Mary's College—at that time a West Coast baseball powerhouse—to sign with the Oakland Oaks of the Pacific Coast League in 1935. That was the beginning of a 73-year career in professional baseball. He spent all or parts of six years in the majors between 1938 and 1946 playing for the Philadelphia A's and the Chicago White Sox, primarily as a third baseman. He lost three seasons while serving in the Army Air Corps in the South Pacific between 1943 and 1945.

When an elbow injury cut short his big league career, he returned to the Pacific Coast League, playing for Oakland and San Francisco from 1947 to 1951. After managing in the minors for two years, he coached for the Indians and Athletics and scouted for the White Sox for more than forty years. He was still employed by Chicago at the time of his death in 2008 at age ninety-one. The team awarded him a World Series ring following its 2005 win. In 2006, he was elected to the Pacific Coast League Hall of Fame.

Here he recalls his experiences with such legendary figures as commissioner Kenesaw Mountain Landis, Connie Mack, Casey Stengel, and Ted Williams.

* * *

My father was from a little town called Broni, south of Milan, and my mother was from a town in the province of Pavia. My father was a baker in San Francisco at the time of the earthquake. He went back to Italy, stayed for five years, married my mother, then came back to San Francisco. He knew when he got here he'd get a job right away. My brothers and I all spoke Italian with our parents. When I went away to play ball, my dad would write to me in Italian, and I'd write back in Italian. Everybody in North Beach spoke Italian, at least the dialects their parents spoke. We spoke Milanese; the DiMaggios were Sicilian. The Puccinellis were from Lucca, so they spoke Tuscan.

I remember when we were kids playing at the North Beach Playground. At that time we were just a bunch of friends playing, not knowing that we were going to have one of the most famous players of all time playing with us, Joe DiMaggio. His brothers, Vince and Dominic, also used to play with us. I went to school with the DiMaggios. I played with Joe on our junior high school team; Joe was the shortstop and I was the second baseman. Then I played in high school with Dom. I lived four blocks from the DiMaggios, on Grand Avenue.

We used to go out to Funston Playground. No matter what park you went to there was a ballgame going on. They started at eight in the morning. If you showed any kind of ability, you always had a place to play. The first time I ever wore a uniform was for the San Francisco Boys Club. Then from there to junior high to high school, then semipro baseball. There were people like Spike Hennessey, the old baseball coach. He used to be around Funston Playground and used to help kids, teach them how to slide and how to bunt, and that helped you get a little better.

Many Italian major leaguers came out of the North Beach Playground and the Funston Playground. Ping Bodie was the first one, then Tony Lazzeri and Frankie Crosetti. Ernie Lombardi and Cookie Lavagetto were from Oakland and Billy Martin from Berkeley. Dolph Camilli, Italo Chelini, later on Gino Cimoli, Dino Restelli. But the Pacific Coast League was really the big thing out here when we were kids. That was the big league out here, and they were our heroes. We never thought of New York, Philadelphia, or Chicago.

The reason so many ballplayers came from San Francisco was that things were kind of tough. We played a lot of ball; there was nothing else to do. A lot of us couldn't afford the price of going to different places, so we stuck around Funston Playground, North Beach Playground, and the different playgrounds around San Francisco.

I knew Ping Bodie when I was a young kid. I was playing ball with Francisco Junior High School and he was the coach at St. Ignatius College, which is now the University of San Francisco. I used to go out there when he was coaching, and he let me work out with them. Every once in a while he'd let me sneak in there and take a few swings. He kind of took a liking to me, and I got to know Ping real well. He was a fun-loving guy and very personable. He was a short, stocky guy; he was built like a six-footer that somebody dropped a safe on. But, geez, he had tremendous power and he hit the ball a long way. He was Babe Ruth out here.

Of course I knew of two players and their records for a long time, and I got to know them real well when I went to the American League: Frankie

Crosetti and Tony Lazzeri. Lazzeri was a great ballplayer, an outstanding second baseman, and a good hitter who hit with power. He was the most underrated player on that club and a pretty sharp man on the ball field. Lazzeri ran that club on the field, not Gehrig. He was my manager when I played for Toronto in 1940. He was a good manager, really a cagey guy. We roomed together because he was an epileptic. My mother was kind of an epileptic, so I knew what to do if he had a spell. His wife, Mary, was the one who asked me, and I said, "Sure."

For years, Frankie Crosetti and I would go duck hunting every Wednesday. Frankie said that Babe Ruth—you know, with Ruth every night was Saturday night—he'd come to the ballpark and wash his eyes out with Murine. But Lazzeri would pour all that stuff out and fill it with water. Then Ruth would use it and say, "This is great stuff, makes you see that ball," and the big guy didn't know he was using water. Tony was kind of a trickster. You had to watch him; he'd nail your shoes down in the locker.

There were so many good ballplayers in San Francisco in those days, and it wasn't easy to get a start. Especially in the Italian neighborhoods, the parents wouldn't let you go. I had to beg my mother to let me go to spring training. My father said, "What do you want to do, become a baseball player? You'll become a bum." My father thought that bocce was the national pastime; he didn't know anything about baseball. But when I was playing for Oakland, he would listen to the games on the radio. One time I came home after a game and he asked me, "What's this poppa-up I hear on the radio?"

"Pop," I said, "that's when I hit the ball under the center, and it goes straight up in the air."

Then he said, "I know what you do. Put one of those inner soles in your shoe; then you'll be taller and you'll hit the ball in the middle."

I was going to go to St. Mary's College; I had a scholarship. That was during the Depression, and I thought, *If I take a chance and don't make it, I lose the scholarship.* As it was, fortunately, I played 21 years, so I sent a lot of checks home. I played with Oakland my first year out of high school. I hit .286 and made $150 a month. I was tickled to death. Dad was hesitant about my not continuing school and playing ball, but when I got to the point where I was making more money than he was, he said, "Boy, you've got a good job."

It was a big change, going east, but I got used to it. Chicago was a tough town, playing on the South Side for the White Sox. I played for the A's for three years. The old saying was, if the show went to Philadelphia and proved a success, it would be a success anywhere. If you played in front of those Philadelphia fans, the toughest fans in the world, you could play anywhere. They had these cups filled with ice. They'd suck the lemonade out of it and if you made a boot, *whoom!*, it would come down on you. One day I made an error late in the game and somebody took off his shoe and threw it at me. I went over and picked it up, and it was a brand-new Florsheim, size 8 1/2, and I thought to myself, *Throw the other one down and I've got a pair.*

They didn't call you a "wop" or a "dago," they called you a "guinea." I didn't know what a "guinea" was; what the hell's a "guinea"? But "wop" and "dago," you never heard that.

They called me "Lodi," using part of my last name. When I first went to Philadelphia, some of the writers wanted to shorten my name, but I said, "No, use the whole thing; you'll get used to it."

The only person who couldn't pronounce my name was Connie Mack. If he wanted to talk to me he'd say, "Young man, come over here." But he was great. Playing for Mr. Mack was like playing for your father. If you made a mistake he would never say anything at the time, but he'd write it down in his notebook. Then the next day he'd call you over and let you know about it in a quiet way.

Dario Lodigiani (right) with Connie Mack, manager of the Philadelphia Athletics. *Courtesy of Diane Lodigiani.*

South Philadelphia had the big Italian settlement, and they'd invite me down there to the different functions they had, and Chicago the same way. I remember one time I was invited to an Italian sports club in South Philly, and I got into a bocce ball tournament with them. They'd have a sports night and they'd invite the Italian ballplayers.

Every year in San Francisco after the end of the season we used to play a CYO benefit game at Seals Stadium, and we'd have the major leaguers against the minor leaguers, all the players that came from the Bay area. Somebody got the bright idea of having an all-Italian team play against an all-nation team. We had Dolph Camilli at first base, Harry Lavagetto and Art Garibaldi at second base, Frankie Crosetti at shortstop, and Joe Orengo and I at third base. In left field we had Vince DiMaggio, Joe DiMaggio in center field, and Dominic DiMaggio in right field. The catcher was Ernie Lombardi, and the pitchers were Italo Chelini and Joe Cascarella. That was about in the early '40s, and we won something like 14–3.

When I played for Oakland in the Coast League in 1948, we were known as "The Nine Old Men." We had Lombardi, Lavagetto, [Billy] Raimondi, [Les] Scarsella. There was a writer in Seattle who wrote, "The only way to beat Oakland is to get the Italians out of there." We were all in our thirties and Lombardi was in his forties, the oldest on the team. Even then he was a great hitter. Come the seventh, eighth, ninth inning, if it was a close game and we had a chance to win, Casey Stengel, our manager, would send Ernie up and it seems he'd always come through.

Casey was the greatest in the world. In all the years I played ball, the most enjoyable year I had was in '48. He kept everyone loose. They all thought he was some kind of *pagliaccio*, but he was one of the smartest managers I ever played for. He knew how to handle the players. If we had a big game to win he'd say, "I'll buy you all a steak dinner." If we won he'd peel off the five dollar bills.

I've always said that Ted Williams was the greatest hitter I ever played against. But the best all-around ballplayer I ever played against was Joe DiMaggio. I mean, Joe could beat you so many ways; he could beat you on the bases, he could beat you in the outfield. In my book, in a jam he was a better hitter than Ted Williams.

When I'd walk out of the clubhouse in New York some guy would say, "Lodi, Joe wants you to wait for him." I'd wait and he would always be the last guy out of the clubhouse. He was staying at the Mayflower Hotel at the time. We'd sit around with some friends and we'd have a couple of beers. Then room service, and up would come a steak dinner or something. And that's what he would do most of the time because if he went anywhere, they'd mob him.

One time we were in Chicago and here come the Yankees with Crosetti and DiMaggio, and I went to talk to them. In those days, when Judge Landis was commissioner, he had a rule: no fraternization. You couldn't talk to players on the other team. That day Judge Landis was sitting in the front row, and he signaled me to come over. I went over and he said, "Did you read that bulletin about no fraternizing? The next time I see you talking to those fellows it's going to cost you some money."

I told him they were friends at home, and he said, "I don't care where they're from, you don't talk to them at the ballpark."

I began playing professionally in 1935. I played in the Pacific Coast League, then the American League. Then I came back, and I was a player-manager in the minor leagues. I began scouting with the White Sox in September '54, then between 1959 and 1962 I was with Cleveland and Kansas City as a coach. In '63, I went back to scouting with the White Sox and I'm still with them, but I'm semi-retired. This is my sixty-seventh year in pro baseball; I've always got a check every two weeks for sixty-seven years.

Baseball has been great to me. It's given me a job that I've loved all my life, taken care of me and my family. Fortunately, I get a good pension every month, so I've been very, very lucky. I still get a big kick out of sitting in the stands and watching those high school and college kids play. I'd give anything if 1935 could roll around again and I could play again.

Sibby Sisti

*S*ebastian *"Sibby" Sisti was signed in 1938 by the Boston Braves (then known as the Bees) during his senior year in high school and made his major-league debut the following year at the age of eighteen. He was a starter at third and short over the next three seasons before losing three years while serving in the Coast Guard during World War II.*

In 1946, he was named Minor League Player of the Year by The Sporting News *after hitting .343 for the Indianapolis Indians. He returned to the Braves in 1947 but was hampered by a series of injuries and played in more than 100 games in only two of his last nine years. Yet, even though he was a lifetime .244 hitter, he was so valuable as a utility man that he was one of the first four players inducted into the Boston Braves Hall of Fame. He played a key role for the 1948 pennant winners as a late-season replacement for injured second baseman Eddie Stanky. His versatility and relentless work ethic earned him the respect of his peers and the adoration of fans.*

Following his release in 1954, Sisti managed in the minors between 1955 and 1959, then returned for one more season in 1969. He would later revive his managerial career, this time on film. Serving as a technical advisor for The Natural, *Barry Levinson's 1984 adaptation of Bernard Malamud's novel, much of which was shot in his hometown of Buffalo, New York, Sisti appears briefly onscreen in the role of the Pittsburgh Pirates' manager. He passed away in 2006 at age eighty-five.*

* * *

I grew up in an Italian neighborhood on the west side of Buffalo. I stayed there for twenty-seven years until I got married and moved out. My grandparents were born in central Italy. My father was born in New York City and my mother in Youngstown, Ohio. I was an only child and they never spoke Italian around the house, so it was tough for me to pick it up. I used to go and visit my grandmother. She'd speak to me in Italian, and sometimes I knew what she was talking about, sometimes I didn't.

I grew up playing organized ball in the Buffalo area. I was playing a lot of baseball in high school and muni ball and amateur ball. My parents were very happy that I wanted to play ball professionally. One day, I'll never forget it, I came home from school and my mother, who never saw me play baseball, had the radio on. She was listening to the Buffalo Bisons game, which was rather odd for her. So she got interested in baseball, and naturally, my father was.

My father was a pretty good athlete when he was younger. He signed my contract with the Boston Braves. I was underage, only about seventeen years old, still going to high school. My father went to Boston and signed me. He called me up and said, "In case you don't know it, you are now a Boston Brave." I was just going into my senior year of high school. When I graduated, I went right to Hartford in the Eastern League. I played two half-seasons in Hartford, then in the middle of the second season, Eddie Miller, who was the shortstop for the Braves, ran into Al Simmons in the outfield. Miller broke his ankle and I had been to spring training, but just on a look. The club wasn't going any place; they were a seventh-place ballclub at the time. In 1939, Casey Stengel, who was managing, called me up from Hartford, so that's how I got my start in the big leagues.

Casey used to start on one story, not finish it, go to the next story and not finish it, then go to the third story and not finish it. Then all of a sudden he'd go back to the first story and finish that story. You never knew what he was going to say or what he was going to come up with.

Phil Masi, the catcher, came up to the Braves the same year I did. He was a terrific ballplayer and a great guy. In fact, we roomed together my first year. We got along great. He was a year or two older than me. We were just like two immigrant kids, you know, green as apples. We just paid attention to the other guys on the ballclub to see what we could learn.

In the 1948 World Series, Phil was on second and I was on first when Feller and Boudreau pulled off that famous pickoff play. The photos show that Masi was sliding back into the bag and Boudreau was tagging him on the head and you could see that Phil wasn't into the bag yet. But he was called safe. I was on first and I had a good angle to look at the play. Johnny Cooney was a coach with us at the time, and I turned and said, "John, we got a lucky break there." And as it turned out, Tommy Holmes got a base hit to drive in Phil, which was the only run of the game. So Johnny Sain pitched a four-hitter and beat Feller. Feller pitched a two-hitter and lost. That was the first game of the World Series.

One of the three or four guys who helped me most in my career was Tony Cuccinello. When I came up to the Braves they wanted to make a second baseman out of me; I usually played third or short. Tony was the second baseman and they wanted to move Tony to third. He was at the end of his career and he wouldn't have to move as much at third. So Tony took me under his wing and we'd go out there every day. Somebody would hit ground balls to us, and he'd work with me on five or six different pivots you could make at second base. So I owe a great deal of my career to Tony Cuccinello.

I played against Ernie Lombardi, and I played with him in 1942 when he was with the Braves. When I played against Ernie I played deep on the grass, as well as every other infielder. When Ernie came to play with the Braves, I noticed they played him the same way. And it was amazing to me that a guy could hit so well and couldn't run a lick. He was the slowest man I've ever seen in baseball. It was terrific that he could hit .300 and do one terrific job. I remember him getting a ball back from the umpire and rubbing the thing up with one hand. He didn't have to put two hands on it. He had hands that made three of mine. He was a great guy. I mean, he was so relaxed all the time, easy going. For the big monster he was size-wise, he was just like a little lamb. He certainly didn't look like a ballplayer, but he was a terrific athlete, believe it or not.

I saw Dolph Camilli about four years ago and he looked great. I know he passed away recently. He was a great-fielding first baseman, and he was the one Pee Wee Reese thanked for making him an outstanding ballplayer because he was a real fancy-dan around that bag at first base. And he was a good hitter.

Sibby Sisti
*National Baseball Hall of Fame
and Museum.*

I lost three years to service during World War II, like many other guys. It was tough because usually when you go into the service, you're in the prime years of your career. You're in your early twenties, and those were the years when guys can develop and progress.

When I got released in the middle of 1954, Braves general manager John Quinn offered me a job as a coach with the ballclub for the last half of the season. Then in the winter he offered me a job as player-manager at Québec. I managed in the Braves organization for several years. I never went to the same place twice. I went to Québec, Corpus Christi, Jacksonville, Austin. The highest I got was Sacramento in the Pacific Coast League; then I went back to Jacksonville again. So I got a good education as a player and as a manager. I never liked scouting because I liked to be more active on the field and work with the players.

A friend of mine told me to get involved with the trucking industry, so I was a truck driver during the offseason. After I quit managing, I stuck with driving all the time. Driving a semi was easy; loading and unloading that thing, that was a load of work. I still live in the outskirts of Buffalo. I was born and raised there, went to school there and grew up there. I'm eighty-one years old now, so there's not much family around, but I've been married sixty years and have five children, ten grandchildren, and eleven great-grandchildren.

Baseball earned me a living and it earned me recognition throughout the United States, and I'm very proud to be Italian and represent the Italian heritage. I was very happy to have the ability to play the game and play different positions, which kept me around for 12 1/2 years. You had to love the game. The money wasn't really there, to be very frank with you. My first year in the big leagues my salary was $400 a month, and I got a big raise my second year; I made $450 a month. When you talk about the salaries these guys are making today, it's enough to make you sick.

Every year after the season was over, I'd go back home to Buffalo and lay around for about a week. Then I'd have to get a job because I didn't make enough money during the summertime to put a lot away. So what would happen, every time I went to work I'd get the same question over and over again. Guys knew I was a major-league ballplayer and they'd say, "Geez, what are you doing working?" So I used to have a stock answer every time they said that. I'd say, "Well, I've got a very bad habit; I like to eat in the winter like I do in the summer."

1940–49

Dom DiMaggio

D̲om DiMaggio was the youngest and, at 5-foot-9 and 170 pounds, the smallest of three brothers to make it to the major leagues. Vince, the oldest, was a two-time All-Star in his 10-year career, and Joe was a Hall of Famer considered the greatest all-around player of his era. Of the more than 350 brother combinations that have played major league baseball, few if any have equaled the combined achievements of these three sons of Sicilian immigrants.

Like his brothers, Dom, who spent his entire career (1940–42, 1946–53) with the Boston Red Sox, was an outstanding outfielder. He led the American League in outfield assists three times, and his 503 putouts in 1948 stood as the AL record until 1977. He also compiled a lifetime average of .298, primarily as a leadoff hitter, was often among the league leaders in runs scored, walks, hits, and doubles, and still holds the Red Sox record for hitting in consecutive games: 34 in 1949. Known as "The Little Professor"—he was one of the few players at the time to wear glasses on the field—he was beloved by Sox fans, who enjoyed singing these lines from a popular song: "He's better than his brother Joe / Dominic DiMaggio." In 1995, he was inducted into the Red Sox Hall of Fame. He passed away in 2009 at the age of ninety-two.

For all he achieved, his career has always been overshadowed by the towering figures of two contemporaries: his brother Joe and his Red Sox teammate, Ted Williams, considered by many the greatest hitter in history. Nevertheless, one measure of his ability is that, at a time when his brother and Williams were virtual locks to start in the All-Star Game, in his 10 full years Dom was a seven-time All-Star and was in the starting lineup three times. In a 2006 interview with me, Red Sox shortstop Johnny Pesky said of his teammate, "Dominic never made a mistake. He was the perfect ballplayer and had one of the brightest minds in baseball."

* * *

When they first arrived in this country, my family settled in a little town across the bay from San Francisco, then eventually moved to San Francisco. I believe I was the only child born in San Francisco. Everyone in the family spoke Italian with Mother and Dad. Dad spoke some broken English. Mom spent most of her days raising the family, so she didn't get involved with Americans all that much. Mother was a schoolteacher in Sicily in Isola delle Femmine. It took five years for Dad to earn enough money to send for her. Our oldest sister, Nellie, was the only member of the family born in Italy.

We first lived two blocks from St. Peter and Paul Church on Filbert Street, then we moved a block away to 2047 Taylor Street, the bottom flat of a three-flat home. We stayed in that residence until 1937, the first year I broke in with the San Francisco Seals baseball team. I remember picking up the cable car a block away from the house to go to Seals Stadium. At the end of the '37 season, we moved to Beach Street, a block and a half up from the Palace of Fine Arts in the Marina district. We stayed there until Mom and Dad passed on, then Joe retained possession of the home, and when he passed on, it was sold by the estate. We kept improving, from Filbert to Taylor and then out to the Marina. There we had one of the nicer homes in the San Francisco area.

We spent a good deal of our time at North Beach Playground, right where I took the cable car. We played a lot of baseball and Joe played a little tennis. There was basketball, soccer, a swimming pool, and we played a little checkers. I was about twelve or thirteen years old when I was the champion checker player for a few years. I even played the playground director, Helen Williams, and I beat her. The playground had blacktop and we weren't allowed to play hardball during the hours when the playground was open, but we would go on Saturday and Sunday mornings before the playground opened and we'd play hardball, without gloves. We'd play until nine o'clock, then the playground would open up and we had to stop. The hardtop would tear the cover off the baseball, but we had a general store across the street and we'd buy nickel tapes, and we'd tape the balls up. As soon as the tape would tear apart, we'd tape it up again. As soon as the playground opened at nine, there was no hardball allowed so we'd get softballs.

The first organized team I played for might well have been the San Francisco Boys Club. Then there was the North Beach Merchants who supplied the uniforms and caps, and we had a club called the Jolly Knights, and we had a baseball team. I played one year of American Legion baseball. We had a whole slew of baseball fields around the San Francisco area. Funston Playground had three baseball fields on it. The main one had stands, and when we got a game there, we thought we were doing pretty well. Games were scheduled by the people who ran amateur baseball in San Francisco. Then when we went across the Bay to Mill Valley, Santa Rosa, Vallejo, we thought we were traveling! We'd take the ferry and go across the Bay and we were really playing it up big.

There was an old gentleman who traveled all through the sandlots, Spike Hennessey. He had a big top coat and a hat. He used to go to the parks and watch kids' games. He'd teach kids how to slide. He was just a lover of baseball.

If he saw somebody making a mistake, he'd say, "Come over here, I want to teach you something." He was a nuisance to an awful lot of kids, but he stayed with it and was pretty persuasive.

Vince, being the oldest, was playing around the sandlots. Dad didn't particularly enjoy his playing baseball; he thought he was wasting his childhood. The Italian families always had the work ethic uppermost in their mind and they thought you should be working. As fast as Dad used to take Vince's gloves and spikes and throw them in the trash can, Mother would go back and retrieve them and hide them until Vince played again. Finally, Vince signed a minor-league contract and went to Tucson and Dad said, "You mean they pay you for playing this game?"

After one year in Tucson, Vince came back to San Francisco to play with the Seals. Before the last two games of the season their shortstop, Augie Galan, left to play in Hawaii, and Vince said, "I've got a brother who can play at short." Joe was an outstanding ballplayer practically from day one. So Joe played the last two games of the season; that was Triple A, remember. He came right off the sandlots and never even signed a contract. He then played some winter ball and signed with San Francisco. Vince was traded to Hollywood, and after Joe went to the Yankees, one day Dad came to me and said, "And when are you going to start playing baseball?" So you see how the pendulum swung.

I didn't play any high school baseball until I was a senior. I wasn't very big and I was still an infielder. After graduating from high school in 1934, I went to work in a box factory, then at the Simmons bed factory. They had a team and I played with them. I broke into baseball from the Simmons bed factory team. I guess I was twenty years old at the time. The Cincinnati Reds and the San Francisco Seals ran a baseball camp in San Francisco. By this time I had started to wear glasses in the field. Prior to wearing glasses, I couldn't hit anything. One day I decided to wear glasses even though there was a danger of getting hurt; I was a shortstop. You weren't supposed to play baseball wearing glasses, but I was tired of not hitting well. The first time I wore glasses I hit the ball like I never hit before. I hit everything they threw me, so I wore the glasses. I took a ribbing about wearing glasses in the minors and the majors: "Four eyes! How many balls do you see?"

At the camp, San Francisco had the first choice, and they picked me; Triple A! That's how I broke into baseball. Right after they selected me they put me in center field. Right from the start I decided to play center with my back to right field. I felt I would get a better break coming in for line drives and ground balls and going back on the ball I'd have a jump there. The only question was if I was standing facing left field, could I go to my left going to right field? And I had no problem with that whatsoever. I used to be running before the pitch got to the batter, based on where the pitch was going. If the batter didn't swing at it, I don't know what the people in the stands must have thought, but here I was running like hell in the direction I thought the ball was going to be hit.

There was a columnist on the *San Francisco Daily News*, Tom Laird, who thought that Joe was the greatest ballplayer that ever lived. He would write something outstanding about Joe, then, in italics, he would give me a needle. "This kid can't play baseball," he'd write. "He's just in there on his brother's name." He said how could I possibly turn to my left and go toward right field playing the way I did. He took me over the coals. So that changed me from wanting to play one year of baseball to saying, "I'm going to make him eat his words, and I'm going to go to the majors." One night we were playing up in Portland and a guy hit a shot to right center and I got a hell of a jump on it and made the catch. The next day Laird wrote, "I take it all back."

We had quite a few major-league players from the San Francisco area, where you could play baseball twelve months a year: Ping Bodie, Tony Lazzeri, Frank Crosetti, Ernie Lombardi. And guys I played with in the sandlots who played in the minors or major leagues. There were the Raimondi boys from Oakland, Dario Lodigiani, "Rugger" Ruggiero.

I met Tony Lazzeri a few times during the offseason. He was kind of shy and wasn't very talkative, but he was a very, very knowledgeable baseball player. In fact, everybody thought he was one of the smartest baseball guys they'd seen. Let me tell you a cute story. One time the bases were loaded with one out and Lefty Gomez was pitching. The batter hits the ball back to Gomez, and he starts to throw home but he didn't think he'd get him, so he turned to throw it to Crosetti, who was covering second base, but he was afraid he wasn't going to get a double play, so instead he threw it to Lazzeri, who was between first and second. Lazzeri was surprised and caught the ball in self-defense. Everybody was safe. So he walked in and gave the ball to Gomez and said, "What are you throwing the ball to me for?" Gomez said, "I didn't know whether to throw to home, third or first and they tell me you're the smartest guy in baseball so I figured you'd know what to do with it." I don't think it's true, but it's a good story.

Frankie Crosetti really got on me when I first came up to the majors. Oh boy, he gave it to me pretty good. He called me all the names a guy who wore glasses could be called, and a few more. It was good-natured, but everybody could hear it, so it wasn't all that great to hear it. Of course, I got it from the other teams the same way. Frankie, who was an outstanding shortstop, was kind of an isolated individual, even long after he retired. He never traveled very far from Stockton, California.

I knew Ernie Lombardi because he lived in Oakland. We played some exhibition games after the season for the benefit of the Catholic Youth Organization. At the end of my third season with the Seals, we played an exhibition game with Oakland and Lombardi was catching. Joe Cronin, who had come out to scout me, was playing short. I was on first and a pitch bounced in front of Lombardi, about six or eight feet in the air, and I took off for second. I slid in safely, and Cronin said, "Nice going, kid." I didn't know what he meant until later on someone told me you don't run on Lombardi. Nobody dared to steal on Lombardi; he had a great arm, a wonderful arm. They tell me he used to catch pitches barehanded.

For my first spring training, we drove across country, Joe Orengo, myself and, oh, I can't remember the third guy. We had a barrel of fun. I hadn't driven cross-country before. It was Route 66 across the southern part of the country, into Biloxi. The Red Sox camp was in Sarasota. I met everybody in the clubhouse and they were all very nice. Johnny Orlando, the clubhouse custodian, took me around to meet the players. Jimmie Foxx came right over to my locker, shook my hand and said, "Glad to have you aboard, welcome to the big leagues, kid."

I was rooming with Moe Berg. One day, when I was confined to my room with a sprained ankle, Tom Yawkey and Joe Cronin came to talk to me, and there were stacks of newspapers all over the room. Moe Berg only had one hat, one topcoat, and one pair of shoes; the guy never had a wardrobe. Mr. Cronin wasn't about to have Mr. Yawkey stand up while we were talking. So he took a stack of newspapers from the chair and tossed them on the floor. Later I went down to dinner, and when I came back to my room all the newspapers were gone, the closets were empty, and there was a message from Mr. Berg. It said, "Roomie, you're too popular and my newspapers are too important to me. I'm going to have to move." I roomed with him for two and a half to three weeks.

When I came up in 1940, the players couldn't have been more pleasant. Cronin told me he wanted me to hit in batting practice before exhibition games whether I was playing that day or not, and the guys never resented it. When I arrived in Sarasota, I was in shape. I didn't need any spring training, and I never did. I came up rather heralded. I had hit .360 in the Pacific Coast League and was named the Most Valuable Player, so I think they were expecting great things from me. So I decided I was going to take it easy in spring training; swing easily in batting practice, jog down to the bases, let long fly balls drop. After about ten days of this, Johnny Orlando came to me and said, "Kid, you feeling all right?" I said, "Fine. Why do you ask?" He said, "Geez, people are worried. Anything bothering you?' I said, "No, I'm as happy as a pig in manure. Everything's fine."

I was inducted into the Navy after the 1942 season. I did boot camp at Treasure Island where I got an infection in my right eye. I entered the Navy as a coxswain and I wanted to become a chief petty officer. They assigned me to a stripped-down PT boat; everything was gone except the gun turret. I was in San Francisco and I knew the San Francisco Bay like the back of my hand. They put me in charge of the PT boat to run errands around the Bay area. People would see this PT boat scooting across the bay, and they'd say, "There goes Dom!"

Eventually I went to Norfolk, Virginia, and I went to physical instructors school. I wanted to come out of there as a chief petty officer. We had two good ball teams there, one on the Naval training station where I was assigned, and another on the other side of the fence where the Naval air base was. The chief warrant officer, who'd been in the Navy thirty years, wanted me to play baseball. But I said I didn't want to play baseball; I wanted to finish PI training and become a chief petty officer. He told me that if I didn't play baseball, I'd be assigned to a destroyer escort, which was the most horrendous duty. I still said no, so he went to talk to Captain McLure, who told him, "What are you waiting for? Why don't you give him his chief petty officer's rating and have him play ball?" and that's what they did. So I played baseball and got my chief petty officer's rating. Then they sent me to Australia for a year, then we went to the Philippine Islands. I missed three full years of baseball: twenty-six, twenty-seven, and twenty-eight years old. We all came back in '46.

Dom DiMaggio
Boston Red Sox.

My first encounter with Ted Williams was when I broke in with the San Francisco Seals in the Pacific Coast League. This was in 1937, and Ted was playing for the San Diego Padres. We knew of each other because we had played against each other, but I didn't meet him until I arrived in Sarasota, Florida, when he had already been playing for the Sox in 1939. I spent my entire career playing next to Ted. There was a lot of talk about him not being a very good fielder, but I thought Teddy was a good outfielder. I may have taken a few in his part of the territory. I don't think he minded that very much; in fact, he encouraged it.

Ted was an excellent teammate; I got along beautifully with him. There was no animosity between him and any of the players at any time. Whatever problems he had were with the media. Back in those days, we had eleven newspapers in Boston, so the competition was terrific. The media blamed Ted for not being cooperative, and Ted thought the media was doing him an injustice. So they had a problem getting along with each other for a long period of time.

I was the leadoff man and he batted third, so I would cross him as he was coming out of the dugout on numerous occasions. I wasn't on base every time I led off a ballgame. When I got back to the dugout, he was waiting on the top step and he would ask me, "What's he got today, Dommie? Is he fast? Is his curveball good?" One or two times when I'd pop up a pitch and was so angry at myself because I didn't hit it well, I was annoyed when he asked me. I'd say, "I don't know what he threw me." I'd go into the dugout, and he'd turn around and say, "What kind of dumb hitter are you? You don't even know what the pitcher's throwing you?"

For him to hit .406 in 1941 was quite an outstanding achievement then, but it was not truly recognized until some years had passed. Then the .406 season got bigger and bigger and bigger, and now after all these years it still stands. The second thing that comes to mind on the ball field was the 1941 All-Star Game when he came to bat with two outs in the last of the ninth. He hit the homer and drove in three runs that brought us from 5–4 to 7–5 and won the game. I was in the on-deck circle at the time and they had a big powwow before the pitch to Ted. I assumed they were talking about walking Ted to get to me. I was surprised when they pitched to him. I thought they should have walked him and pitched to me. They made a mistake.

And I remember Ted as a man, not as a ballplayer, when he served his country not once but twice, and we all felt that was unfair because a ballplayer's career is limited. He went and almost got killed in action in Korea.

Sure, there was a friendly competition with my brother, Joe, but I think I was competing against the New York Yankees. I had a great desire to beat the Yankees, and Joe was part of them, so I guess in that respect you might say I was competing against him. But I knew there was a big difference. Joe was much bigger than I was and he hit the ball harder than I did. Did I get less recognition than Joe? Well, not only Joe but because of Ted Williams. I've got Ted on one side of me in the outfield and Joe's my brother. I was privileged to be Joe's brother and be a teammate of Teddy my entire career, and I loved both of those guys. You've got to remember, when management and/or the public voted for All-Stars, there was only one outfield position open because those two guys monopolized two of the positions. I was very pleased; I started three times with those two guys next to me, meaning, in effect, that of the remaining players, I was the guy who was entitled to play with them. I don't think there's a doubt that people have now been saying for some years that I have been grossly underrated. It's been a common saying in recent years.

Then there was the incident when they honored Joe on his day. He wasn't feeling well, and he had his baseball jacket on and was standing before the mike. They called me up to stand next to Joe for photos, and he put his arm around me. I accused him of leaning on me to get me exhausted for the game. My mother was standing on the first-base side, and she came across, went right past Joe and came to me, and the crowd roared. She went to the baby.

I know how important Joe was and I've never ever felt I was all that important. I don't know exactly how to say this, but instead of being in a position of being subservient, I feel now that I'm in a position to act, for lack of a better term, as an executor in my life. I guess I've had a tendency to be a great deal more independent and call a spade a spade. I liken my position to that of Ted Williams. When he first came up, in '39, he admired Joe, and even in his last days, he thought Joe was the greatest all-around baseball player he had ever seen, justifiably so. And Joe admired Ted; thought he was the greatest hitter he had ever seen. As the years went by, Ted felt he kept creeping up on Joe, and I know he felt on an equal plane with Joe in his last days. So I think that's maybe what I'm trying to say. I've been honored by the Italian American Hall of Fame in Chicago, I've been inducted into the Bay Area Hall of Fame in San Francisco, and I'm in the Red Sox Hall of Fame, and so I'm represented across the country. All that's left is Cooperstown.

Baseball was a springboard for my future. I'll forever be grateful that I was privileged to be able to play baseball in the major leagues. There were only 400 people in the United States playing major league baseball; that's quite an honor. I was in an enviable position, not only because I was capable of playing to the extent I did, but the fact that I had a brother and teammate who were two of the greatest players in the history of the game. So I was very grateful. Anybody that does anything detrimental to baseball might as well be doing it to me. That's why I've often said that if the Players Association is negligent to the extent that when one of its members does something that is detrimental, instead of backing him to the fullest extent, I think they ought to call him on the carpet and let him know in no uncertain terms that if his actions are detrimental to baseball he should be punished accordingly. The Players Association should do that along with Major League Baseball.

Am I proud of my heritage? Absolutely, I certainly am. I didn't encounter any prejudice against Italians when I was playing. There were all kinds of ethnic differences, and we all needled each other. In our own clubhouse, we would use all kinds of names and pay no attention to it. We'd call each other all kinds of names, but it was all in fun. For example, they'd say, "Hey, get your program. Don't let the 'dago' by without a program." On occasion someone would call me a dago, but it was not a slur or insult. There were times I heard slurs when people spoke about various ethnic groups: the "wops," the "micks," and all that sort of thing. There's still some of that. Later, when I applied for membership in a country club in Massachusetts, I was blackballed by two members. I was a jock, an Italian, and Catholic. The club was embarrassed so they asked me to reapply, and I was let in.

Phil Rizzuto

*A*t his first major league tryout, Phil Rizzuto was told to "go out and get a shoeshine box; that's the only way you're going to make a living." The diminutive 5-foot-6, 150-pound shortstop known as "The Scooter" not only made a living in the big leagues, he was a five-time All-Star, a mainstay of the postwar Yankees dynasty that won nine pennants and seven World Series in his 13-year career, and is enshrined in the Hall of Fame.

By 1941, one year after he was the MVP of the Triple-A American Association, the Brooklyn native was in the Yankees starting lineup, replacing longtime shortstop Frank Crosetti. He made the All-Star team the next year before his career was interrupted by three years of service in the Navy. After finishing second in the MVP vote in 1949, he was the runaway winner of the award in 1950 when he had career highs in several offensive categories, including hits, average, slugging percentage, on-base percentage, RBIs, and runs. In addition to being an outstanding shortstop, Rizzuto was one of the most skillful bunters of his era and an excellent base runner.

When his playing career ended in 1956, Rizzuto began what would be a 40-year run as a Yankees broadcaster. He was no less successful in the booth than he had been on the field as his stream of consciousness style and trademark call of "Holy Cow" made him a fan favorite. By the time he retired in 1996, the man once dismissed as too small to make it in the big leagues had been with the Yankees for 53 years, longer than anyone in the history of the franchise. In 1994, Rizzuto was inducted into the Hall of Fame following his selection by the Veterans Committee. He was eighty-nine when he passed away in 2009.

* * *

My family came from the province of Cosenza in the Calabria region. All of my relatives on both my mother's and father's side came from there. They came over, it had to be 1912 because my sisters and I aren't more than a year or two apart. I was born in 1917. I had two sisters older than myself, and all of us were born here. They came to New York because there were already some family members there.

When they did migrate to the United States, it was amazing. They all moved into these three family houses in the Ridgewood section of Brooklyn that were connected to each other with a little alleyway and a backyard. Everybody would come out. It was one of the greatest times of my life because they all played musical instruments. They'd sing, they'd tell stories in Italian, they'd make wine. As long as there was food on the table, everyone was happy. But our neighborhood wasn't just Italians. Our little niche was all Italian, but there were German and Irish, a great mixture of nationalities. I was so lucky; they all played sports, all different sports.

In those days it was very easy to pick up Italian because everyone talked Italian when they first came over until they'd been here for ten years or so. But I spoke English because my mother and father had learned English and spoke it in the house all the time. They wanted me to retain my heritage, but they knew that in school it would be difficult for me if I just spoke Italian. It worked out for the best because with all the relatives living right there they still got their Italian in. I didn't move from that section until I got married. I went to New Jersey and I lost that daily communication in Italian. It's amazing how soon you can forget.

There were people who would go to Italy and try to sell the natives on the idea that the streets in America were paved with gold and when they got here they put them in those sweatshops. It was terrible. My relatives happened to be a lot luckier than that. They came here and were able to do what they knew how to do. They were laborers. They built homes; they built sidewalks; they built garages in New York City and out in Long Island.

My father was very fortunate; through one of the men he knew, he got a job as a motorman on a trolley car. My mother was so happy because he didn't have to travel to all these distant places and stay overnight when he was building. That lasted until the trolley cars became extinct. I think that was one of the biggest mistakes the cities made, taking out the trolley cars and taking up the tracks. Now they could really use them with all the cars and all the traffic. Then he ended up working down at the docks as security, which was a job which at his age was just perfect for him. A lot of people to talk to and, of course, with the ships that went to Italy and came back, he'd be one of the interpreters if they needed one.

We never asked for or wanted things like the kids today. They get it so easily. And we were out playing ball every day; we never sat still. We'd come in and eat and go out and play. In the baseball season we played baseball and the football season we played football. In between we played all those games on the street: steal the white flag and kick the can. We used to play a game with a tennis racquet and a tennis ball, and you had to keep it within the streets. You'd hit it as high and as far as you want, or you hit those hard skip grounders. I tell you, it was the greatest experience for eye and hand coordination.

Then my mother, to keep us from breaking windows, she'd take the cover off an old baseball. The baseballs would wear out on the streets; we didn't have many baseball fields around. She'd stuff the cover with rags and sew it back up again and we'd play with that. You could throw curves and things. I'm sure it helped me with my eye and hand coordination and helped me do as well as I did as a kid and later on. You could play box ball and triangle ball under the streetlights right on the corners there, so there was always activity. We'd form teams and you'd have to get up early because they had three or four fields you could play on and the first ones there got to play on them. It was just great getting out there. We never had uniforms when we were kids, but we beat a lot of teams that had uniforms.

I would get frustrated quite often because in those days the way they'd pick teams to play, they'd have two captains and they'd flip a coin. Whoever won would have the first pick from all of us standing around. More than 50 percent of the time nobody would pick me because I was so small and I'd have to wait, and if somebody had to leave, I got to play an inning or two. They tried to put me in right field, but I always wanted to be an infielder for some reason. Then gradually, you know, they saw I could do things they didn't think I could do.

When I went to Richmond Hill High School, I tried out and I made the team. Just before my last year of high school, I got to play with a semipro team, and that was better than any minor league experience. I was still in high school, so I had to play under an assumed name or they'd have to forfeit all those games. My name was Kennedy. I batted against Satchel Paige, the House of David, the Black Yankees, the Homestead Grays, all those guys, a lot of them in the Hall of Fame now. And don't forget, this is 1935 and 1936; we played under portable lights in those days, trying to hit off Satchel Paige who was in his prime then. I mean, that was some experience, and it helped me get through the minor leagues the first couple of years because I knew the fundamentals of the game. Those guys, they knew how to play the game. So many of them could've been in the big leagues, but because of the color line . . .

I had a lot of tryouts when I was in high school. My mother was all for me playing ball. She thought you had to give the kids a chance to get away and be on their own, to see what they can do. My father was dead against it. He wanted me to get a job, to follow in his footsteps. "You can't make a living playing baseball." But he didn't hold me back because he knew my mother really wanted me to go, thank goodness.

I always wanted to be a ballplayer. I was like the kids today who collect cards. I read everything, every line score of every game, and I used to make little crystal sets. Not many games would be broadcast on radio, but the ones that were, I'd be able to get. I wake up in a cold sweat sometimes wondering if I had not been a ballplayer what would I have been? I was not one of the smart kids in school because I was always thinking, *Oh boy, we'll get out of school soon and I can play ball.*

I idolized more people on the Yankees, but only because they were more well known and they were winning at the time, and the Dodgers were not. The Yankees had a lot of Italians at that time. The name Frank Crosetti right away stuck with me, and Joe DiMaggio. They also had Marius Russo, a left-hander who was one of the top pitchers then and who lived right near me. As a matter of fact, he drove me to Yankee Stadium my first year; I didn't have a car. And naturally they had Babe Ruth and Lou Gehrig. My uncle used to take me to see those great ballplayers.

My first tryout was with the Dodgers, and that's when I had the problems with Casey, who was managing them. In 1936 we had these tryouts in Ebbets Field. It's not like the tryouts you have today. They'd line you up and you'd run from the right field foul line to the left field foul line and the first fifty they keep. I was so fast I was always one of the first fifty. You get five swings and then go out and field your position. This kid who was trying to impress Casey hit me right in the middle of the back with his first pitch. I stiffened up, and I couldn't hit. I'll never forget what Casey said: "Hey, kid, listen. You go out and get a shoeshine box; that's the only way you're going to make a living. You'll never make it in the big leagues."

About a week later my high school coach got me a tryout with the Giants. Bill Terry was the manager, another Hall of Famer. And he didn't even let me work out. He said, "We're looking for guys who can hit home runs." And then the Red Sox, they were going to sign me, but they said they were looking at another kid. They had just signed this kid who lives in Louisville, and he looks like a great one, and it was Pee Wee Reese. Geez, I wanted to play with the Red Sox. I'd heard about that short left field fence and all of that. But then the Dodgers bought him from Louisville, and so he became a Dodger. So eventually I might've gone with the Red Sox, but who knows?

Then the Yankees, they were the last ones. Whoever thought you could get with the Yankees? They had this unusual tryout for a full week. Every day you played a game and different situations would come up. They'd ask you to bunt, to hit-and-run, try to steal, and you'd play third, you'd play second, you'd play short. And I just happened to have a great week; I couldn't do anything wrong.

I was working in Bush Terminal, factory work, and I was getting $15 a week. They said, "We've got a team in Bassett, Virginia, and we'll give you $75 a month." Now, I had never been away from home. When I had to leave to go there, my father, because they didn't give you any money, no bonuses, or anything, he pinned a $20 bill to my undershirt. I'll never forget how beautiful the train ride was, riding through Washington and Richmond. We stopped at Richmond and I had my first taste of Southern fried chicken and grits and all that. So then we get to Bassett. Now don't forget, I've never been away from home. I got off the train and there's nothing there. I said, "Where the hell is the town?" There was a drugstore, a post office, and a diner. That was the whole town and I couldn't believe it. And it was very hilly. They used to say, "This is a very unusual place. All the cows, their front legs are shorter than the back legs so they can climb." And I believed everything they told me. The people were so nice, but they couldn't understand me with my Brooklyn accent, and I couldn't understand them with their Southern accent.

My rookie year in 1941 was unbelievable, with DiMag hitting in 56 straight and Williams hitting over .400. That's when I saw my first live president. We opened in Washington and the history was that the president used to throw out the first ball. DiMag told me, "Now look, don't get too close 'cause people get spiked, they dive for that souvenir." They had to help Roosevelt stand up and he threw the ball and everybody dives for it. I mean these monsters. I didn't come close to it, but I tried, just to see the president. I didn't think I'd ever see a live president. Plus, a whole contingent from Norfork, Virginia, came up. My second year in professional ball I played in Norfolk, in the Piedmont League. I met wonderful friends there, Italian friends. I lived in the home of a barber in Norfork, and he was my best man when I got married. Jerry Priddy was with the Yankees and he had played with me in Norfolk. They gave us gifts. Here it was opening day, and at home plate they're giving us gifts, two rookies. That was a big thrill.

I grounded out my first time at bat. My knees were shaking. Bill Dickey had warned me before the game. He said, "You're going to have butterflies. If you don't, you're not a good ballplayer. As soon as you get your first time at bat, your first chance in the field, it'll go away." And sure enough, it did.

Prior to that at spring training I had a rough time. Crosetti was so well-liked by the players and a great guy, and here I was a fresh rookie trying to take his job. But if it hadn't been for Crosetti, I'd have looked like a bum in my first series because the Washington Senators had three left-handed hitters and I didn't know where they hit. Crosetti said, "You watch me in the dugout and I'll move you." He'd move me towards third base, and I'd think, "What's he trying to do, make me look bad?" And every one of them hit toward left field, and he made me look great, a guy whose job I was trying to take. And then he'd do that for every team we played. I didn't know the guys and he knew them like he had a book on them.

That was a phenomenal year. I think we clinched the pennant by the Fourth of July. Not really, but we won by 16 or 17 games. That was a great team. Henrich, Keller, DiMag in the outfield, Dickey catching, and we had so many great pitchers; no one won more than 15 games. I hit .307, so then they took me in as one of the members. My dad was proud; he was telling everybody that he taught me how to play ball. I wouldn't trade it for all the money in the world. Great memories.

I went into the service '43 through '45. I ended up in New Guinea and the Philippines, but I was lucky; I came back. A lot of guys didn't come back. I got married in 1943 while I was in Norfolk, Virginia, going through boot camp with the Navy. I met my wife through Joe DiMaggio my rookie year. I was supposed to go to a communion breakfast in Newark, New Jersey, where Joe was to be the speaker. That day his baby boy was born, and he called me up and says, "I've got to go to the hospital; you've got to fill in for me." I said, "Joe, they'll shoot me, they'll run me out of town. You hit in 56 straight games, were the most valuable player in the American League, and I'm a rookie."

I had never given a speech before and, oh, I was lousy. No applause. Some of them actually booed when they announced me because everyone was expecting to see DiMaggio and I walk up. The man who was to become my father-in-law, who was a friend of DiMaggio, said, "That's a shame," and took me to his house for a cup of coffee and to relax. When I was there having a cup of coffee, I saw this vision of loveliness come down the stairs, and you know how they say in the movies, it was love at first sight.

Holy cow, I was struck. I'd come over every night and I'd take her out to dinner, and I asked her to marry me in November, and she said no. Just like that. In January I asked her again, and she said no. I went to spring training and I didn't see her for a while. About the middle of the year I asked her again, and she still said no. Three times. I didn't know that all this time she was taking Catholic instruction and became a convert. Her family was Protestant. Unfortunately, it was after I had gone into the Navy when the World Series was over in '42. She came to Norfolk where I was in boot camp and said, "Well, if you still want me . . ." And sure enough, we got married while she was down there. I was in my sailor suit and we had a one-day honeymoon. We got married in June, and in March of the next year, just three days after our first child was born, I got shipped overseas.

Phil Rizzuto
AP Photo.

In 1950, I won the MVP Award. I couldn't believe it. I never thought I'd get it. I mean, with guys like DiMag and Williams and Yogi was having his great years then. When you got to be a Yankee, the pinstripes meant so much then. It was something to live up to and live for, and once you got in the habit of winning, that's one reason they won so many times. A lot of clubs never experience the thrill of winning a World Series. I mean, to us it was almost automatic. You figure, in my 13 years, only three times we didn't get in the World Series. I played in nine World Series, and the tenth I would've played in but that was the year they released me on the last day of August 1956. In my late years, Casey had all the kids—Mantle, Martin, McDougald—and he wanted to get rid of all the veteran ballplayers.

Lennie Merullo

A native of East Boston, Leonard Richard "Lennie" Merullo was the ninth of twelve children of Italian immigrants. His outstanding prep school performance in baseball earned him a scholarship to Villanova University, where he was captain of the baseball team. He became ineligible to play during his senior year after signing with the Chicago Cubs.

Exempt from military service during World War II due to color blindness, Merullo made his debut as a late-season call-up in 1941 and was then a Cubs shortstop through 1947, when a back injury forced him to retire at the age of thirty. In six-plus seasons, he hit .240 in 639 games. On September 13, 1942, in the second game of a doubleheader in Boston, Merullo set a major-league record. It was the day his first child had been born, and after playing the entire first game on little sleep, the Cubs shortstop made four errors in one inning, booting two grounders and then making errant throws on both. As a result, Len Jr. would forever be known as "Boots."

Merullo also enjoyed a long and successful career as a scout, working for the Cubs from 1950 to 1972 before joining the Major League Baseball Scouting Bureau. He retired in 2003, ending a 64-year career in professional baseball. In 2006 the Boston chapter of the Baseball Writers Association of America presented him with the Judge Emil Fuchs Memorial Award for his contributions to baseball.

As part of the events celebrating the 100th anniversary of Wrigley Field in 2014, Merullo, who at the time was only three years younger than the ballpark, was honored by the team on June 7. He threw out the ceremonial first pitch and led the crowd in singing "Take Me Out to the Ball Game" during the seventh-inning stretch. At the time of his death on May 30, 2015, at age ninety-eight, he was the last living Cubs player from the 1945 World Series.

Merullo's son, Len Jr., aka "Boots," played in the Pirates minor league system for three years, and his grandson, Matt, had a six-year major-league career with three teams, mainly as a catcher.

* * *

My parents, Carmine and Angelina, were born in the same village outside Naples, in the province of Avellino. Three brothers married three sisters. My father came to this country to work on the Canadian Railroad. He made three trips, and after the third trip he married my mother and brought her over.

They settled on Franklin Street in East Boston with his brother, then my father bought a house on Byron Street, and that's where we were all born and raised. There were nine sons and three daughters. I was very proud to be the son of Italian parents. People had respect for you if you came from a good, hard-working family.

I started playing baseball from the day I knew what the game was all about. We played in the streets; we played all the time. Whatever was in season: football, basketball, hockey. My mother could never understand how we could spend so much time playing; she thought we were wasting our time. But we never got out there until our chores were done.

Every kid wanted to be a professional ballplayer. Any kid that had a glove on his hand, that's what he wanted to do. My parents didn't understand at the beginning. They didn't understand baseball because we didn't have the heroic ballplayers then. DiMaggio was just breaking in at the same time I was. I used to go out and talk to groups—Kiwanis, Rotary, gatherings like that—when they couldn't get a big name. I loved to tell that story about growing up. My mother never could understand how you could spend so much time playing ball. She'd have jobs for us; go with the milkman, delivering bread, things like that. But we always found time to play and she could never understand. But when I got a scholarship . . . .

Ralph Wheeler, sports editor of the local paper, saw me play in high school. I was a fifteen-year-old senior, captain of the ballclub. Back in those days they'd give you a promotion to get through high school early and go to work. I was taking the commercial course because I didn't want to work in a factory; I wanted a job where you go to work in a white shirt. He told me he was going to come to the house to talk about a scholarship. I said, "Please don't; they'll throw you out of the house." They had no plan for me to go to school.

I was one of those lucky boys who was able to get a college education because of baseball. I got a scholarship to St. John's Prep, and then I went to Villanova University. I came to an agreement with the Cubs my senior year, so I was ruled ineligible to play my senior year. After my first year in baseball I went to Boston College and got my BS in Education.

My father didn't have time to enjoy the game until myself and my brother Manny played college baseball—he was captain at Holy Cross—and the coming of more Italian players. He became a great fan of Joe DiMaggio, Phil Cavarretta, Crosetti, Lazzeri, later Malzone and Petrocelli. It was great to watch him enjoying the game with excitement for the Italian players.

When they took me out to Chicago my senior year at Villanova and I met Mr. Wrigley, he said, "You've got a fine future in baseball." They paid for my ticket, but he told me not to tell anybody. That's the way they did things in those days. And he said, "Now, you promise me before you accept this check, you go back to school and come back to me in June and I'll have another check for you." It was a $1,500 check, more money than I'd ever seen in my life. Then, before they put me on the train, they bought me an overcoat, a hat, and a pair of shoes, and put me on the train back home.

When I got home I just threw the check on the table. They didn't know what it was; they couldn't read or write. My older brother picked it up and read it to them. He said it was a check for $1,500 from baseball. From that day on my mother kicked the others out of the house: "Get out and play ball!"

My first full year with the Cubs was with Tulsa, Oklahoma, in the Texas League. We had a good young team, plus Dizzy Dean. He was fresh out of the big leagues. That was 1940. The next year I was at Los Angeles, the Cubs Triple-A club.

When I joined the Cubs I roomed with Phil Cavarretta. We were two Italian kids about the same age and we got along great. Our teammates called me and Cavarretta "the grand opera twins." Of course, he lived in Chicago so it was only on the road that we roomed together. To Phil, I was known as "Moose," for Mussolini. That didn't bother me at all. The only thing that would bother you was if somebody called you a "guinea." This is what I understood from the players that came from California. If you called them "guinea" out there, it didn't bother them. If you called them a "dago," that bothered the hell out of them. Other players called me "daig," never "dago." It was not downgrading if it came from a person you knew and had respect for. "Hey, "Daig," how you doing?"

I called him Buck, which was short for *baccalá*. If he'd be at the plate and start to come out of his crouch, I'd yell from the bench, "Come on, Buck," and that would mean "stay down." If I wasn't watching and he didn't get a good piece of the ball, I'd get hell when he got back to the bench: "You weren't watching."

I had a little confrontation with Jackie Robinson. He was on second one day and we put on a pickoff play, and it worked. When he slid into the bag his leg hit me on the shoulder. My reaction was to tag him a second time, harder. He got up and started to come at me. He was big, a football player, and he looked at me as if to say, "I could take you." But Branch Rickey had told him he had to control himself, so he just turned around and walked off the field. I admired him for that. I wasn't like a lot of southern players that had animosity toward him. I could see the torment he was going through. It seemed like everybody was pulling against him and it shouldn't have been that way.

Lennie Merullo
National Baseball Hall of Fame and Museum.

My wife gave birth to our son Len Jr. ("Boots") the day I went out and set the major-league record for most errors in one inning, September 13, 1942. One of the Chicago writers had a headline: "'Boots' is born, Merullo boots four." That's my claim to fame.

When I got through, I had a good opportunity to go with the Prince Macaroni Company. I got to know the owner through baseball. I did a favor for him once when he couldn't get a room in New York. I heard him talking Italian to the bell captain. I gave up my room to him and shared a room with Peanuts Lowrey. He never forgot it. We got to be good friends and he offered me a job. But the Cubs told me they needed a scout in New England, and that's how I got started. I'm still doing it. I'm working for the Major League Scouting Bureau as an area scout for New England. I *should* be retiring.

I've enjoyed every minute of my career, and I'm still learning. My gosh, baseball has been my life. It's meant so much to me. I've traveled everywhere. The most important thing I've got out of baseball is the relationships with so many friends. I'm a people person.

Yogi Berra

*B*orn in the Italian "Hill" section of St. Louis to immigrant parents, Lawrence Peter "Yogi" Berra was an unlikely candidate for baseball immortality. At 5-foot-7, 185-pounds, he was both short and ungainly. Even Cardinals general manager Branch Rickey, one of the most astute judges of baseball talent, thought Berra was too slow and clumsy to be a big leaguer. But Yogi confounded the skeptics by having one of the greatest careers in baseball history.

Following service in World War II, in which he was a gunner on a rocket ship during the D-Day invasion of Normandy, he made his major league debut in 1946. In his 18 years with the Yankees, he won three MVP Awards and a record ten World Series rings, holds numerous Series batting records, was an All-Star for 15 consecutive years, had his uniform number 8 retired by the Yankees, and was honored with a plaque in Yankee Stadium's Monument Park. He also led both the Yankees and Mets to the World Series as a manager, and was inducted into the Hall of Fame in 1972.

Like Joe DiMaggio, Berra transcended baseball to become a cultural icon. For a half century he was a highly visible part of American popular culture, as a television spokesperson for various products, as the namesake of the cartoon character Yogi Bear, and as one of the most frequently-quoted American personalities. Thanks to his visibility, his unintentionally witty sayings, known as "Yogi-isms," and his unassuming and endearing manner, he became one of America's most beloved figures. In his eulogy of Berra in 2015, former Yankees manager Joe Torre said of his friend, "He was so good and so honest and so real and so human." Those in baseball knew him as a man with an exceptionally keen baseball mind. Hall of Famer Craig Biggio, who played for the Houston Astros when Berra was a coach, told me, "He's the smartest baseball man I've ever been around."

His son, Dale, was a major league infielder for 11 years (1977–87) with the Pirates, Yankees, and Astros.

The Yogi Berra Museum and Learning Center, located on the campus of Montclair State University in New Jersey, both perpetuates Berra's legacy and provides sports-based educational and public programs for K-12 schoolchildren.

* * *

My dad came over first, then my mother and my two brothers. I had two brothers born in Italy: Tony and Mike. My father didn't know anything about baseball. He liked soccer; he was from the old country. He wanted me to go to work, get a job. My brothers made my father change his mind. My mother didn't have anything to say about it. My oldest brother was the best one of all of us, but he had to go to work.

We called our neighborhood "The Hill." Others called it "Dago Hill," but we never found that offensive. We would use terms like "low-class dago," "high-class dago," but that was among ourselves because we all lived there. We were very close-knit. If someone else said "dago," it might bother me; it all depends on how he says it.

We played whatever was in season. I played a lot of soccer. But a lot of the kids on "The Hill" played baseball. Soccer was played in the winter; baseball was played in the summer. I used to play softball in the morning, then baseball in the afternoon. We also went to the YMCA. I followed baseball pretty good. I used to listen to it a lot on the radio. I thought it was a good game. I knew about Joe DiMaggio and Tony Lazzeri from reading the paper. I used to like the Cardinals and Browns. I used to go watch in the "Knothole Gang" section. Joe Medwick was my idol. I think it was 1934; the Browns won. I don't think we had an Italian player on the Browns. Maybe Frank Crespi and Oscar Melillo, the shortstop.

Yogi Berra
AP Photo.

I enjoyed playing baseball, and they said you could make a living at it if you are good enough. I probably started thinking about playing it professionally when I played American Legion ball, when I was like fourteen, fifteen. See, we had our own clubs up on "The Hill" in St. Louis. We formed them ourselves and we paid dues. I played with the Stags A.C. We had about twenty members in our club and they were all Italians. Then you had the Nightingales, you had the Wildcats, the Panthers, and we played against each other. That started when my older brother was in a club called the Hawks. I used to watch my big brother; he played against Satchel Paige.

When I got to the Yankees, the other Italians treated me very good. I don't know if it was because I was Italian. We didn't talk about that much. We never used the term *dago* when I was there. I didn't relate to the Italians in a way that was different than with the other players. I just worried about playing ball. We were all ballplayers who were happy to be in the big leagues. It's the best game in the world, baseball. You get to go out there for three hours and make that kind of money. It was fun; I enjoyed baseball. I got to meet a lot of people, all different kinds of nationalities; they were all nice.

I feel proud to be an Italian. In about '50, '51 they wouldn't let me into a country club in New Jersey. They didn't like Italians then. I went to an Italian club; I got in there real quick.

Johnny Antonelli

*J*ohnny Antonelli was one of baseball's first "bonus babies." The Bonus Rule, which went into effect in 1947, was designed to prevent wealthier teams from signing all the top prospects and stockpiling them in the minors. On June 29, 1948, the eighteen-year-old phenom, fresh out of high school in Rochester, New York, was signed by the Boston Braves for a bonus reported by various sources to be between $52,000 and $75,000. Whatever the actual amount, it eclipsed the salaries of all other Braves players.

On July 4, five days after signing, Antonelli made his major-league debut but would appear in only three more games the entire season. The pennant-bound Braves, with Johnny Sain and Warren Spahn anchoring their staff, had little need for the untested youngster. He continued to languish on the bench for the next two years, making 42 appearances. It wasn't until 1951, when he was drafted into the Army, that he was able to get consistent work by pitching for his post team at Fort Myer, Virginia.

Traded to the New York Giants in 1954, the twenty-four-year-old southpaw suddenly flourished. He posted the best record of his career that season, winning 21 and losing 7, leading the league in ERA and shutouts, making the first of five All-Star teams, finishing third in the MVP vote, and winning The Sporting News Pitcher of the Year Award. In the stunning Giants sweep over the Indians, who had won a then AL record 111 games, Antonelli pitched a complete-game, 3–1 win in the second game, then notched a save in the Game 4 clincher. After the Series, he received a hero's welcome in his hometown as well as a new car from the Italian American Businessmen's Association.

He won 20 games in 1956, beginning a string of four straight All-Star appearances, and averaged 17 wins in his first six seasons with the Giants. Antonelli split the 1961 season between the Indians and Braves, then decided to retire when he was sold to the Mets. In his 12-year career he compiled a record of 126–110 with an ERA of 3.34. Between 1969 and 1974, he managed at the Double- and Triple-A levels in the Mets minor-league system.

* * *

I was born in Rochester, New York, April 12, 1930. My father was born in Casalbordino, the province of Chieti in the Abruzzi region. He came over in 1913. His father was the first immigrant from their hometown in Italy.

My mother was born in Buffalo, New York, of Italian parentage, of course. Her father and mother were both born in Italy. The only time my father and mother spoke Italian was when they didn't want us to understand. My mother didn't speak Italian, but my father taught her. He spoke perfect English. You'd think he was born in this country. He never had an accent whatsoever. He was a foreman on the New York Central Railroad and an engineer before he went into business for himself as a railroad contractor. In fact, his father was brought here from Italy to be a foreman on the New York Central. If you had a factory and you needed a siding, my father would switch into the main line and bring the track right to your loading dock. I worked with him myself when I was younger.

My father was a baseball fan. He never played baseball but he would go to spring training every year when the Braves were in Bradenton. When I started playing in Rochester he'd bring my writings to Florida, and that's how I got involved with playing this game of baseball. Had it not been for him I probably never would've made it to the major leagues. He really pushed me and got me what I've got today.

In those days if you received, I think it was more than $5,000, you were called a bonus player. To protect from everyone going to the Yankees or other teams with money, they had to limit how many players you could sign. I was one of the fortunate people to have received the money. I think '47 was the first year because Robin Roberts and Curt Simmons both signed in '47 and I signed in 1948 when I was eighteen.

It was exciting because I was flown in by Lou Perini, the owner at that time. He had a Beechcraft twin-engine airplane, and he took my father and I and brought us into Boston. The first night we went right to the ballpark and, of course, they were fighting for the pennant. I saw 38,000 people in the stands and I thought that was all the people in the world. I'd never really been out of Rochester so consequently I was very impressed.

The only resentment about the bonus signing was never against me. Johnny Sain came up to me at the fiftieth anniversary of the '48 Braves and said, "I want to make something clear. I never said a thing against you nor was I ever against you for receiving the money. My only problem was I wanted a raise and they wouldn't give it to me, and they gave you the money, so I want to thank you for getting my raise." Spahn was the same way. They weren't paying big money in those days.

It was a big disappointment when I got traded to the Giants in '54 for Bobby Thomson because I felt the Milwaukee team was really going to go somewhere. We had a great team in '53 and we probably could have or should have won it, but you knew there were good things to come. Nobody knew about Aaron up to that time. That's why they traded for Bobby Thomson. Then a fellow by the name of Hank Aaron, who was playing second base somewhere in the minor leagues, came to Milwaukee. Bobby Thomson broke his ankle that year and never really played for the Braves, then he came back to New York and we became very good friends and roommates.

Everyone asks me what was the most exciting thing in baseball. I say 1954, and I'll tell you why. When you're growing up and you're in baseball, you want to be on an All-Star team; I was chosen that year. You want to win 20; I won 20. You want to be in a World Series; I was in a World Series. You want to win a World Series; I won a World Series. You also want to become pitcher of the year, and before they had the Cy Young Award, they had *The Sporting News* Pitcher of the Year Award, and I won that. So really I did everything that a lot of pitchers, even Bob Feller, never accomplished in one year. He was a great pitcher, we know that, but he never won a World Series game. So I was very thrilled with that.

Sal Maglie won 14 games that year. I don't really know why he started the first game in the World Series except that he was a seasoned general, so to speak, on our pitching staff. I may have been what they considered the ace of the staff that year, but I think Leo Durocher, who played a lot of hunches, wanted to start Sal. I couldn't disagree with him. He had beaten the Dodgers that year, I think, eight times, so we saved him for those people. He was used to pitching important ballgames.

Sal was a good friend. When he pitched in Milwaukee he had a favorite restaurant, which was a Chinese restaurant on the second floor. I only remember that because I was twenty-three or twenty-four and, of course, I didn't drink. But he, after pitching, would enjoy a few martinis. He let me taste one once, and I told him, "You know what, Sal, that's like Aqua Velva aftershave lotion."

But anyway, he was a great guy. You wouldn't meet a nicer person than Sal Maglie. On the field he was "The Barber." He taught me to pitch with a little aggressiveness. You can't let them walk over you. He only knew one way; shave them back, then throw that curveball low and away. And he did it on a regular basis. He didn't wait until somebody hit a home run off of him. He did it because that's how he pitched.

He was from Niagara Falls, which was only about ninety miles from us. If they had a banquet, I would go there; if we had a banquet in Rochester, he would come there. We always got together. In fact, we lived, for two years, in New York in the same complex. So we were pretty close. I called him Sal, and he called me John.

I didn't really get a nickname. I got the name "Lefty" for a while, but all lefthanders get that name. In New York the writers called me "Anty" for whatever reason. They just shortened the name a little bit. The *Mirror* and the *Post* were small papers, very narrow, and to write Antonelli across there would be something else. So they called me "Anty."

I think Italians, like all nationalities, seek each other out. It's kind of an unwritten law or whatever. We do get along pretty well. They would call me "Daigs" or "Dago," but coming from them, it wasn't a slur. Joe Amalfitano was my roommate. He came up with the Giants, another bonus player. Of course, Tom Lasorda, a good friend of mine. He was really a devout Italian. In fact, he's a devout Abruzzese; it's unbelievable. There were others. Sibby Sisti. We had Phil Masi on our team, the Braves. He was our catcher. He caught doubleheaders, day after night games. He was never tired and he always did a great job. I once asked him after he caught, say, 146 games, "What was the best salary you ever received?" He said, "I got $8,500 one year."

Baseball meant everything to me. I met my wife; we've been married fifty years. We had our family: four children, ten grandchildren. I was able to get

Johnny Antonelli
*National Baseball Hall
of Fame and Museum.*

into business because of baseball. I became a Firestone dealer in the Rochester area in 1954. The players would say, "You're lucky, you've got a business." I said, "What do you do when you go home?" "Oh, I go hunting and fishing." I said, "Well, I go home and change tires." We worked hard at it and we did grow a pretty good-sized business. We had twenty-eight stores. We never made a lot of money, but we were comfortable. Without baseball, I don't know what I would have achieved in life.

1950–59

Tommy Lasorda

*T*homas Charles "Tommy" Lasorda was never one to hide his feelings. His passion for the Dodgers was such that he was said to bleed Dodgers blue. He was no less open about his pride in his Italian heritage. Prior to Italy's game against the heavily favored Venezuela squad in the inaugural World Baseball Classic in 2006, the seventy-eight-year-old former manager addressed the team in the locker room. Appealing to the players' sense of pride in their heritage, he said, "Each and every one of you has that Italian blood. Italy gave me the greatest gift that any man can ever receive; Italy gave me my father. I want to give something back to Italy today: a victory."

It was a moment that captured the essence of the man, combining his showmanship, his ability to motivate, his love of baseball, and his devotion to his Italian roots. He addressed the Italian squad as underdogs, a role he was familiar with all his life. The son of an Italian immigrant who drove a truck in a sand quarry and an Italian American mother, Lasorda, along with his three brothers, grew up poor in Norristown, Pennsylvania, with few, if any, prospects for a better future. With a combination of street smarts, competitiveness, humor, and bravura, he willed himself to unimaginable success.

After eight seasons in the minors, the left-handed pitcher compiled a major-league record of 0–4 in 26 games over three seasons (1954–56) with the Brooklyn Dodgers and Kansas City Athletics. Beginning in 1965, he spent eight years managing in the minors before becoming the Dodgers third-base coach in 1973. He succeeded Walter Alston as manager for the final four games in 1976 and went on to lead the team for the next 20 years, winning four pennants and two World Series. When he retired in 1996, only Connie Mack, John McGraw, and Alston had managed one team for more years, and only Casey Stengel had managed in more postseason games. Lasorda was lauded by some and criticized by others for his habit of showing his emotions so openly, including hugging his players on the field.

In 1997, he was elected to the Hall of Fame by the Veterans Committee, and in 2000 he managed the USA team to a gold medal in the Olympics. His fame increased after his managerial career ended as he became one of the most recognizable and popular ambassadors the game has ever had.

* * *

My father was born in Tollo, Abruzzo, and came to Pennsylvania after serving in the Italian Army in World War I. He met my mother in the United States. She was American born but also of Abruzzese origin. My motto is, "I'd walk a mile to shake the hand of an Italian, but I'd crawl two miles to hug an Abruzzese."

As far back as I can remember I wanted to be a major-league ballplayer. My father drove a truck in a sand quarry. He was thinking we had to go out and work to help support the family, but he also wanted me to go to school. I was supposed to clean the house on Saturday morning, but I'd sneak out and play ball all day at the local park. When I'd come home, my father would whack me because I hadn't done my chores. He said, "I want you to go to school. I'll work two jobs to help you do that." But all I wanted to do was play baseball.

In high school I made the varsity, but the coach said I had to have baseball shoes. My father didn't know what the hell the varsity was, and he said he could barely afford regular shoes and he wasn't going to buy me baseball shoes. I cried, and the next day when I came home from school, there was a box on the table. It was a pair of baseball shoes with yellow laces. They were three sizes too big. My dad said he wasn't going to buy another pair in a year, so I had to pack them with cotton.

Growing up was different than playing baseball. In baseball they didn't care what you were. They didn't worry about a guy being Italian, or a guy being Polish, or anything like that. But associating with people, that's when it was really tough. Where I grew up, in the East End of Norristown, we were all Italians, practically everybody in that entire area were Italians. But the people in the West End, they were prejudiced. They didn't like Italians, and they weren't even going to associate with Italians. We'd go to dances and the girls wouldn't even dance with us because we were Italian. So it wasn't easy. When you went to Catholic schools it was different, but if you went to a public school some of the teachers didn't like Italians. I played on a team when I was in high school, and I think the coach didn't like Italians.

See, when we were growing up the Italian people were jealous of each other. If some Italian family did good, other Italians resented it. In that town, boy, if you made good, they resented you. But today it's different; we stick together. We see a guy do good, we're proud. We're proud when we see Italians do good in any field, politics, anything. There's so many good doctors, so many good politicians, everything, and it's helped to make this country strong.

There were some people in town who changed their names. Some of them did it when they came over because a lot of times the immigration people misjudged their names, and they wrote what they thought it was. And that was the name they had to stand by. But there were a few people who changed their names because they didn't think they could get in anything, which was true. They couldn't speak the language, they took the dirty jobs. They would make the sacrifice, but they were making it for their families. They knew their children could grow up to be anything they wanted to be. So they took the slop jobs, they did anything to survive, to be able to raise the family.

But we had all the pride in the world in our name. Our name meant something to us. Our name was gold as far as we were concerned. So why would we change our name if we loved our father's and mother's heritage?

I knew every big leaguer when I was growing up, but Joe DiMaggio was my hero. He was our hero; he was everything we Italians wanted to be. I think Italian players learn from day one to always be at your best, do the best you can with anything you undertake in life. I think that's one of the top ingredients that our fathers and forefathers poured into us. They showed us what it's like to have pride; they are proud people. I think that alone was why you saw Joe DiMaggio and all those great Italian players do good, that driving feeling they had about making it.

Tommy Lasorda
*National Baseball Hall
of Fame and Museum.*

I didn't go to college, but I got six honorary doctorate degrees. I didn't go to college, but I have a hospital named after me, the Tommy Lasorda Heart Institute. I didn't go to college, but I had an asteroid named after me. I didn't go to college, but I have baseball fields named after me. I didn't go to college, but I got a big job with the Dodgers. I spoke to many, many groups of people that had gone to college, graduated college, but they would be sitting there listening to me. It's really amazing when you stop and think about those people listening to *me*. I've spoken where there were fifteen, eighteen generals in the room. They came up and wanted to take a picture with me. I spoke to thirty-seven United States senators in the VIP room; they wanted to take a picture with me. You look at your life and all that has rolled by, it's great, unbelievable. I only wish my brothers could have lived like I did. They worked hard; they were great guys.

Joey Amalfitano

*B*y the time John Joseph "Joey" Amalfitano was signed by the Giants in 1954, the bonus rule required that "bonus babies" be kept on the twenty-five-man roster for two full seasons. Not surprisingly, the twenty-year-old infielder from San Pedro, California, spent most of that time warming the bench, with 25 at-bats in 45 games. In his rookie year, he roomed with Johnny Antonelli, the Braves' "bonus baby" of 1948 who had just been traded to the Giants.

Following his two-year initiation, Amalfitano spent four seasons in the minors before returning to the big leagues in 1960, when the Giants were in San Francisco. That proved to be his best offensive year in the big leagues with a .277 average in 106 games. Over his 10-year career (1954–55, 1960–67) with the Giants, Houston Colt .45s, and Cubs, the utility infielder compiled a .244 average in 643 games.

As it turned out, Amalfitano's major-league career was just getting started. Between 1967 and 1977 he coached for the Cubs, Giants, and Padres. In 1978 he returned to the Cubs coaching staff, served as interim manager for the final seven games in 1979, then took over as manager 91 games into the 1980 season. He managed again in 1981 but was let go after the Cubs finished last and next to last in the strike-shortened split season. After coaching for the Reds in 1982, he began a 16-year stretch as the Dodgers' third base coach, the first 14 with Tommy Lasorda as manager. Ending his long tenure as a big league coach in 1998, he then moved into various front-office positions with the Dodgers and Giants.

* * *

I grew up in Southern California. Up until I was five I spoke nothing but Italian. Then they threw me in school and I forgot it, but I could understand it. I have to think about it too much to say it in a conversation. When Tommy Lasorda was here, that was fun because he'd just yell out the signs to me in the coach's box in Italian; hit and run, steal, whatever he wanted. He'd laugh like hell. If he wanted to repeat a sign, he'd say, *un'altra volta* (one more time). We had some fun. Now you talk about a guy with his heritage; he's a guy that wears it very, very proudly. Oh my God!

I was a Yankee fan because of DiMaggio. I became aware of him growing up, and I used to listen to games being recreated at the time in California. As a youngster, I went up to Wrigley Field in Los Angeles. The Yankees played an exhibition game and I went to watch DiMaggio in particular. I can remember like it was yesterday. I took the red car, which was a streetcar, with a relative who was a baseball fan. He was from the old country and his name was Tony Amalfitano. Luckily I got to see Joe get two hits; he went 2-for-4 with a home run. Then I got to meet him. I consider us to be on a first-name basis, and we're sort of friends. We had lunch together, and I've spoken to him on the phone a few times.

As a player I wasn't a household name, but if there is recognition, it's because of the length of time I've been in the business. I've been in it a long time and more of my recognition came after I played. I managed for a couple of years, but I didn't get too much notoriety there. But as a coach, I think I've probably received some because of the longevity. Frank Crosetti was Italian and he coached the Yankees for many years. As far as length of service on the lines, I've gone by him, which is important to me because I knew who he was. I know all the Italians. I never knew Lazzeri, but I read about him.

Johnny Antonelli was my roommate my first year, and Sal Maglie looked out for me like a father. He took me under his wing and nobody messed with me. The veterans tried to play a few practical jokes on me, but he put them straight right away. I was very protected by him. They sized me up. I got there because of a rule, not my ability, because I received over X amount of dollars as a youngster, so I had to stay on the twenty-five-man roster. Nobody warmed up to me right away because here's a new kid that got this money and he's not proven. I mean, what did I ever do? So they watched me closely. I paid attention and, Lord knows, I didn't have an ego. I think Sal saw what I was about and he took a liking to me and I was very fortunate. And Antonelli, he chose me as a roommate. He was a bonus player and he went through quite a lot more than I did.

It was a nice foundation for me because I was young and inexperienced, and I got to go to all these major-league cities with a major-league ball team. I never played because I wasn't ready to play, and I could've had just one heck of a nice time away from the field, just go goofy. I didn't do that. I think my sense of values and the way my parents raised me were in place. I truly enjoy the game or else I wouldn't be in it as long as I have now. I respect it and feel it's done an awful lot for me, and by the same token, to be honest with you, I think I've done something for it.

It's a little different today. The players are very talented and I don't think playing the game is any easier. It's still a difficult game, but I think they make it more pleasant for them. They are catered to, and rightfully so; they are in the entertainment business. I think because of the way the industry is today that

Joey Amalfitano
National Baseball Hall of Fame and Museum.

the player has a great deal more protection because of the Players Association. It's a union, and when you have a union, it protects its members. Those years when I first started, talking about Maglie and Antonelli, that's a different era in that the association wasn't as strong as it is today. It started when I first came along in '54, but it was nowhere near where it is today. I'd heard of strikes on the docks by the longshoremen or the cannery workers or fishermen. I never thought that would happen in this industry; it's happened not once but several times, which is sad, in my opinion, because it doesn't separate us. I thought this game was always something special. It's still special, but it's been tarnished. I've got some friends I grew up with and we meet every Saturday morning and we go to breakfast. San Pedro's kind of a blue-collar town and those guys are still scarred by what happened.

My dad was a commercial fisherman in San Pedro. He was from the island of Ischia, near Naples. He owned his own boat and, by the way, he was a Hall of Famer. You know like Ted Williams and those guys could hit .300? My father hit .300 every year. He drove in a lot of runs too. He didn't want me to go fishing, but I finally got an opportunity when a deck hand got injured. And when I did go and had a chance to play baseball on Saturday and Sunday as an amateur, no matter where he was he would bring the boat in so I could play. He'd wait, and then I'd go back out. He realized that I was very interested in baseball.

When I signed my contract, it's a very interesting story. He was working on the engine of his boat. The two scouts from the New York Giants, Evo Pusich and Dutch Reuther, came to the house and I'm going to sign this contract. But I'm a minor and I have to have my mother and father sign it. So I went down and brought him home. My dad spoke broken English; his name was Frank, Francesco. We sat there and he didn't ask how much it was, nothing. Then he said in Italian, "Is this what you want to do?" I said, "Yeah, this is what I want to do." So he signed it. Then the three of them had a little glass of wine; I didn't get any. Then I took him back down to the boat, and this is the best part about it. He asked me, "How much money did you sign for?" I told him, "$35,000." He looked at me and said, in Italian, "Isn't this a great country?"

Ken Aspromonte

O *ne of many future major leaguers who grew up playing baseball on the*
famed Parade Grounds in Brooklyn, Ken Aspromonte was an infielder who
played for the Red Sox, Senators, Indians, Angels, Braves, and Cubs. In
his seven-year career between 1957 and 1963, he hit .249 with 19 homers and
124 RBIs. He then spent three years (1964–66) playing in Japan for the Chunichi
Dragons and the Taiyo Whales. From 1972 to 1974 he managed the Cleveland
Indians, compiling a record of 220–260.

His brother, Bob, was a major-league infielder who played for the Dodgers,
Astros, Braves, and Mets. Over the course of a 13-year career between 1956 and
1971, he hit .252 with 60 home runs and 457 RBIs.

Ken became very active in the National Italian American Foundation, serving
as executive vice president, a member of the Board of Directors, and as regional vice
president for the Southwest.

Here he reminisces about an unusual batting tip he got from Hall of Famer Ted
Williams, playing against the all-time Japanese home run king Sadaharu Oh, and
a brawl in which players of the two opposing teams fought together against unruly
fans at a ten-cent beer night.

* * *

My grandparents came from Calabria and Basilicata in the southern part of
Italy in the late nineteenth century. They lived in New York City and eventually
moved to Brooklyn, where my mother and father were born. They died when I
was about ten or twelve years old. My mother didn't speak Italian with us; she
only spoke Italian when she was talking to her mother and father.

Brooklyn had close to a million and a half people; about half were Italian
Americans and the rest were primarily Jewish. Then the Hispanics came along,
and now there are Chinese people in Brooklyn. So we had Italian Americans
in our high schools and we played against each other for many years. Joe Torre
and his brother, Frank, played against us. Then we went to Long Island and
played against Whitey Ford. I even played against Mario Cuomo in what they
called the Queens Alliance League, a league with much better players than what
I was facing with the Brooklyn Royals. We were just seventeen years old at the
time. In my high school, Lafayette, we had a number of major-league ballplayers.
The greatest one, of course, was Sandy Koufax. It was just a great school.

The Parade Grounds in Brooklyn was our Ebbets Field. We had to get up at five o'clock in the morning to get the Number 1 field, which was a caged diamond. We had a great ballclub called the Brooklyn Royals, a neighborhood team not affiliated with any league. My brother Bob and I owe our major-league careers to Gabriel Verde, an individual that held a large group of teenagers together for five years to play over one hundred baseball games a year. I think my brother and I were the only ones that went to the major leagues, but there were a lot of minor leaguers that didn't make it. I played with them from about fifteen to seventeen. That's what really made us pretty good ballplayers, because we were playing three or four times a week. We were in Bensonhurst, and we played clubs in Williamsburg and Park Slope, then we went to Long Island and New Jersey. Everybody wanted to play us. This was after the high school season, which was only 20 to 25 games.

Then I signed a contract and went to the Red Sox. I don't know where Sandy's first contract was. At school he couldn't hit a ball to save his life. He threw the ball very well, but he couldn't throw a ball in the ballpark for a while. Then the Dodgers signed him, and after about six or seven years of banging around in the minors he just found the right rhythm, and he was unbeatable.

My father was out there helping us all the way through, and he was just a good, hard-working individual who loved sports, and he drove us around to all the games. When I got the contract from the Red Sox, he was thrilled about that. Bob got his contract with the Brooklyn Dodgers, and part of the contract was that he would stay with the Dodgers for about two months. So he was an original Brooklyn Dodger, with Jackie Robinson and Pee Wee Reese. Then he went on to the minor leagues. My older brother, Charles, played minor-league ball, I think with the Yankee chain, and he left after three or four years. He decided he wasn't going to make it, so he went back to school.

I was kind of worried about my big-league debut coming up from the Pacific Coast League in 1957 after leading the league in hitting. I didn't think I got a fair shot with the Red Sox. I guess their catcher got hurt and they needed a catcher. Washington wanted me, and I was really devastated when I got traded within one year. I thought the Red Sox were not up to par with the young guys. They traded away more talent than what they had. You know, when a guy leads the league in hitting you've got to give him at least a year in the big leagues before you make a decision. That's the only thing that bothered me. You work so hard to get to the big leagues with the club you want to play for and you're gone within half a year.

The time I was with them I lockered next to Ted Williams for some reason; I don't know why. We talked a lot and his conversations revolved around hitting all the time, nothing else. He was very much to himself. He didn't participate with most of the guys. He traveled alone and had a very bad temper. But we just seemed to hit it off. When I was traded, he said, "I don't know what kind of ballplayer you're going to be, but I think you should have stayed with us."

I batted second and he batted third. I was in the on-deck circle waiting to hit, and I was looking around at the fans. After we got back to the dugout, he said to me, "Don't you ever do that again. You look at the grass in front of you because the ball will come in to you whiter. Don't ever look at a white shirt, always look at the grass."

I said, "Thanks, Ted, I appreciate that very much."

He knew everything about hitting. "Build up your forearms, don't worry about your chest. You hit the ball with your forearms and your wrist action." And he was a skinny guy; there was no bulk to him. But he knew what to do with that bat. I'm just sorry he had such a tough life outside of baseball. I didn't like what the children did to him. Very sad, very sad.

I played in the years of Mickey Mantle and Roger Maris. Hank Aaron and Warren Spahn were teammates of mine in Milwaukee. I tell you, I played with more superstars than you've got hair on your head; it was a great era. I was just so awed and lucky to put on the same uniform that they did. Mickey used to slide into me and knock me down, then say, "How you doin'?" Roger Maris didn't say much; he just hit home runs. In 1961 I was playing against him all the time. He was like a troubled ballplayer. He just didn't act like a baseball player should act as a superstar. Hank Aaron used to hit home runs like I'd hit singles. Of course, Eddie Mathews was at third base, and we just had a great ballclub. There wasn't a weak link on the whole team.

As for pitchers, Whitey Ford was tough in New York; Jim Bunning was another one that was just terrific. There were a number of pitchers that were hard to hit, hard to pick up. Bob Gibson in the National League. If you stood too close to the plate, he'd knock you down. You had to give him his seventeen inches, otherwise he'd knock you down. He'd throw the hardest sinker on your hands and break your bat. He was a great one. I faced Sandy Koufax when I was with the Chicago Cubs. I'd tell him, "Sandy, just throw me fastballs, don't throw me any curveballs." He'd laugh, then strike me out with a curveball. The ballplayers we had in those days were all great competitors.

Today they're very protective of young pitchers. I managed against Billy Martin. I can remember when he had this youngster with the Texas Rangers, David Clyde. He pitched the kid every third or fourth day. The kid was drawing crowds of 40,000 because he was local. Then all of a sudden, he hurt his arm and he was out of there. The kid wasn't ready for that kind of pitching.

I played in Japan for three years and that was a great time. They paid me more money than I made in the big leagues. I could've stayed longer, but my wife wanted to get back. She said, "Either we take out Japanese citizenship or go home." It was different over there. What really struck me was that there was no violence in their play, none whatsoever. It was like getting a group of guys in New York for a softball game. They had the big pot of tea in their dugout and they'd all bow to one another.

Very seldom you'd see a pitcher throw at anybody. It was always an American pitcher throwing at a Japanese guy. On slides into second base, there's no knocking anybody down. It's just a very calm game and they just honor one another. It's getting a little different now though because the ballplayers get too much instruction from the Americans. We've had American managers over there and they teach these kids a little differently. I don't know if the Japanese want to play as well as the Americans; they just want a good time and enjoy it. If they win, fine; if they lose, fine. There is no animosity toward anybody.

When I was there, hitting was like Double A, pitching was like Triple A. I played against Sadaharu Oh, the Japanese superstar. Boy, he could've played in the big leagues, no doubt in my mind. I asked him about playing in America. He said, "Aspro San,"—they called me Aspro San, Mr. Aspro—"why should I come to your country? I don't speak the language, I don't like your food, and I make $1 million over here. It doesn't make sense for me to go over there. I don't have to prove to you all that I can hit a baseball."

He was absolutely right. This guy hit like 850 home runs, and they weren't pop flies; they were 400, 450 feet, way out of those stadiums. He was a nice guy, a wonderful man.

I had an interpreter, and I learned a little Japanese. But the Japanese the ballplayers taught me was all bad Japanese, a lot of cuss words. I had to watch myself. Every time I had to say something I looked at the interpreter and said, "Is this okay?" It was a great experience and I really loved my time there.

Becoming a manager was more or less an accident. I was home in Washington, DC, when one of the sportscasters, Warner Wolf, was doing a game for the Washington Senators against the Cleveland Indians one night. He called and said, "Kenny, why don't you come up and do the broadcast with me tonight?"

So I gave my commentary about the ballclubs on the air. Lo and behold, it was broadcast back to Cleveland. Hank Peters was the general manager at the time and he called me the next day, and said, "Do you have any interest in coming back into baseball?" I told him I wasn't sure what I wanted to do. I just got back from Japan.

He said, "Look, we have a rookie league down in Florida and we could use you for three months." So I said to my wife, "Let's go to Florida."

I worked with young kids who had just signed out of high school and college. I enjoyed it, and the next year they moved me to Reno, which was Class A. I didn't like the bus rides, but I had a good time. Then I went to Triple A, so I must have opened up some eyes. I stayed there two years, then Gabe Paul called me and said, "It's your time."

I managed the Indians for three years. The minor leagues were good training for me, and I just believe that the managers of today that don't go to the minor leagues are going to have trouble. It's not because they don't know how to play the game, it's how they handle twenty-five personalities. You've got to have some psychology major in you because there are all kinds of thoughts going through these kids' heads and you've got to talk to them. If they don't have that experience, they're going to have trouble, and they usually don't last very long.

Ken Aspromonte
Courtesy of Ken Aspromonte.

I managed against Ted Williams when he was with Washington. We'd talk around the batting cage, and he'd say, "These guys can't hit." My pitching coach was Warren Spahn. He had a difficult time talking to my pitchers with the Cleveland Indians; they weren't as good as he was. He meant well, he tried to help them, but they didn't have the ability he had and he didn't get along with some of them. "Why can't you get the ball over with two strikes? Why can't you get the slider over?"

The greatest challenge to a manager is the front office. The ballplayers will play the game for you; they know what they have to do in the major leagues. It's the front office and the press and the fans that you have to answer to, but mostly it's the general manager and yourself that disagree. Of course, he's your boss, and if he doesn't like you, you don't get your contract renewed. The front office is run by people who are not baseball-oriented. They're mostly business people who are successful. I can't blame them because it's their money, but they don't bend enough. Very rarely do the ballplayers get the manager fired. I was a little bit depressed because I didn't deserve to not be hired again by the Cleveland Indians for the job that I did. But I had a falling out with the general manager and he decided to go with Frank Robinson.

Billy Martin was a great tactician. He knew the game; he just couldn't control his temper. That's what got him into a lot of trouble. And [Yankee owner George] Steinbrenner, whom I knew very well, thought Billy was a good showman and he drew the fans. But the time Billy had it out with Reggie Jackson, that was uncalled for by a manager. It didn't help either one of them. But that's the way he was. We all knew he was going to have a tough time outside baseball.

We got along very well together as Italian Americans. One time I was managing the Indians and he was managing the Rangers and we did what I can only call a stupid promotion in Cleveland. They had a ten-cent beer night. I think it was '74, and I said, "No, you can't do this. You're going to draw 30,000 and they will be drunk in the first inning."

They went ahead and did it, and we had very little security. In the ninth inning they jumped out of the stands in right field and went after Jeff Burroughs. All of a sudden about 100 of them came out and the Texas Rangers started fighting. Then I brought my team out there. We had fifty ballplayers fighting about a thousand hoodlums, and we knocked them down like they were bowling pins, they were so drunk. Then we couldn't get them off the field. The umpires waited about an hour; then I lost a forfeited game. It was just ridiculous. Billy thanked me for helping him out by bringing out my team, and he sent me a bottle of scotch. We were friends before, but after that we were like brothers.

1960–69

Joe Torre

*J*oe Torre is best remembered as the manager who led the Yankees to four World Series wins between 1996 and 2000. But while it was his managerial success that led to his 2014 induction into the Hall of Fame, his outstanding career as a player should not be overlooked. In 1971, he was the NL MVP, leading the league in average, RBIs, hits, and total bases. Over the course of his 18-year career (1960–77) as a catcher, first baseman, and third baseman for the Braves, Cardinals, and Mets, he hit .297 with 252 home runs and 1,185 RBIs, won a Gold Glove, and was a nine-time All-Star.

When the Brooklyn native was signed by the Milwaukee Braves in 1959, his older brother, Frank, who played a significant role in Joe's development as a player, was in his fourth season as a first baseman with the Braves. After five seasons in Milwaukee, he played his final two years (1962–63) with the Phillies.

Before beginning his stint as the Yankees manager in 2006, Torre had managed the Mets, Braves, and Cardinals for a total of 14 seasons between 1977 and 1995, making it to the postseason only in 1982 with the Braves, winners of the NL West division. In his 12 years as manager of the Yankees, the team went to the postseason every year and played in six World Series. He then managed the Los Angeles Dodgers for three years, leading them to the NLCS in his first two years. Twice named NL Manager of the Year by the Associated Press, Torre ranked fifth all-time in wins when he retired in 2010.

The following year, commissioner Bud Selig appointed him Major League Baseball's executive vice president of baseball operations. Also in 2011, Torre was a recipient of the Ellis Island Family Heritage Award, which celebrates the extraordinary achievements of Americans who trace their ancestry through Ellis Island.

* * *

My mother, whose maiden name was Rofrano, was born in Naples. My dad was born in New York. I think his family was from northern Italy. He had blue eyes, the only one in the family with blue eyes. By the time I was ready to play ball, my two older brothers were more of a father to me than my father was. My mom and dad separated when I was about twelve years old.

I guess I was what you'd consider first and a half generation. I grew up in Brooklyn, the youngest of five children. The other four of my brothers and sisters were born in my grandmother's house, so there was more Italian spoken at that time, but when we moved into the house in Brooklyn where I was raised nobody spoke Italian and it's sad. I didn't speak Italian. I certainly would have liked to speak another language and learn more about your past and the family tree. I knew what nationality I was on both sides of the family, but mainly I was American.

I did have a sense of ethnic identity when I was a kid. But I'll never forget; when I asked my mom, "What are we, Neapolitan, Calabrese?" she'd say, "We're American." I sensed that unless you were American you had something to be ashamed of in those days, and it was sad, in retrospect. My mom wanted to Americanize everything because of all the prejudice against Italians. And my dad made her feel inferior because she was born in Italy. He really didn't allow her to be proud of her heritage. I came to find out later that my dad both physically and emotionally abused my mom. Part of it was telling her she came from the other side and she wasn't smart enough. So she was, in essence, American because that's the way everybody would perceive her in a better light, unfortunately.

I'm proud of my heritage; I'm proud of my mom. She came over to this country when she was eight years old. But I don't feel any more closeness to anyone because they're Italian as opposed to anybody else. And I feel fortunate about that because I know the Italians were prejudiced against for a time, as the blacks were and still are in certain circles, and the Jews, obviously. I didn't like any of that. I didn't encounter any of that prejudice as a kid. I was pretty well protected, or naive, whatever you want to call it. I never looked for any prejudice so maybe that's why I never recognized a lot of it if there were subtle things that happened. I grew up not having any prejudice, going to school with blacks, going to school with Jews. Looking back, it's probably the greatest exposure I had as a child.

I'm very proud to be Italian. I've been there a number of times. I went with Rudy LaRusso; he used to be a basketball player, and he was an agent for some basketball players. We started in Rome and went north, and I drove the whole way. We went to Forlí, Bologna, San Marino, Venice, and finished up at Lake Como and Milan. I knew how to say red or white wine and ask for the check, and my wife got a kick of how we would go in and bargain for one thing or another while shopping. That was half the fun. You didn't really care what you spent; it was the bargaining. You know what's funny, you go to an Italian restaurant and you feel like you're in somebody's house. You're just very comfortable. I enjoy Italy; I love the warmth, the sort of organized disorganization.

As a kid I was a Giants fan, which was dangerous growing up in Brooklyn, but I did it anyway, basically because my older brothers and sisters were Giants fans. Willie Mays was my hero. When I was growing up I was aware of Italian ballplayers like DiMaggio and Furillo. Of course, when I was growing up I was also aware of Saul Rogovin and Sandy Koufax, Jewish ballplayers. We were very ethnic in our neighborhood. There were a lot of Italians and a lot of Jews. I didn't like the Dodgers, but Carl Furillo was okay, and I guess the fact he was Italian must've been the reason why. Johnny Antonelli is more a guy I was rooting for because I was a Giants fan, and Sal "The Barber" Maglie, of course. He was mean. He was a favorite for sure when he pitched for the Giants.

My father discouraged my oldest brother Rocco from playing baseball; he wanted him to go to college. He only got involved in baseball because when my brother Frank signed in high school he was too young to sign his own contract. In getting my brother the bonus with the Boston Braves at the time, he got a job as a scout. That was part of the deal. He went on to learn about baseball and became a scout for the Baltimore Orioles also. He was a retired New York City policeman.

I signed with the Braves. The same scout that signed my brother Frank, "Honey" Russell, signed me. I was playing in C ball at Eau Claire and I was being interviewed on the bench and Bob Scheffing, who was one of our coaches, was sitting there. The interviewer asked me, "What are your goals?" I said, "I want to play in the big leagues." And Scheffing said, "No, no, you want to *star* in the big leagues. That's what your goal should be." And that always stuck with me and sort of helped the motivation.

When I had my first full year in the major leagues in 1961, the one guy in spring training who took me under his wing was Billy Martin. He used to call me "Daig," affectionately. He always felt a closeness; I think because we were both Italian. He taught me a lot of baseball. I guess he was the only Italian player I was close to in those days. Of course, he was a lot older than me; I was like twenty, and he was in his thirties, which was a big difference at that time.

I played for the Braves in Milwaukee and Atlanta and I was very immature, probably irresponsible. I know I was irresponsible. It was a very turbulent time I had the last year or so in the Braves organization. I got traded to St. Louis, a very successful franchise that went to two World Series in a row in '67 and '68. You realize you've got to grow up and it was a big influence on my career going to St. Louis and being surrounded by the people who had just come off of two successful years. I became friends with the McCarvers and Maxvills, Bob Gibson, and Lou Brock. I learned how to behave, I learned what competing was about, and I was very thankful for that experience.

The Dodgers boast how family-oriented they are; I have that sense. When we had our first meeting at Dodgertown in Vero Beach, all my coaches were around the table, all the scouts, all the minor league managers, chefs from the town, people in the housekeeping department. I was so taken by that, where everybody was taken to be so important, which to me is the way I like to do things. It made me feel very welcome at that time coming in from another organization. They made me feel not only welcome but that I could help.

Tommy Lasorda did some things that I gave him credit for but at the time I cursed him for. I said, "Tommy, you invented the hug in this game. We had a lot of macho people playing this game and all of a sudden you humanized it." I give him a lot of credit for that because you realize the passion you need, not only to compete in this game but to win. He did that, plus he had his team out there loosening up all together and they used to run as a unit. You really scoff at it as an opposing player or manager, but you certainly understand how necessary it is to have a team help each other along the way.

Baseball has been my whole life. As a youngster it was always something that was being talked about in your family, how much fun it is, fun to watch. All of a sudden you find yourself the kid brother of Frank Torre, who's playing on World Series teams, wondering if it's possible to have two members of

Joe Torre
National Baseball Hall of Fame and Museum.

one family in the major leagues. What are the chances of that, to have an opportunity to be in the big leagues and to really have a very successful career as a player? It was always something you did in your spare time, then you find yourself getting paid to do that. So I feel very fortunate. I never had to look for a job.

I enjoyed the playing, though while I was playing, I didn't enjoy playing as much as looking back on it and knowing how much fun it really was. Everything was work to me. I always felt growing up that I was under a great deal of pressure, which I think comes from our ethnic background. There's such a need to succeed and to accomplish a lot of stuff. I had older brothers who both played baseball ahead of me: Frank professionally, my brother Rocco in school. Everybody pretty much knew what family I belonged to while playing in the sandlots, and I just felt a lot of pressure to live up to whatever it was I had to live up to. So maybe the baseball end of this thing, it was a lot of work, which is what it's supposed to be, but I don't think I enjoyed playing as much as I could have. And I think it was based on the fact that I had low self-esteem, based on probably a lot of abuse that was going on at home. Dad was abusive to my mom, never physically abusive to me, but I think my self-esteem was based on how I did on the baseball field.

Ron Santo

*T*he childhood and adolescence of Ron Santo were anything but idyllic. His father was an abusive alcoholic, his parents divorced when he was six, and he was diagnosed with diabetes at the age of eighteen. Nevertheless, a combination of iron-willed resiliency and natural talent enabled him to overcome these adversities and become one of the greatest players in Chicago Cubs history and a Hall of Fame inductee.

Ronald Edward Santo grew up in the Italian district of Seattle known as "Garlic Gulch." As a senior in high school, he was selected to play for the US All-Stars in the Hearst Sandlot Classic in New York City against a team of New York All-Stars (one of whose players was Joe Torre). Signed out of high school in 1959, a year later, on June 26, 1960, the twenty-year-old third baseman was in the Cubs starting lineup, where he would remain for 14 seasons. Traded to the Chicago White Sox in 1974, Santo retired at the end of that season.

In spite of playing his entire 15-year major-league career while afflicted with diabetes, Santo was a nine-time All-Star and a five-time Gold Glove winner who hit 342 homers and drove in 1,331 runs. He was one of only four players over that span who had 2,000 hits, 300 home runs, and 1,300 RBIs. The public remained unaware of Santo's illness until he revealed the news on "Ron Santo Day" in August 1971, when he began a lifelong commitment to raising funds for the cure of juvenile diabetes.

Following his retirement, Santo became a successful businessman before returning to the Cubs in 1990 as a radio color analyst. Beloved by fans for his unbridled enthusiasm and blatant rooting for the Cubs, he held the job until his death in 2010 at the age of seventy. In 2003, the Cubs retired his uniform number 10, and in 2011 they erected a statue of him outside Wrigley Field. Santo was elected to the Hall of Fame by the Veterans Committee in 2012.

No less impressive than his on-field achievements was the way he responded to a series of health issues that plagued him over the last decade of his life, which included heart surgery, amputation of both legs below the knee, and cancer. We would often speak during those years when the Cubs came to Milwaukee, and I was always impressed by his positive attitude, courage, and self-deprecating sense of humor. There was no hint of self-pity, even in the face of afflictions that would have kept most people at home.

* * *

I grew up in Seattle, Washington. My father, Louie Santo, was born in Foggia, Italy, and came over when he was about sixteen. My mother, Vivian Danielson, was born in Sweden and came over when she was twelve. They met in Seattle. So I'm half Swedish, half Italian, and all American. But I absolutely think of myself as Italian American. My mother, even though she was Swedish, could speak Italian with my dad. But my dad left so early in my life that they never talked in Italian to my sister and me. But I wish they had. Tuesday, Thursday, and Sunday we had spaghetti and gravy; at Christmas, linguine and calamari; tuna fish on Friday because we were Catholic. So we were definitely an Italian family.

My mother and father got divorced when I was six years old. He was an alcoholic and an abusive man. I remember vividly. He owned a couple of taverns, and he was a mean drunk. He'd come home and he'd be pounding the walls and I'd jump on his back. I'll never forget the day he didn't come back and I could finally sleep through the night.

He left when I was six years old. He picked up my sister and I three weekends in a row, then I didn't see him until I was nineteen. In the time I didn't see him, he became a Merchant Marine and traveled around the world. We played a minor-league exhibition game in Tacoma, Washington. I walk into this minor-league clubhouse and there he was. I recognized him. I grabbed him and I walked him outside, and I told him, "Don't you ever, ever come back here again."

Seven or eight years later my uncle called from Seattle and said, "Your dad's dying." I saw him before he died, and I asked him the question, "Why did you leave?" He said, "I was an alcoholic. I loved your mother, but I couldn't help myself."

When I was nine, John Constantino, my stepfather, came into my life. I loved him. He always came out to watch me play and he never criticized me. He was a wonderful man and took very good care of my mother. In 1973, they were killed in a car accident coming down to see me in spring training.

I first thought about playing professionally in high school. Baseball was my first love and I always had aspirations. I played football and basketball and had a couple of scholarships in football. At that time they were looking for a six-foot quarterback that could throw. I remember sitting down with a friend of mine in high school. We talked about what he was going to do, and I said I'm going to try to go into professional baseball early, right out of high school, if they're interested. I'll give it four years, and if I don't make it, I'll go to college. I signed out of high school and went directly to Double-A ball in San Antonio, and in those days that was big.

I didn't get off to a good start. They were going to send me down, but I said to [manager] Grady Hatton, "Give me another week. I know I can play here." And he did. I knew I had a great arm, so I'd let a runner get down the line then fire it. I had a lot of young kids in San Antonio sitting behind the first baseman because they got a lot of balls up there. I think my first year I made something like 35 errors. Grady helped me with that. He taught me that I had more time, and I knew I did, but it was like showing off just letting it go. At the end of the San Antonio season, I was brought up to Triple A to play in the playoffs. Then that winter I got married. I was in Palm Springs for my honeymoon when I get a call from my mother who said the Cubs called and have invited you to spring training as a non-roster player. I was very excited and, in fact, I cut my honeymoon short.

I had a very good spring and Charlie Grimm, the manager, told me the last week that I'd break with the major-league club. Then at the hotel, I got a call from John Holland, the general manager, and I thought I was going to Charlie Grimm's room to sign a major-league contract. When I walked into the room, I knew something was wrong. They had just made a trade with the Dodgers for Don Zimmer. I was so emotional, and I didn't want to cry there, so I said, "I quit. You promised me, Charlie, that I'd make the big leagues. You lied to me." And I walked out the door. I went to my room and called my wife of about two months and said, "I just quit. I'm coming home."

I was packing and there was a knock at the door. It was John Holland. He said, "You can't quit, you're so talented. You'll be in the big leagues before the end of the season for sure. Go down to Triple A and get off to a good start." So he convinced me. I went down and did have a good start. The Cubs were doing horseshit; I mean, they were terrible. They were in a nine-game losing streak. Then on June 24 I got a call to be on a plane in the morning. I played against the Pittsburgh Pirates on the 26th and went 3-for-7 in a doubleheader.

I'll never forget meeting Billy Williams. I was just out of high school and they had a three-week rookie camp for all the best talent. Billy and I became friends. He was very friendly and very nice, and we just kind of hit it off. Rogers Hornsby, who was a minor league hitting instructor, was our batting instructor, which was unbelievable. After three weeks he put everybody on bleacher benches and he stood in front of us. We had thirty guys and he started in the lowest row. Billy and I were in the second row. He told the guys in the first row that nobody would make it above Double A. Now I'm starting to sweat. If he tells me this, it'll kill me. To make a long story short, he gets to Billy and he says, "You can hit in the big leagues right now." And now he comes to me and he goes, "And you can hit in the big leagues." Of all those other guys, he just picked a pitcher. And he was right. Not one other player made it to the big leagues.

Hornsby was great as a coach. The only thing he ever told me was to move back in the batter's box. He told me, "You'll see the curveball better and you have a little more time for that fastball." That was it. No mechanics, no nothing. He talked about stride. The shorter the stride, the quicker the bat. He would put a bat in the batter's box and if you took a stride and stepped on the bat you'd break your ankle. Can you imagine, Rogers Hornsby? I was in awe.

I came up in '60 when we were a second division ballclub. But when Leo [Durocher] came in '66, I don't know what it was, but I just remember going on the field and all of a sudden having respect from other teams. In '66 he said, "We're not an eighth-place team," and we ended up tenth. But the next year we ended up third. That's when we had Kessinger, Beckert, Hundley, Fergie, Ernie Banks, and Billy Williams—three Hall of Famers.

When I got to the big leagues I was only twenty years old. There were only sixteen major league teams. I was in awe and I was just trying to stay. When you get to the big leagues that early in life your only concern is going across those white lines and getting the job done so that you stay. I have to say, though, that after my first year I felt that God had given me a special talent, because baseball was easy for me.

The only thing that happened to me was that I contracted diabetes when I was eighteen years old. I wrote a book about my life, but it was more an inspirational book about growing up with diabetes. When I finished that book—it was the first time I ever thought about this—I said, "The numbers I put up with this devastating disease!"

I had to take a shot every day; I had to worry about my sugars dropping; I had to regulate my insulin. I have to believe that I was out there playing ball so many times with my sugar being at a level where I was thinking I was functioning with all my faculties, but I probably wasn't. Anybody that's a diabetic can understand. In fact, all diabetics say to me, "How did you ever do it?" I still don't believe my career was shortened because of it. I retired at age thirty-four after 15 years in the big leagues. But I wonder what kind of numbers I could've put up. I knew I had the ability, and it's what you make of your ability. A lot of players I see coming up, they've got all the ability in the world, but they don't have it here [touching his heart].

When I first came up, my nickname was "Daig." Even to this day, if I run into Billy or Fergie, they all call me "Daig." It never offended me. I have Italian friends at home that I call "daig" or "paesan." But I have to say that "wop" really offended me. It's just the sound of it. I think they called me that because I have that Italian personality. I have a quick temper, I carried my emotions on my sleeve. Nobody was my friend when I crossed those white lines, and when the game was over, even the fans couldn't relate because they thought the way I played the game was the way I was off the field. But I was completely different. I had a lot of compassion for people, even though I got upset quickly and might have reacted, I forgave. And if I was wrong, I would apologize.

I never thought of any racial thing with Italians. I was so proud to be one. When I got to Chicago, I thought bodies fell out of closets, with Al Capone, because I'd never been there before. You know what I mean? Then one day I'm coming out of our clubhouse and I'm walking with Ernie Banks, and one of the ushers came up to me and said, "There's a gentleman in the box seats who wants to say hello to you." You know, in those days we related to the fans. So I walk over and he's got two big guys sitting with him; they were Italian. Then this guy says, "I'm Sam Giancana." I knew who he was because when I first came to Chicago, I was very close with an Italian family in Elmwood Park. We would go to this Italian restaurant and Sam would always be in there with the McGuire sisters.

So he came to five ballgames, and every time he came to a game he would sit there and yell at me, "Hey, Ron." I'd go, "Hi." And every time, I hit a home run. Five times. So he invites me over to his house for dinner. It was an old house in Elmwood Park. He made his own spaghetti gravy; excellent. And he had the wine like my grandfather, the muscatel, the white wine. I go to his house for dinner and they find out, the commissioner's office. Bowie Kuhn brought me in and never asked me about the Cubbies or anything. He just said, "You can't associate with him." So I had to go back and tell him, and that was tough. But he understood.

Being in Chicago and being Italian was unbelievable. I remember watching the Cubs on the TV *Game of the Week*. I used to watch the Yankees; I was kind of a Yankees fan. Joe DiMaggio was one of my favorite ballplayers because he was Italian. The Cubs weren't on that much, but when they were, there was something about Wrigley Field that I loved. I was very short, about 5-foot-2 my first year in high school. This kid in my neighborhood who was about the same size moved to Chicago for three years. When he came back, he was about a foot taller than me. So I would think that you grew taller in Chicago. It's funny how I remember these things.

When I got out of the game, I went into business. They wanted me to stay in baseball, but I said no because I was vice president of an oil company and I was making as much money off the field as I was on the field. I retired on my own. I still had a couple of years left, physically but not mentally. When we didn't win in '69 and '70 and '71, it really took a lot out of me. And then when I got traded to the White Sox thinking that was going to be a great move,

Ron Santo
National Baseball Hall of Fame and Museum.

it was a horrible move. Now I'm retired; then I started my own business and became very successful. I left that oil company and started my own, bought fuel in the Gulf Coast and brought it up by barge. Then I bought a company called Interpoint, truck stops throughout the country.

Then, when I was forty-seven, the Cubs called me and said, "Would you be interested in color commentary?" I never thought of myself as a broadcaster, but I fell in love with it. And that's the only reason that I got into the game. I sold my business and now I'm doing something I love.

Here's how I feel about the Hall of Fame. Sure I wanted to get in. What was more upsetting to me than anything else, when I became eligible five years after I retired, I didn't get 5 percent of the vote. So I don't even get on the ballot. I was devastated. I couldn't believe it, with my numbers. I didn't say a word. How in the hell did that happen? So right away I figured it was going to be tough. There are only nine third basemen in the Hall of Fame, and there are only two with numbers better than mine: Eddie Mathews and Mike Schmidt. After games when the writers would come in, it wasn't the time to get me sometimes. I spoke my mind. I don't think I ever insulted anybody, but maybe they didn't like me.

I don't know what happened. All I know is that's all they talked about when I was getting out of baseball: the Hall of Fame. I was an impact player; I put up big numbers. I was the only position player that ever played in the big leagues with diabetes. Nobody knows what it's like to take insulin every day and go out there and bust your ass. I missed 23 games in 10 years, and the only reason I missed, I got hit in the face with a pitch and busted my cheekbone. I was only gone a week.

I've been very lucky, considering I came from "Garlic Gulch," which is what they called the Italian neighborhood in Seattle where I grew up. I never expected to be where I am today or to be in the big leagues. My stepfather had a lot to do with the reason I'm in the big leagues. I've overcome a lot of adversities; a lot, believe me. I was lucky that when my real father left another father came into my life. Otherwise, I don't know what the outcome would have been.

Jim Fregosi

*J*im Fregosi did just about everything a person can do in big league baseball. *Originally signed by the Boston Red Sox, the San Francisco native was drafted by the Los Angeles Angels in the 1960 expansion draft. In 11 years with the Angels (1961–71), he was a six-time All-Star shortstop before moving on to the Mets, Rangers, and Pirates. In his 18-year career, he compiled a batting average of .265, with 151 home runs and 706 RBIs. At the time of his induction into the Angels Hall of Fame in 1989, he led the franchise all-time lists in games, at-bats, hits, and triples. In 1998, the Angels retired his uniform number 11.*

At age thirty-six, while still an active player, Fregosi was hired as manager of the Angels. He managed the team from June 1978 until May 1981, leading them to their first-ever Western Division title in 1979 and finishing second in the Associated Press voting that year for AL Manager of the Year. He went on to manage the White Sox, Phillies (winners of the 1993 NL pennant), and Blue Jays, compiling a 15-year record of 1,028–1,094. He later was a special assistant to the general manager of the Atlanta Braves, serving as their top advance scout. In 2010, he received the George Genovese Award for excellence in scouting from the Professional Baseball Scouts Foundation. He died following complications of a stroke at age seventy-one in 2014.

* * *

My mother was Irish and my father, Archie, was Italian. His father came from the old country in northern Italy, actually Toscana. Basically, he grew up in an all-Italian neighborhood in South San Francisco. He was in the produce business, and my father ran an Italian deli in South San Francisco for many, many years. There was a very large Italian community there. I have an older brother and an older sister. Dad spoke Italian, but he didn't want us to speak Italian. He said, "You're American, you speak English."

But the customers who came in the store were mostly all Italian, so at that time when I was younger I understood a great deal of Italian because I knew when they were yelling at me they wanted something. Every time I hit a home run in the big leagues, at six o'clock in the morning when the door opened up, all the old-time Italians came in and had a shot of whiskey with my dad.

I grew up as a fan of the Pacific Coast League because there wasn't major league baseball, of course. Everybody knew Joe D and all the great things that he did throughout his career. I kind of grew up as a Yankee fan because of DiMaggio. My dad was a great athlete himself, but he got married, I think, when my mother was fourteen and he was sixteen or eighteen, something like that. He was a worker. He worked sixteen hours a day. The store was open six to six, six days a week. When I was a little kid, I used to go with him to the produce market in San Francisco all the time. He was always a big baseball fan; he loved the game and played a lot. In fact, there's a park in South San Francisco named after him. He coached softball in South San Francisco until he was eighty-three years old. He was always part of that community. He was a captain of the volunteer fire department.

I grew up with Y. A. Tittle with the 49ers and Bill Russell at the University of San Francisco. And it was a big thrill for me when the Giants came out there. I went to Serra High School in San Mateo. Barry Bonds, John Robinson, and Lynn Swann all went to that high school. And there's a young guy that's a quarterback for New England right now named Tom Brady.

My mother wanted me to go to college and my dad wanted me to play baseball, so they left it up to me. I had a lot of scholarship offers for football, but it was a choice I eventually made to play pro baseball. I signed a professional contract when I was seventeen with the Boston Red Sox. Then I went in the first expansion draft to the, at that time, Los Angeles Angels. My first year in the big leagues, I weighed 163, 165. I was thin; I came up at eighteen or nineteen and was still growing.

One of my real heroes was Rocky Colavito. I played with Tony Conigliaro; after his eye injury he came to the Angels. I played on some All-Star teams with Rico Petrocelli, who is really a fine man. But really, all the Italians kind of hung out and kind of rooted for each other. And there was such a great heritage from San Francisco of Italian players that came out of there. Being in the National Italian American Sports Hall of Fame means a lot to me.

I didn't encounter any prejudice. Well, they'd call you a "dago" or a "wop," but mostly it was an endearing term. One time, Bud Furillo, who was a sportswriter for the *Herald Examiner*, had a headline about me, "Super Dago," and he caught a rash of criticism for that. Growing up in California, it was different because there was not a lot of prejudice towards anybody. It was much more difficult for the black player going to the East Coast or training in Florida at that time. When I first went to Florida, they still had black and white drinking fountains. I mean, it was much more difficult for a young black player leaving the atmosphere they had in California and going to the South to play. A lot of places they wouldn't let them in restaurants. But I never really encountered any prejudice towards Italians.

Playing on an expansion club, we weren't so good, but I remember back in the early sixties we fought the Yankees for the pennant. I was fortunate enough to play in six All-Star games. Being around the great players that were playing then was really a special time for me. I had the opportunity of knowing some of them. Mickey Mantle was great, Brooks Robinson, Elston Howard, and Yogi Berra.

I played for Yogi; he managed me when I was with the Mets. He was just a wonderful man, a great, great guy. When he was catching I used to have to tell him to shut up because whenever I was hitting, he'd be talking to me all the time. I couldn't concentrate on what I was doing. He was quite a character. The thing that amazed me was his size. He was really a small guy to generate the kind of power he did. He could hit a ball off his shoe tops or over his head.

I was fortunate to play at a time when it was still a game. I loved the years that I played in the sixties and seventies. It was not a lifelong career at that time. You were thrilled to death. You had to get five years to get a pension. Every time somebody got five years they'd throw a big party. You never thought of it as working in a game that would enable you to retire at the end of that time. The game has changed a lot, and the money has changed the game. There was a different type of camaraderie. We spent more time with newspapermen, more time with umpires, more time with other players. It was really a family. There were sixteen teams; now that there are thirty teams, guys are spread all over. And there were more kids playing baseball then than there are now. It wasn't all organized. They just played the game. I think that's the biggest difference.

When we played, we were all fans of the game. And the organization you were with, that's the one you wanted to stay with your whole career. There wasn't the free agency involved. Hell, I've been in the game for 40 years and I need a scorecard to find out where everybody is. It's a little bit unfortunate. When kids grew up as fans, they had the same heroes for ten, fifteen years. And now that's not true anymore. Today, younger players don't have the loyalty to the organization that they had in the past. It goes back to when agents got in the game and the money. I don't blame the players; make as much money as you possibly can. I made the All-Star team four times before I got to $20,000. Unfortunately, some of them think they're worth the money they're getting. It's great that they can play ten years now and not have to work another day in their lives.

While I was still playing, Buzzie Bavasi and Gene Autry called me on the phone and asked me if I was interested in managing the Angels. I said, "The way I'm hitting, I'll take any job I can get, for Chrissakes." I was with the Pirates in Cincinnati on an offday, and I can remember going up to my room and getting the phone call. I came back downstairs and said, "Well, I'll see you guys later." They said, "Where are you going?" I said, "I'm going to manage the Angels," and they said, "Yeah, sure."

And I managed the Angels the next day. I had managed in winter ball down in Puerto Rico at a young age, in '69 when I was still playing. The Angels were bringing somebody back that had a name in the organization, that had some feeling for the organization, and had some leadership qualities. That's why I think they wanted to bring me back. But I had no idea and I was surprised. I was fortunate. We finished second the first year I managed, and we won the division the second year.

When I went to the White Sox I replaced Tony La Russa. He's had a fantastic career; he's going to be in the Hall of Fame as a manager. It's well deserved. I mean, just the longevity of managing as many consecutive years as he has managed is quite a feat. I managed against Joe Torre. Joe was the perfect guy to manage the New York Yankees. The fabulous run he's had is unheard of. And besides that, he's a class guy. He's also had a great career.

I played for Billy Martin in Texas, and I managed against Billy. I loved Billy. He asked me to go to work for him a number of times. Probably overall the best between the white lines of anybody I've ever seen. I learned a lot of what to do, and I learned a lot of what not to do. His intensity level; he was a rambunctious little guy, I'll tell you that. Tough guy. We got along great, though. I really cared a lot about Billy. I loved playing for Billy. We used to fight and argue all the time about this and that. He kept me around for a few years just because he liked me and what I did in the clubhouse.

I don't think that anybody that ever was in the game that was Italian did not make it known. I have a little ten-year-old daughter that goes around and tells everybody that there are only two kinds of people in this world: those that are Italian, and those that want to be Italian. So she's indoctrinated too. I have five children. My oldest son is the national cross-checker for the Philadelphia Phillies. He made All-American at the University of New Mexico. I have five grandchildren. A very fortunate man.

For five years now I've been a special assistant to the general manager of the Braves, John Schuerholz. Basically what I do is cover all thirty major-league clubs for free-agent signings at the end of the year and for trades. I live in Tarpon Springs, Florida. I moved out of California in the mid-to-late eighties; no state taxes and the fishing's good.

The toughest transition for me when I got into the front office was, what do you do from noon until the start of the game? I was always in the clubhouse.

Jim Fregosi
AP Photo/Ed Reinke.

Being around the players keeps you young. You know, I've been very fortunate to have managed in four different decades.

I feel as fortunate as anybody could ever be, to be involved in something you love and care about. I kid once in a while by saying I've got to go to work, but it's never been work for me. It's been a labor of love. I had the opportunity to play at the major-league level, to manage, to work in the front office. I've done just about every aspect of the game. I enjoy the camaraderie of the people that are involved in the game. I'm talking about people who care about the game. I've always thought about baseball as two circles. One is the circle of concern, and the other is the circle of influence. Most players and people who have been involved in the game are always in the circle of concern, but very seldom do we ever get in the circle of influence. Ownership money constitutes that circle.

Growing up where I grew up, the people that helped me throughout my young career, and being around the people I have has been very satisfactory for me. I've been fortunate enough to be in the game as long as I have. The ballparks you go to across the country, you're always going to run into someone you know. It makes for a very nice lifestyle.

Tony La Russa

A major-league infielder with three teams, Tony La Russa appeared in 132 games over six seasons between 1963 and 1973. He also spent all or parts of 15 seasons in the minors. Inquisitive as well as competitive, the native of Tampa took advantage of all that experience by closely studying the intricacies of the game and becoming a major-league manager. He learned so well that by the time his managerial career ended in 2011, only Connie Mack and John McGraw had won more games.

In 1973, when La Russa was in his twelfth year in professional baseball and aware of his limited future as a player, he began to pursue a law degree. Taking classes during the offseason, he obtained his degree in 1978. But that same year the Chicago White Sox hired him to manage their Double-A affiliate in the Southern League. One hundred and six games into the 1979 season, he was named manager of the parent club at age thirty-four, beginning an uninterrupted string of 33 consecutive seasons as a major-league skipper. As manager of the White Sox, Athletics, and Cardinals between 1979 and 2011, he led his teams to 2,728 wins, six pennants, and three World Series titles. Voted Manager of the Year four times and finishing second five times, he is one of two managers to win the World Series in both leagues and the only one to win one in three different decades.

La Russa was an innovator in a game that treasures tradition. Intensely focused and detail-oriented, he was driven to find even the slightest edge over his opponents. No less significant than the wins and titles he accumulated was his lasting impact on the way the game is played. His best known, and most enduring, influence was his modification of relief pitching, using specialty relievers in late innings to take advantage of situational match-ups and defining the role of closer as a ninth-inning specialist. While his relentless competitiveness, not to mention frequent pitching changes, made him a polarizing figure at times, his innovations and strategic brilliance earned him the respect and admiration of his peers and baseball analysts. Widely recognized as one of the game's greatest managers, in 2013, his first year of eligibility, La Russa was unanimously elected to the Hall of Fame by the Expansion Era Committee.

* * *

Both my parents were born in the States. My dad's parents came from Sicily, the Catania province, I think. My mother's family came from Spain, Asturias.

That's how I was raised; Latin American, Italian American. There was no differentiation for us. My dad, Antonio La Russa, spoke Spanish and Italian; my mother, Olivia Cuervo, spoke Spanish but not Italian. So we spoke Spanish in the house; in fact, Spanish was my first language. My nickname was "Tonin." I had to learn English to go to school.

I grew up in a community with a bunch of people that really loved baseball. My father was a fanatic about baseball. My mother is more into education, but she recognized that athletics is good for a young person. They both gave me every opportunity they could to play baseball.

The big hero in our town was Al Lopez. He lived in Ybor City, where I was born and raised. In fact, my father knew him and the guys there always admired him because, as he became a big-league catcher and then later on became a big-league manager, he never changed. He always came back and never put on any airs. He was really a good guy who never let his success get to him. So I always admired him. He was the first major leaguer that I paid attention to. When I was at his house, he was already a manager.

I was fortunate because Cincinnati and Chicago trained in Tampa, Florida, and the Yankees and St. Louis in St. Pete. On weekends, my dad would take me very often to Tampa, and once in a while, we'd go to St. Pete. He was a big, big baseball fan. The story back home was that he was a pretty good catcher who was never allowed to play much because his father required him to do chores. He worked so hard. At the end, the last thirty years, he was a wholesale route milk salesman for a company called Florida Dairy. He'd get up early, work late, six days a week. We never had a lot of extra money, but he made it a point to always give me every opportunity to play because he didn't want me to be frustrated like he was.

I can remember the first time I got on second base, Rocky Colavito, who was with the Detroit Tigers at that time, said, "Hey, it's nice to have another Italian in the league." With the Kansas City A's, you had Gino Cimoli and Bobby Del Greco, so they were all kind of protective. Actually, Terry Francona's dad, Tito, was on that Kansas City club. I roomed with him on a trip to Chicago; he was a real gentleman. Joe Torre I know a lot better than I do Terry; I think he's a wonderful guy, a great man. So are both of them; I just happen to know one better than the other.

I pursued the law degree because at the end of my playing career, when I was a Triple-A player-coach, I knew I wasn't going to make it as a legitimate major leaguer, so I needed to find something else to do. I always loved reading and problem-solving and I had friends who were lawyers, so I said, *It looks like things add together and that would be a good thing to do.*

I started managing when I was thirty-four and there were giants in the league then. They were very kind to me. Guys like Sparky Anderson, Billy Martin, Chuck Tanner, Earl Weaver, John McNamara; all these guys over the years answered a bunch of questions I had. Later on, if you're still around, you realize just how great their instructions, the teachings, the advice was really important.

As far as managing, I just check myself and as long as I get excited and get nervous, I figure that's what I should be doing, as long as somebody wants me. For me, the anxiety is every bit the same. I haven't lost any excitement or nervousness whatever; not a bit. It's probably worse than ever because you know how good it is to win. When you're younger, you're wondering. Now you know, so the losses are harder to take, and you appreciate the winning more, maybe, a little bit.

The importance of having the third most wins of all-time, the importance of that versus Ned Yost in his sixth or seventh year is nothing. We both start out with the score zero to zero. All that stuff has just happened. The key is, you've got a responsibility and an opportunity to do something to put the right people in place to try to win games for the team you're with. It's that simple, and as long as that excites a person, then you should keep trying to do it if they want you. If the fire's burning, I like what I'm doing. If it isn't, then I'd be cheating, and I don't want to cheat. Then it's time to do something different.

Tony La Russa
*National Baseball Hall of Fame
and Museum.*

Rico Petrocelli

*B*orn *in Brooklyn on June 27, 1943, Americo Peter Petrocelli was the youngest of seven children of Italian immigrants. Signed out of high school in 1961 by the Boston Red Sox, by 1965 he was their starting shortstop at age twenty-one. Unlike the typical slick-fielding, light-hitting shortstops of the era, Petrocelli was a power hitter, twice finishing in the top five in home runs in the American League. In 1969, he set an AL record for shortstops by hitting 40 home runs, a mark that stood until 1998 and remains the single-season record for Red Sox shortstops. That same season he tied the record, since broken, for fewest errors by a shortstop and finished seventh in the MVP vote. Then, when he moved to third base in 1971 following the arrival of future Hall of Fame shortstop Luis Aparicio, he set a then-major-league record for third basemen with 77 straight games without an error.*

In 1967, beginning with a three-run homer on opening day, he played a key role in the "Impossible Dream" season of 1967 when the Red Sox won the pennant after finishing in ninth place the previous year, an event that is credited with launching a new era of success and popularity for the struggling franchise. In his 13 years with Boston, the two-time All-Star hit 210 home runs with 773 RBIs. After his playing career ended in 1976, he became a Red Sox broadcaster then managed in the minor leagues for four years between 1986 and 1992. Petrocelli was inducted into the Red Sox Hall of Fame in 1997.

* * *

Both of my parents were born in the Abruzzi region of Italy. I'm the youngest of seven kids: four brothers and two sisters. Pretty big disparity in age. My father was fifty-one when they had me; my mother was forty-three. So I was kind of a late arrival. Lots of cousins, lots of relatives all over the country. When I was growing up, my parents didn't speak much Italian. They were speaking very good English by that time. My mother spoke perfect English; my father had a bit of an accent. They very seldom spoke Italian to me. My older brothers and sisters understood and could speak pretty decent Italian.

My mother and father met right outside Pittsburgh; they migrated there from Italy because they had cousins there. My father started in a foundry, working for very little money in those days. One thing about him, he always provided food and shelter. But then he left and got a job with the Pennsylvania Railroad, and he was there for twenty-three years as a fireman. At that time, they used coal and wood, so probably because of that he developed tuberculosis in one of his lungs. He thought he was going to die, so he went back to Italy. He kissed my mother and all the kids goodbye and said, "I'm going back to die with my family." He went back and saw some doctors, in Naples, I think. His sisters and other relatives were there and they kind of nursed him and he was healed. So he came back, after over a year. Then they decided to move to New York. They moved to Mulberry Street, then to Brooklyn, and that's where they had me. I think I was a surprise to them at that age.

We were a very close family and did a lot of things together. My brothers took me to ballgames all the time and that was great: Ebbets Field, Yankee Stadium, and the Polo Grounds. Plus, they had good teams, and usually there was one team at least in the World Series. So it was great to grow up and see the great players. So that's what I wanted to do; I wanted to be a great baseball player.

One day my brothers took me to Yankee Stadium, and we're out in the bleachers. Joe DiMaggio was still playing. I'll never forget this. I looked around, and here the pitcher was throwing the ball, but everyone in the bleachers was looking at Joe DiMaggio. No one was even looking at the ball or the hitter. He was such a hero. And when he'd go to catch a ball he'd just lope after it; it was just beautiful to watch. My father, the only thing he knew about baseball was Joe DiMaggio and Yogi Berra and Rizzuto because he could relate to them, players that made it.

But I was fortunate to be able to go out and play ball. My brothers and sisters worked; they had to make money in order for us to survive. By the time I was growing up, I took to baseball and sports overall. I was able to go out there and do pretty much what I wanted. The place I grew up in Brooklyn was predominantly Italian. Then we moved and I went to Sheepshead Bay High School, which was in a mixed neighborhood, all nationalities and races. That's where I really started to play sports seriously and wanted to be a professional. I became a pretty good athlete, played a lot, practiced a lot. My idol was Mickey Mantle, and what kid doesn't want to be like his idol? So I wanted to be a baseball player. My father would say, "Hey, go out and get a regular job. What's baseball? Are you crazy? There's no money in that." I told him I loved it, and he said, "All right, go ahead."

I signed with the Red Sox right out of high school, three days after I graduated. I went to Winston-Salem in the Carolina League. Then I went to the Eastern League, and Triple A was in Seattle. When I was in the Carolina League, there was a big, heavy guy. It seemed like every ballpark had someone who'd take up two seats and yell at everybody, loud as anything. So this guy, he got on the blacks. We only had one black player, a utility player. Any time he got in there, this guy would get on him and he would say every derogatory word to him. One day a guy named Joe DeCandido was at third base, Rico Petrocelli at shortstop, and other Italians at second and at first. Four Italians in there. So this guy says, "Well my, my, look at that; we've got an all-guinea infield." Then he wouldn't let up. "Hey, the wops are coming out," stuff like that. I was ready to go after him, but Joe DeCandido, who was from the Bronx, said, "That's it!" He threw his glove down and ran into the stands. The ushers had to stop him or he was going to kill this guy. After that, he kept coming to the games, but he didn't say anything ethnic-wise, to us or to Tom, the black player.

Early on, when I first got to Boston, I heard things from the stands once in a while: "Petrocelli, you wop." If that happened, the worst thing you could do was to come back and say something, acknowledge that. So you just kept your mouth shut. But it wasn't anything close to what the black players had to go through, like Jackie Robinson.

Growing up in New York in really mixed areas, with Irish, Jewish, Italians, I never heard my father or my brothers talk about any other race or nationality in a derogatory way. I guess my father went through some difficulties in the foundries when he first came over. He said the people that ran those places were tough on the workers, who were making nothing. But in New York, I didn't hear anything about prejudice. Maybe because I played ball so much. Sports really bring people together. You don't look at color. If a guy's a jerk and he's Italian, that doesn't mean all Italians are jerks.

Rico Petrocelli
Boston Red Sox.

I felt a bond with other Italian players. Tony Conigliaro was a close friend of mine. We were proud that we had the ability to play in the major leagues. We knew about the heritage of Italian Americans who had struggled in other fields. They were proud of us, and we wanted to acknowledge that and also go out there and do a good job. We'd see other Italian players on the other teams and you kind of got a little bit friendly with them. You know, you had that common Italian American heritage. The Italians in the North End and the Sons of Italy, they were fantastic. I just loved to go to the North End; they were all Italians from the old country. I'd go in to have a beer with a friend of mine from the area and, geez, the whole place would come over. "Hey, how you doing?" They really made me feel good.

Al "The Bull" Ferrara

*A*l Ferrara, the son of Al Ferrara Sr., a New York City fireman, and Adele Paulucci Ferrara, grew up on East Second Street in Brooklyn. His maternal grandmother, Assunta Paulucci, as well as an aunt and several uncles, lived in the same building. Then, after his mother passed away when Al was seventeen, Assunta moved into the Ferrara's apartment to help care for Al and his twelve-year-old twin siblings. When Al was eight years old, and preferred to play baseball, Assunta insisted that he take piano lessons. Despite his initial reluctance, by the time he was sixteen, he was good enough to play a recital at Carnegie Hall.

But that was just the beginning for Alfred John Ferrara Jr. He appeared in several films and television shows between 1953 and 1978 and played on two World Series-winning teams with the Los Angeles Dodgers. His Dodgers uniform number 20 is retired, though only because it was worn by future Hall of Famer Don Sutton after Ferrara opted to switch to number 9 in honor of Ted Williams.

Nicknamed "The Bull" for his muscular build, Ferrara was one of several Brooklyn-born major leaguers who got their start in baseball playing on the Parade Grounds at Prospect Park. He spent five years with the Dodgers between 1963 and 1968 before being selected by the San Diego Padres in the 1968 expansion draft. After two seasons with San Diego, he split his final season between the Padres and the Cincinnati Reds. In his eight-year career, the 6-foot-1, 200-pound outfielder hit .259 with 51 home runs and 198 RBIs. In his one World Series game (against the Baltimore Orioles in 1966), he hit a single in his only plate appearance.

* * *

My grandmother, Assunta Paulucci, came from Italy with her best friend and her best friend's husband, Guido Morvillo. He was the piano teacher who taught her, taught my mother, and taught me. My grandmother spoke perfect, beautiful Italian, but I couldn't say a word. So when I went to high school, I took Italian for three years. I still couldn't speak it.

Grandma and all her sons, my uncles, were a great influence on my life. I was more influenced by my mother's side, the Paulucci side. The Ferrara side were completely different from the Paulucci side. The Ferraras were well educated, disciplined, where the Pauluccis were partiers. We lived on East Second Street in Brooklyn. The Pauluccis lived on the ground floor, and we lived on the fourth floor. We had one bedroom with five people in it; there was my mother and father, and we had bunk beds with me on the top and my brother and sister on the bottom. I remember on steamy hot nights I'd sit up on the fire escape; there was no such thing as air-conditioning. You learned how to play on the streets; stickball, punchball.

So grandma would be down on the first floor and she used to make the sauce. Sunday afternoon all the uncles would come over; she had eleven children. My mother was very saintly. She worked at the rectory and would cook for them, clean up. She was the level-headed one, the voice of reason, because the rest of them, they were wild. I remember the long table where we'd sit on Sunday afternoons. They'd bring the homemade pasta from Mulberry Street, from up in New York. All the uncles would be around the large table and on one side was the baby grand piano, which I played. That's where I would practice and take my lessons from Mr. Morvillo.

In this red-blooded Italian family, invariably somebody would get in an argument. Brothers and sisters, that's what it was. And there'd be a beef, usually before the antipasto was there, and my mother would try to be the peacemaker, but somebody would always walk out. Then during the week, mother would go and try to bring them back, and the next week the same thing would happen, with two other brothers fighting. We were a typical Italian family and grandma was the leader. My mother was the facilitator. She was the glue that held the family together, and when she passed away when I was seventeen, some of the aunts and uncles didn't come over anymore. It wasn't the same.

My grandmother was a tremendous influence on me because she wanted me to learn to play the piano, because of her friend Morvillo's influence. So I did. Being from Brooklyn and having absolutely no ear, I would sit down and what I would do was strictly classical music. I would read it, memorize it, and play it, exactly the way Bach or Beethoven played it. In Brooklyn, the kids would say, "I want to hear 'Rock Around the Clock,'" and I'd say, "I can't play it."

One of my aunts, my godmother, sent me to my first rock-and-roll show at the Paramount: Alan Freed's Tribute to the Stars. The featured player was Little Richard, and I sat there thinking, "Why can't I do that?" and I couldn't because I couldn't play "Happy Birthday" by ear. And if Morvillo ever found any popular music in the house, he had the ruler and he'd whack you.

The neighborhood was mostly Italian and Jewish, and school was almost completely Italian and Jewish. The Italian ethnicity was there. My father took me to Avenue U, which is where I learned how to eat a lot of the ethnic foods, like cappozell, which is the sheep's head. You'd have a baked cappozell, and they were absolutely fantastic. It was fearsome looking, but I learned how to eat that, and scungilli salads, tripe. When you went back to the area where

I went to school, if you went to Avenue U, there was nothing but Italian restaurants, Italian delis, pizza parlors, and bars. Some of them are still there today. The place that I got my cappozell and scungilli salad, Original Joe's, is still there and they've got a picture up on the wall. It's a newspaper clipping of when Marciano knocked out Joe Louis.

When I was a kid growing up, DiMaggio was just going out. But of course, I heard all these marvelous things about what a great player he was. To an Italian in New York, DiMaggio was the man, OK? No ifs, ands, or buts about it.

There was no video in my day. There were pictures in *Sports Illustrated* of players swinging the bat. I remember there was a picture of Al Kaline, and I tried to duplicate it, on the roof in Brooklyn. In the sandlots as I came up, most of the managers were Italian. Actually, at Lafayette High where I went to school, almost the whole baseball team was Italian, and the whole basketball team was Jewish. The football team was a mixture of both.

I had a terrible senior year in high school; I hit .083. It looked like everything was over. I went to work on an assembly line, and one day a kid I worked with said that the next day there was a tryout at Ebbets Field with the Brooklyn Rookies, which was not a professional team but a barnstorming team sponsored by the Dodgers. They would barnstorm up and down the East Coast. He said, "It beats this shit," and I said, "You've got that right."

So I went and they made me shag fly balls. I hit two balls into the stands, so they invited me back the next day, and I went 0-for-4 and didn't get the ball out of the infield. I figured that's it, but that night they called me and said I was selected to play on the Dodgers Rookies. Then in 1959, I was signed by the Dodgers.

Several of us who played on the Parade Grounds in Brooklyn went on to play in the big leagues: the Aspromonte brothers, Joe Pepitone, Joe Torre, Sandy Koufax, Tommy Davis, and myself. The best guys I saw as a kid were Pepitone and Bob Aspromonte, who was my teammate at Lafayette High School. There were a lot of Italian American players in Brooklyn you never heard of. Some of those guys, they had to go to work when school was out, so they couldn't play ball. Of course, after me, Rico Petrocelli came out of Sheepshead Bay, and John Franco came out of the same high school as I did.

A funny story about Tommy Lasorda. The first time I went to Vero Beach, Florida, my first year, they used to have a big fence. Of course, I was young and didn't care too much about the curfew. I remember coming in you had to climb over this fence and at that time they had the scouts and the minor-league managers roaming the grounds with flashlights. So who nails me as I'm coming back? There used to be a window that the other players would leave open, and he caught me. He asked me who I was, and I said Al Ferrara.

"Ferrara? You're Italian?" And I said, "Yeah, I'm Italian." And he says, "What the hell are you doing? You know, they can still send you home if you do things like this. I'm gonna tell you what; you're Italian, I'm going to let you off this time. But if I ever catch you again, I'm going to turn you in."

Now about four years later I make the big leagues. I'm sitting in a hotel in Los Angeles, and I get a phone call. "Al, this is Tommy Lasorda. You remember the time when I didn't turn you in?" I said, "Yeah, Tommy. I really appreciated it." And he says, "We've got a Kiwanis Club and I'm speaking there today. I want you to come down, and I want you to speak. Would you do that for me?" I said, "Sure, Tommy." So we go down there. About two weeks later the phone rings again. "Al, you remember the time I let you in? I'm going to the Lions club today. Would you mind speaking?" Still, I can't turn him down. So this happened four times because he's always out in the community. The fifth time he called, I said, "Tom, I wish the fuck you would have turned me in." He laughed like a son of a bitch.

My number one memory is winning the 1963 World Series over the Yankees in four straight. You know, I was a kid from Brooklyn, and the Yankees used to beat us all the time. So to beat them in the World Series my first year to make up for it was a big thrill. I was on two World championship teams with the number 20, but I wanted number 9 because of Ted Williams. When Wally Moon retired, I got 9, and Don Sutton got my number 20, and now that's retired and in the Hall of Fame. It's hanging up in Dodger Stadium and when I go there, I tell people, "Look, they retired my number."

Al Ferrara
Courtesy of Al Ferrara.

Sal Bando

*A*n all-city quarterback at Warrensville Heights (Ohio) High School, Salvatore Leonard Bando chose to focus on baseball at Arizona State University. In his junior year, he led the team to the 1965 College World Series title and was named the tournament's outstanding player. Following his junior year at ASU, Bando was selected by the Kansas City A's in the sixth round of the 1965 draft.

By 1968, the 6-foot, 200-pound third baseman was in the A's starting lineup, and the following year, he was the American League's starting third baseman in the All-Star Game. Recognizing Bando's leadership qualities and his win-at-all-costs approach to the game, that same year manager Hank Bauer named the twenty-five-year-old infielder captain of the now Oakland A's, a team that featured three future Hall of Famers: Reggie Jackson, Catfish Hunter, and Rollie Fingers. Respected by his teammates and management, Bando provided a much-needed stabilizing influence on a team marked by outsized personalities that clashed with some frequency. Considered to be the mavericks of Major League Baseball because of their trademark mustaches and internal squabbles, the A's won three consecutive World Series between 1972 and 1974.

While his on-field performance was at times overshadowed by that of some teammates, Bando was the undisputed leader of the A's and played a key role in the team's success, in part because, as captain, he was the intermediary between the players and their tight-fisted owner, Charlie Finley. While the team flourished on the field, the players had an increasingly contentious relationship with Finley. They even took the unprecedented step of threatening to strike in the midst of the pennant race in 1976 when Finley refused to play three of his star players after commissioner Bowie Kuhn nixed the owner's attempt to sell them. Bando served as a buffer between the players and Finley, but he was also one of his most outspoken critics.

Fed up with Finley's meddling, Bando became a free agent after the 1976 season and spent his final five years playing for the Milwaukee Brewers. A durable player who led the league in games played four times, over his 16-year career he hit .254 with 242 home runs and 1,039 RBIs. A four-time All-Star, he finished in the top four in MVP voting three times between 1971 and 1974.

After nine years as an assistant to general manager Harry Dalton, Bando served as the Brewers GM from October 1991 until August 1999, which Bando describes as the toughest eight years of his life. His brother, Chris, was a major-league catcher from 1981 to 1989, primarily with Cleveland, and his son, Sal Jr., played in the minors.

* * *

My grandparents on both sides came from Sicily, from near Palermo. The original family name was Baudo. The change was a mistake, I believe, made at Ellis Island. Mom was 100 percent Italian; Angela DeFrancisco. My mother's side went to Pennsylvania first, then to Cleveland. I think my mother's father was a barber. My father's father was a bootlegger. My father, Benedetto, was a subcontractor. Our parents spoke Italian when they didn't want us to know what they were talking about. I wish I had paid attention. I wish I would've learned it when they were speaking Italian.

My mother would always ask me when I was going to get married. I'd say, "I just haven't met the right one." So now I meet Sandy, my wife-to-be, down in Puerto Rico where I was playing winter ball. I called my mother and said, "Ma, you'll never guess. I met an Italian girl and I'm in love."

She says, "What part of Italy is her family from?" I couldn't believe that. I was just so stunned. My wife's family is not Sicilian; they're from the Sorrento and Naples area. You'd have to marry an Italian to be able to name your kids Salvatore, Santino, and Stefano.

The first major-league game I remember was a doubleheader against the Yankees in 1954 in Cleveland. The Indians won the doubleheader and went on that year to win the pennant and lose to the Giants in the World Series. One thing I do remember. We sat down near the right field foul pole, and Yogi Berra hit a home run in the ninth inning to send it to extra innings, but the Indians ended up winning. As a kid, as I got older, I'd take the rapid transit downtown and go to games at the huge Municipal Stadium.

When I was a senior in high school, I had to choose between football and baseball, and I thought baseball, long-term, was a better avenue for me. I hoped I was good enough to play, and when I got the scholarship to go to Arizona State, that just confirmed that I had a chance. Being able to compete out there against kids from California who had been playing the game all year and do well, it really got my attention that I had a chance to play professional ball. In my junior year, we won the College World Series, and I was named Most Valuable Player of the tournament.

I was named captain of the Oakland A's by Hank Bauer in 1969, which would have been my second full year. I had been up and down in '66 and '67. I said to Hank, "Are you sure you want me to do this?" He said, "You don't want it?" I said, "I didn't say that. I'm only in my second full year." And he said, "Well, you've been doing the job without the title, so we'll give you the title."

I think Bauer saw my desire to win at all costs and that I was willing to pay the price to win. Sometimes you get players who are just happy to be there. I was honored that he saw that in me and I think that was a big reason, my drive to win. So I was very appreciative and I was captain there, and then when I went to Milwaukee, they named me captain there. It was a nice honor, but I never looked at it as anything I held over the players' heads. I was just like they were. My job was to communicate with them. Because of my position at third base, I was close to the pitcher, so I'd remind him of how we're pitching guys. I tried to encourage guys if they were struggling. I patted them on the back like I would want to be patted on the back when I was struggling. It gave managers and the owner one person to pass on information, rather than go to all the different players at different times. So I was also a vehicle for management to communicate about what was going on.

Sal Bando
National Baseball Hall of Fame and Museum.

There were some strong personalities on the A's, but they were friends, and I think I handled it well enough where there was no animosity or jealousy about it. I never lorded it over anybody. It worked out, and I had different managers who continued to name me captain, so I think that I didn't embarrass the position.

Reggie Jackson and I both went to Arizona State; he was a freshman when I was a junior. We were friends. Look, Reggie was a key to our ballclub. I wasn't taking anything away from him. We all had a different job, and if we did our job right, we would win, and we did. Reggie had a beard, and in those days there was an unwritten rule about facial hair. Finley didn't want to tell Reggie to shave it, so he paid us all $300 to grow mustaches. It just caught on and it became a symbol, and instead of an embarrassment it turned out to be our identity, and we all loved it.

We did have some disagreements on the team, but when you get a handle that your guys are unhappy, everything gets blown out of proportion. When I went to Milwaukee, there were disagreements, but it never got written about because it was no big deal. But in Oakland that seemed to be the focus. At one time Rollie Fingers and Blue Moon Odom got into a fight right before the World Series started, so that makes headlines. We always had episodes, but no different than any other team.

It was mostly players against the owner. We had an owner who, at the very beginning, was very comforting. But as we got successful he became more difficult, and there was a lot of friction between front office and the players. Quite honestly, Finley brought us together as players because we had one common enemy. I think he just wanted things his way, and he wasn't going to give in to anyone. We always complained about not flying charter; we were always flying commercial. When you're out in Oakland, it's a tough way to travel. That was a complaint. He was very cheap. When we found out that other players that were comparable were making much more, that brought upon more disagreements with ownership. Most of the time the issues were not baseball.

He was hands-on, but from Chicago; he was never in Oakland. It was always by phone. We had a situation one time where Reggie had blasted Finley in the paper about flying commercial. It's a Sunday and I'm on the field taking batting practice when one of his errand boys comes out to get me and says, "Mr. Finley wants to talk to you on the phone." So I go up to his office and got on the phone, and he says, "Mr. Bando, I read Mr. Jackson's comments. Would you tell Mr. Jackson and the team that I can't afford charter planes."

So I said, "Mr. Finley, I'll tell him whatever you want, but we know you can afford charter planes." There was a long pause, and he says, "Thank you, Mr. Bando," and hangs up. So it was stuff like that.

There was always something. He never wanted to pay you, and at that time, he had all the leverage. When he lost that leverage, when arbitration came into being and you got to see across the board what people were making, he became even more difficult.

In 1976 we came close to having the only strike by one team in baseball. We were chasing the Kansas City Royals and Finley had sold Vida Blue to the Yankees and Joe Rudi and Rollie to Boston. The commissioner disallowed the sale and sent the players back to Oakland, and Finley would not play them because he was going to file a lawsuit against the commissioner's office. We needed those guys to compete. So we had a meeting, and it was unanimous that we would go out on strike. This was a Friday. I called Finley after the game Friday night and told him that if they weren't in the lineup Sunday, we were going out on strike. I cleared it with Marvin Miller, who was the head of the Players Association. He really didn't want us to do it, but said "Let's talk Sunday morning."

After I told Finley what our plans were after the game Friday, and after he called me every name in the book, he went on radio and blasted us. We played Saturday's game and lost. I talked to Marvin Sunday morning. He asked us to have another meeting and let them know how he felt. We had the meeting, and I won't use the language the players did, but it was, "Screw him." So I called Marvin and said, "We're going out."

After batting practice—it was about quarter to one, before a one o'clock game—we started taking our uniforms off. [Manager] Chuck Tanner was on the phone communicating with Finley, and Tanner wants us to strike because he wants those players to play. All of a sudden, he comes running in and posts the lineup. Rudi was in the lineup, and that ended the threat of a strike. The fact was, we had writers from all over the world because this would've been the first time. A sidebar to that was, we got out there a little late and [Minnesota Twins manager] Gene Mauch was going to protest the game because we came out late, but he forgot to put the DH on his lineup card, so he couldn't protest it, and so we played the game. We ended up losing the pennant by two games, and we didn't have those players for about a week, plus the time to get back into baseball shape. So I think we could've won our division again that year.

I think winning the first World Series is always the biggest thrill. You're excited when you get there, but then it's more games. And then you deal with the media and everything, and it really starts to weigh on you because it's not just playing a ballgame anymore, so you've really got to keep your focus. To beat Cincinnati without Reggie and Knowles, our number one left-handed reliever, speaks volumes for the type of talent we had. We beat Cincinnati in seven games, and six of them were one-run games, so they were all tense games. When you win, the first thing you feel is relief; it's over. Then you realize what you've accomplished.

There was always something a little special, having the same bloodline as a teammate or a guy on the other club. Gino Tenace and I just kind of hit it off, and that was in the era when you didn't have rooms by yourself. We roomed together for most of our time in Oakland; I was there ten years, and I bet eight of them Gino and I were roommates. We were good friends. We were both from Ohio, both Italian. Gino was soft-spoken, kind of new to the major leagues, so I kind of took him under my wing and we just grew real close. I think he became more Italian because we roomed together.

Over the years, even as you play against guys who are Italian, there is that common bond. Billy Martin was a piece of work. He'd always call me "Daigs." One way I got to know Billy was I would take the lineup card out as captain and exchange with him. This is my favorite story with Billy Martin. We'd gotten into a big fight with Detroit on a Friday night, and Saturday we come out to exchange cards. On his lineup card under "Extra Men," he's got Rocky Marciano, Carmen Basilio; he's got all these Italian fighters written down there. I laughed, and he had a good laugh.

Billy was fiery. He liked to intimidate you if he could, but he was a good manager. I think he took away from his reputation as a good manager by the crazy things he did. His drinking got out of hand, but he knew his baseball.

I knew Frank Crosetti when I played third base and he coached the Yankees. He talked all the time; I mean, he was nonstop. He was a good guy but a nonstop talker, in between innings or whenever there was a lull. Rico Petrocelli and I would always talk. A real quiet guy, but a good guy.

My dad would always talk about Joe DiMaggio. Joe was the hitting coach for two years when I played for Oakland. You know, hitting coaches in those days were not like the hitting coaches today, with video. They were somebody that knew a little bit about hitting. They just didn't have the specialty that they have today. The problem with Joe, he was such a natural as a hitter that he didn't have to think about it or break it down. It just came naturally. Joe was mostly a theory guy—look for this or, if you're not comfortable back off the plate—but not in the mechanics of hitting. He was there as a hitting coach, but he was there because he was Joe DiMaggio.

Joe took me under his wing somewhat, but he was a quiet man, a reserved man; he wasn't always outgoing. I got to know him better than most because there was the common thread that we were both with the A's. I thought he could have been a little more helpful, with everybody, not just me. But, you know, he was a private person. He ate a lot of sunflower seeds, sat there on the bench, didn't try to manage or anything. I know he got paid at that time a lot of money, $100,000. That was a lot of money in 1968. He was a hitting coach, but he was also a vice president of something or other. But his presence was unbelievable. The aura that he had with visiting players, coaches, the media; they held him up as a god, and we got to know him just as a coach. So that was a great experience.

I thought this was a cute story. We were going into Cleveland for the first time and my dad was really excited about meeting DiMaggio. I told him, "Dad, don't go up to Joe because if you go up to him, he won't give you the time of day. But if you sit there in the dugout during batting practice he might come up and sit next to you and start talking."

Well, sure enough, my dad's in the dugout and Joe's at the other end of the dugout eating sunflower seeds. The writers go up to Joe, and he didn't want to talk to them, so he gets up and goes and sits next to my dad and starts talking to him. My dad was in hog heaven the whole batting practice talking to Joe.

After I retired, [Milwaukee Brewers owner] Bud Selig asked me to stay in the organization as an assistant to Harry Dalton. I was offered the opportunity to manage twice; then I was named general manager. That was the toughest eight years I've ever spent in my life. We were a small-market franchise trying to compete and get a new stadium. You can't afford to get your ears beaten and get a new stadium. We did the best we could trying to stay competitive so we could get a stadium. It just was a very difficult time.

Jerry Colangelo was the owner of the Diamondbacks, an expansion team, and Larry Lucchino was with Baltimore, but I don't think there were any other Italian general managers when I was a GM. I got fairly close to Bart Giamatti. He would come in to see Bud, and Bud would always have me either pick him up or take him to the airport, so I had those one-on-one conversations with him. I would confide in him. He had that excitement when you would talk to him. He just lights up a room. Giamatti was just down to earth but yet he could be at that other level. He was just a great guy. He was outstanding. I was sad because he was commissioner for such a short period.

Obviously, baseball was a way of life; it provided for our family. But I was able to do something that my dad was never able to do, and that is do something as a living that you like. My father worked because he had to work. But I was making a living doing something I loved, and I'm very thankful for that. I'm thankful for my parents giving me the opportunity to do that and being supportive. I was really blessed. When I think back how things fell into place and everything worked out, coming to Milwaukee, raising our family here, then becoming a general manager; I wouldn't have thought those things would happen.

Bobby Valentine

A three-time All-State football player in Stamford, Connecticut, Bobby
Valentine opted to play pro baseball when the Los Angeles Dodgers made
him the fifth overall pick in the first round of the 1968 draft. An MVP
in two seasons of minor-league ball, he became a regular at the age of twenty-one.
Traded to the California Angels in 1973, he suffered a career-altering injury when
he broke his leg crashing into an outfield wall. He played six more seasons, mostly in
a reserve role, with the Angels, Padres, Mets, and Mariners.

In January 1977, Valentine married Mary Branca, daughter of former Dodgers
pitcher Ralph Branca. Though he won 21 games in 1947 at the age of twenty-one
and posted a record of 80–58 in 11 seasons with Brooklyn, Branca is best known as
the pitcher who gave up Bobby Thomson's "Shot Heard 'Round the World" homer
in the 1951 playoff with the Giants. He was also one of the founders of the Baseball
Assistance Team (B.A.T.), established in 1986 to help former players who were in
need of medical, financial, or psychological assistance.

Valentine managed the Rangers (1985–92), Mets (1996–2002), and Red Sox
(2012), compiling a record of 1,186–1,165 over 16 seasons. His greatest success
came with the Mets, who had five consecutive winning seasons between 1997 and
2001 and went to the World Series in 2000.

He also had two stints managing the Chiba Lotte Marines in the Japanese
Pacific League, first in 1995, then again between 2004 and 2009. Under
Valentine's leadership, the Marines, who had not won a pennant since 1974, won
the Japan Series title in 2005. Following the Series win, the Sapporo Breweries
produced "Bobeer," with Valentine's cartoon likeness on the can, and a street in
Chiba was named Valentine Way. The first to manage in both the World Series and
the Japan Series, in 2005 Valentine became the first, and still the only, foreigner to
win the Matsutaro Shoriki Award, given annually to the player or manager who
contributed the most to Japanese baseball.

* * *

I think the family name originally was Valentini, with an "i," but I never
researched it. A couple of the aunts had said that my grandparents were from
Abruzzi, on my mother's side, and Calabria. I knew three of the four; I never
really knew my dad's father because he died when I was young. They never
really talked about it much. My grandparents spoke Italian and we ate Italian,

so there absolutely was a connection with my heritage. Neither of my parents spoke Italian. It's true that we spoke only English in the house, but we followed the traditions, like the Sunday dinners. There was a family pride in being Italian, but my parents wanted to make sure that I was American. There was that generational separation, I think. I thought of myself as an Italian growing up, but as a baseball fan, I was next generation so I thought it was all right to root for the Americans.

I met my wife, Mary, when she and her father were in the Dominican on vacation and I was playing baseball there. Ralph Branca was a spectacular person. He lived ninety years, he was intelligent and kindhearted, and he did amazing things in his lifetime. He and Joe Black and Joe Garagiola got together one day and decided to help others by establishing the Baseball Assistance Team (B.A.T.). I was blessed that I had forty years with him.

I got drafted out of high school by the Dodgers when I was eighteen years old. They offered me a contract and I decided to sign it. I played only a few years of football in high school, and I had played baseball since I was in Little League, so I knew the game a lot better. Tommy Lasorda was my manager in the minor leagues. It was the most amazing experience anyone could ever have. Tommy was just starting out in his managerial career, and he allowed all of his players to be part of his life and his career. He wanted to excel, and he wanted all of his players to excel also. It was really fun. He was more than a mentor. In those days, managers had no coaches, so they were everything. They taught you how to play and eat, how to travel, dress, and talk. It was a different world, obviously. He was spectacular in everything he did. I still have a strong relationship with Tommy. He's a very important person in my life.

When I got to the majors, I always thought that I should be playing. The Dodgers were the team I came up with, and it was the major leagues, so I'm not sure that I thought there was anything different from the minors other than the lights were a little brighter. My career came to kind of an abrupt halt when I ran into a wall and broke my leg in 1973. I had other injuries, but that was the one that derailed me, kept me from running like I once ran and hitting like I once hit, playing like I once played. I played a lot of different positions in the rest of my career, but that was only to try to get playing time. It was by necessity, not by choice.

I didn't really have a special camaraderie with other Italian players. Not really. I never looked at people as either Italians or Latins or whites or blacks. I just looked at them as who they were. Sure, I had some Italian friends. Lee Mazzilli was my roommate for a while. There were others, but I don't characterize people like that.

I know the ethnic slurs but I never really heard them, not on the ball field. But they weren't new terms to me. Billy Martin always called me "Daig," which is kind of cool, but I think it was more for him than for me, actually. He wanted people to know that he had Italian in him. I always thought there was more rivalry between Italian ballplayers, more competition. It was kind of like Italian families that don't get along or Italian neighborhoods that wind up competing. I guess that's just the way it was.

I don't really remember when I started thinking about managing. Maybe when no one would give me a contract to play anymore. You sit on the bench and you think about a lot of things. I don't know how to characterize myself as a manager. I gave my best at everything I did, whether it was instructing, managing the game, taking care of my players. I just tried to do my best.

I have no idea what the hardest thing was about managing on any given day: players, media, front office. Probably, on any given day, all of the above were difficult, and on other days they weren't a problem at all. It's a full-time job; you never think there's just one thing that tips the scale. I think you miss the boat if you think that way.

I managed against Tony La Russa and Joe Torre. Tony and Joe had similar personalities. They were both quiet for the most part and well prepared. Tony was a little more animated in his early days. Joe had the right personality, he handled it well, and he won more games than he lost. That's the name of the game. I liked them both because they both did a spectacular job, for the game and for their heritage. They represented their teams in spectacular fashion. I had a good rapport with both of them. We were in it together for years, so it's hard not to have a good rapport, I think. Probably a little better with Joe because I was with him a lot of days when I was in uniform playing for him. I was never in uniform with Tony.

I enjoyed managing in New York. I got to share the experience with a lot of friends and family; that made it real special. New York was a good place for me. I spent a lot of time there, I knew my way around, it kind of knows me.

Two of my Mets players were Italian American: Mike Piazza and John Franco. Mike's a Hall of Famer. I managed half a dozen or so Hall of Famers, but Mike was spectacular at what he did. He worked really hard every single day. And he could compete with the bat as well as anyone I ever had. Johnny was kind of the heart and soul of any group. He always took the ball; he was healthy every day. Johnny's special, and he's still a good friend today.

Another player I had with the Mets was Matt Franco. Matt's a terrific guy. His grandfather is actor Bing Russell, his uncle is Kurt Russell, the actor, and his mom drove race cars. Just a spectacular family. Matty played for me in the

Bobby Valentine
AP Photo/Ron Frehm.

minor leagues with the Mets and then in the majors from 1996 to 2000. Then I brought him to Japan in 2004 and 2005. He was an integral part of that team. He was a veteran, he got a lot of big hits, he got along with the guys, and he did a great job of immersing himself into the culture. He was perfect for being one of the four guys that weren't native Japanese. He was spectacular in representing the other side of the pond.

When I went to Texas, I was a very popular manager; when I managed in New York, I was a very popular manager; and when I went to Japan, I was a very popular manager, so something must have resonated with the fans. I wasn't popular in Boston, but I didn't have much time to get my feet on the ground there.

I was the first foreign manager ever to manage in Japan. It was an amazingly enlightening experience filled with everything imaginable. I learned to speak Japanese because necessity is the mother of all great things that happen. Of course, not many stayed as long as I stayed. It's hard to survive in a foreign country without eating the food and speaking the language. Tuffy Rhodes learned to speak it pretty good; he was there about eleven years. A lot of the Latins learn to speak it pretty well because it's similar to Romance languages.

I spent two thirds of my life in professional baseball, so it fulfilled a lot of my time, my energy, my expectations, my joys, my sorrows. It made my life pretty much what it is. Baseball's been very good to me. I've returned to my hometown because I'm familiar with it and I like familiarity. There was a big Italian community in Stamford. I have some family in the area. I didn't come from a big family. I only have one brother; he still lives part-time in Darien, Connecticut. I have a couple of aunts and uncles, a couple of cousins. I feel really fortunate about not only when but where I grew up. There were Italians that took care of me, if you will. I had coaches and teachers who were Italian. But it wasn't like we had to pound our chest that we were Italian; we pounded our chest that we were friends, family.

1970–79

Larry Bowa

*L*arry Bowa embodies the definition of a baseball "lifer." The son of a minor-league infielder and manager, he has spent his entire adult life in the game, as a player, coach, and manager. Not blessed with exceptional talent, Bowa was a quintessential hard-nosed ballplayer and overachiever. Through determination and tireless effort, the 5-foot-10, 155-pound infielder from Sacramento became a five-time All-Star and two-time Gold Glove winner in a 16-year big league career (1970–85) with the Phillies, Cubs, and Mets. Beginning in his rookie season, he was a starting shortstop for 15 consecutive years, 12 with the Phillies and three with the Cubs. His best season came in 1978 when he finished third in the MVP vote. Bowa ranks second all-time in NL fielding percentage and games played at short.

He managed the Padres in 1987 and part of 1998, then managed the Phillies for four years (2001–04). After leading the team to its first winning record since 1993, he was named NL Manager of the Year in 2001. He also coached for the Angels, Mariners, Yankees, Dodgers, and Phillies. In 2017, his 43rd season in the majors and 33rd with the Phillies, Bowa was in his fourth season as their bench coach.

Always candid and outspoken, he pulls no punches in expressing his old-school opinions about the way the game should be played, how it's changed since his playing days, the skills and attitudes of current players, and the importance of fundamentals and hard work.

* * *

Our family name on my dad's side was Bua. It was changed way before my time, say in the late twenties, early thirties. Growing up, I very much had a sense of being Italian. My great-grandparents came from Italy. My great-grandmother and my grandmother spoke a lot of Italian. They lived a long life, they raised a lot of kids, and they worked hard. I think the Italian generation never took anything for granted. You have to work and earn your way; no one was going to give you anything. To this day I respect that. I want to go to Italy; there's a lot of tradition there from my family. Hopefully that will come about.

My work ethic came from my dad, no question. He had two and three jobs he had to do. He didn't come from a lot of money so I'd see him get up at five in the morning and come home at eight at night, every day. Yet on the weekends, he always had time to go to the park and play. If I said, "Dad, let's go hit and take ground balls," he never said no. Italians are known for working hard and taking care of their families. That was my dad. My mom was Slavic; she was another tough person. She played softball and I got a lot of mental toughness from her too.

My dad taught me how to play the game. He was a third baseman with the Cardinals organization and got as high as Triple A. He played for the Sacramento Solons and the Duluth Dukes. Then he got as high as Double A as a manager. He taught me how to do the little things, how to be a complete player, not just worry about hitting the ball. You've got to worry about defense and stealing bases and bunting. He just taught me everything. My dad used to talk about DiMaggio all the time. He did it all. Not just power, but the way he handled himself, his gracefulness in the outfield. A professional from the word go.

To be honest with you, I wanted to play professionally, but I was small. So I knew the odds were probably against me. I used to watch games on TV. I remember staying home from school and watching the World Series in '56 when Don Larsen pitched a perfect game. My mom and me, we kept score together. When I was growing up, the Yankees were on every Saturday, so that was my favorite team. I idolized Rizzuto. He was one of the guys I watched a lot. Then watching Nellie Fox and Luis Aparicio; they were small guys. You felt these guys aren't really big so maybe something could happen here. I loved watching all those little guys. They were the same type players: scrappers, didn't hit a lot of home runs but helped their teams in different ways, with the glove, getting runners over, bunting, stealing bases, being a pesky out.

My dad always told me you don't have to be big to play this game. You had to be a smart player, moving runners, stealing bases, making routine plays. Whatever you hit is a bonus. Obviously, the game has changed in that respect. My dad taught me fundamentals when I was in Little League. That's why it bothers me sometimes when you watch games; as basic as a bunt is, guys can't do it. It doesn't show you the real meaning of the game. To me, you've got to be able to do everything. And it's not their fault. Guys that own these teams pay for home runs and RBIs; the fundamentals are sort of thrown under the rug.

That's why I like watching Kansas City. They're fundamentally a sound team. I like watching the Giants. They put the ball in play and they don't have six guys that strike out 140 times. When you have the sabermetrics people saying what's the big deal with strikeouts, it's a stupid statement to make, and the people that make those statements, to me, they have no knowledge of the game of baseball. There's a lot about strikeouts. It means you're not putting the ball in play where something bad can happen. Put it in play, the guy could throw it away, there's a bad hop you get a base hit.

I got signed by Eddie Bockman, a scout for the Phillies. I didn't play in high school; I got cut every year. They said I was too small. But I went to Sacramento Junior College, played two years, and I made all-conference at shortstop. Eddie saw me and called the Phillies and said, "I've got a guy who can catch the ball, throw, and run. I don't know if he's going to hit, but in the long run, he'd be a good organization guy." They asked him what it would take to get me to sign, and Eddie said, "I can get him for $2,000."

Bob Wellman, my very first manager, was important to me. My very first game, with Spartanburg in the Western Carolinas League, I struck out four times. I remember sitting at my locker. He said, "Are you all right?" And I said, "If baseball is like this, you guys might as well send me home." And he said, "Well, this guy is going to be something special." And it was Nolan Ryan. I'm playing in Spartanburg, South Carolina, and the lights are about as bright as when you turn on your lamp to read at night.

I was still a right-handed hitter when I went to Bob Skinner, another guy who played an integral part in me getting to the big leagues. I made the team in '69 as a utility player, and he called me in and said, "You can make this team right now as a utility player, or you can go down and learn how to switch-hit in Triple A," and I said, "I don't want to play utility. I'll go down and learn how to switch-hit."

So after all those years hitting right-handed, I had to go to Triple A and learn how to hit left-handed. Obviously, it was very ugly at the beginning. I struggled my first year in the big leagues trying to switch-hit, but I ended up hitting .250. When someone tells you to eat with your right hand and now all of a sudden you're twenty-two years old and they tell you to put this in your left hand and do this, it was hard. I had never tried it before. I look back on that and I say, *What a dope. Why didn't you say, "I'll play in the big leagues as a utility player"?* But I rolled the dice and said I want to play every day. It did pay off.

I think the one guy that probably had more influence on me besides my dad was my manager for three years in the minor leagues and then was my first big league manager, Frank Lucchesi. He would always say "paesan." My first year I was hitting about a buck eighty, and I thought I was going to get sent out. I remember him calling me in like it was yesterday. He said, "You know, there's a lot of rumors about you being sent out." I said, "You're probably going to send me out. I'd have no hard feelings; I'm not doing the job." And he said, "You're my shortstop, no matter what happens." I might never have played in the big leagues if it wasn't for him. He let me stay up there and learn how to play, and I played 16 years. So, besides my dad, he was a real big influence in my baseball career.

The toughest part of major league baseball is the daily grind of playing every day. I used to pride myself on playing a lot of games. Knock on wood, I didn't get hurt that much. I took a lot of pride just going out there, and that starts with mental toughness. When you're working out in the winter, you're working out to play every day, not four days a week or five days a week. You're working out to play a 150-plus games. You're going to get some days off, but your mind-set is, "I'm going to play every day."

As far as who were the toughest guys for me to hit, at first, everybody. There were a lot of them: Ryan, Bob Gibson, Seaver. They're all Hall of Fame pitchers. That's why when some of these kids ask me, "Did you ever face really good pitchers?", I say, "If they had the radar guns they have now, those guys would all register 95 to 98." The only thing different is the mentality of pitchers these days. They don't like pitching inside or they're not taught to, whereas those guys, they were mean. If you took a hard swing or fell down, the next pitch would be up and in. It's one thing facing a good pitcher you know is going to be around the plate, but facing a pitcher who had a mean streak down his back . . . we didn't have all that armor and that stuff. Guys like Ryan and Gibson, they had that mean streak in them. If you got a hit, you just ran down there; you didn't gloat, you didn't flip, you didn't do shit. You just got down there and said thank you for letting me have the ability to get a hit off of them. You didn't stare at them if they threw one up and in. You didn't do that stuff. That's just the way the game was played.

When I was in the minor leagues, I used to watch Rico Petrocelli a lot. He was ahead of me but not by much. You'd always say some stuff to players. If the guy was a pretty good player, you might say, "That's the Italian in you coming out," or something like that. *"Dago"* and *"wop"* are terms you should never use. You respect the heritage and you're not supposed to use things like that.

I used to love watching Willie Stargell play. I was very lucky; my first year, I got to see Roberto Clemente play. That was something special. Johnny Bench, Pete Rose, the Dodgers with that infield. There were a lot of good players when I played. The competition between me and Davey Concepción; he obviously had more power than I did, but it was a friendly competition we had. John Smoltz, when he first started out, he had to have a professional guy take care of the mentality of how to pitch. When he and Maddux first came up they struggled; now they're in the Hall of Fame. Shows you a lot about their mental toughness. I really think that when you go through adversity, this game makes you a better person. And there aren't too many guys that can say they didn't go through adversity when they played baseball.

Today, Syndergaard stands out real big in my mind; four pitches, great velocity, got a little mean streak in him. There are a lot of good pitchers now. I just think that with the philosophy these trainers have now, the information they have, the diets they're on, the conditions are better. I was very fortunate to coach in LA when Kershaw first came up, to watch him go through that maturation process. But you can look at every team and there's some talent on the mound. I love watching McCutchen play, I like the way Bryce Harper plays the game. Trout. I like the way Rizzo handles himself, very professional. Votto, a good hitter. Posey. Mike Piazza, another great catcher with tremendous power. He probably hit the ball the other way better than anybody I've ever seen. There are so many good baseball players now. I just wish that all the players were fundamentally sound. The ones I mentioned are pretty much fundamentally sound; that's why they're such great players.

It doesn't matter in baseball, your size or your weight. If you've got a big heart and you're willing to work—I don't mean an hour a day, I mean a lot of hours—and you want it bad enough, you go out and get it. A lot of guys say "I want it," but do they really want it? Are they willing to sacrifice? In the summer, I was playing Legion ball and stuff like that, not going on vacation all summer, just playing baseball, getting to the park at nine o'clock in the morning and staying till four in the afternoon. You had to get there at nine o'clock because if you didn't get a diamond, you didn't play. I remember my mom packing a lunch and dropping me off and picking me up. That to me is sacrifice, but I wanted to do it. This game's been great to me and I respect the heck out of it. I get a little annoyed at some of the antics guys do now, but again, it's a different game now. It's an entertainment business, so I've learned to deal with the bat-flipping. I think back and wonder if somebody did that to Carlton or Gibson, what would happen the next time up.

I'm all for guys making money, there's no question about that. But you've got utility players making two or three million dollars a year. But, hey, if the owners didn't have it, they wouldn't give it to them. That part doesn't bother me at all. I'm glad for these guys that they can make that kind of money and take care of their families the rest of their lives. It would've been nice to do that when we played, but everything being what it was at that time, we thought it was a lot of money.

I'll tell you one thing I wish I could implement if I could be commissioner for a day. They have these seminars for these up-and-coming kids in the wintertime in North Carolina. They have the speakers telling them this is what you have to do. I would change that and put it in Cooperstown and make those guys go through all the history of the game and learn about Marvin

Miller, learn about Curt Flood, the strikes guys went on, the reason you're making all this money. I think it would be important for these kids coming up. That's how you know what the history of baseball is all about. A lot of players today, if you asked them, wouldn't even know who Rizzuto was, or DiMaggio. I'm telling you, there's no history involved. I'm not saying all of them, but most of them, they just know what's going on right now.

The game has changed. Obviously, the rules are different; the slide rule at home, the slide rule at second. I'm not thrilled with either one of them. The game's the game. The catcher wants to go off the plate, let him go off the plate. If he doesn't want to, he doesn't have to. I'm not in for dirty play, but I was always taught to break up a double play in a clean manner. I don't advocate late slides, but as a middle infielder, once the shortstop turns his back, he's got to know that's not a double play, so to get the out and get out of the way. Things like that. Warnings on a breaking ball; if a guy hits you with a breaking ball, that's a warning. I mean, come on!

I guess instant replay is a sign of the times. Teams can get the wild card by one game. If it means getting the call right, I'm willing to take that. I do think it puts more pressure on umpires. An umpire establishes the strike zone in the first inning and you make the adjustment; that's how it should be. Every umpire is different. But now they're getting graded on whether the ball's in the box. To me, it puts a lot of pressure on the umpire. I'll be honest with you; I wouldn't get any of them right if I was an umpire. You wonder, how did he make that call, because they're right most of the time. Then, on the other hand, we've had some calls already in 20 games where the calls got overturned. If you get it right, I guess that's the bottom line.

I stay in the game because I like teaching, I like trying to help out, even though some guys are set in their ways. The barrier's up; they're in the big leagues and they don't need any help. I never force anything on them. I try to suggest things. If they want to do it, fine; if they don't, that's up to them. I never say this is the way I did it, I want you to do it that way. Everybody's different. I learned that the hard way. I thought everyone should have my work ethic. I tell these guys even in spring training, "Every one of you has more ability than me, but I don't know if you have the drive or the desire." It's more than just ability. It's being able to deal with 0-for-15s, it's being able to deal with making an error in the eighth inning and losing the game. You've got to be able to turn the page. I always wanted every ball to me. I didn't care if I made an error, I wanted every ball hit to me. But again, my work ethic is different. I took fifty to sixty ground balls every day. Now they say don't take too many ground balls, you'll get tired. I just shake my head when I hear stuff like that.

I respect the heck out of Joe Torre. Lou Piniella, Jimmy Leyland, Tony La Russa. What they've done in baseball as managers, to mold teams like they did, to have that instant respectability that they get. Danny Ozark was a great guy for our team. We had a bunch of rabble-rousers, and he was quiet and he let us do our thing. Dallas Green put his foot up our ass when he had to. I learned a lot as a manager by watching them. But you know, if there is a negative in baseball it's that you get labeled, and people don't think that you change. In Philly, I basically took over a team that lost 100 games every year, four or five years. And then every year I managed we were over .500. So I feel a little bit responsible for changing the culture of that clubhouse. Obviously, I wasn't around to reap the benefits. I think that in baseball they label people, and people do change. But that's just the way baseball is.

Looking back, I think you have to delegate coaches. You've got enough to worry about with the media and strategy and pitchers. So, hindsight being 20/20, you'd like to see them do their thing. It's tough to manage a team and not lose players. Dan Plesac would be the first to tell you he loved playing for me, and he said he's shocked at some people saying Bowa was tough. He says it's like these guys who lined up to play basketball at Indiana; they knew

Larry Bowa
AP Photo/Ralph Freso.

what Bobby Knight was all about and they still went there. That was a pretty good correlation. I'm just that way; I wear my emotions on my sleeve whether I'm mad or I'm happy. I've always done that, so it's not a matter of being a frontrunner. When I'm mad, I'm mad, and when I'm happy, I'm happy. I don't like losing. I used to play my daughter in gin. As bad as this sounds, when she beat me, I'd get mad. I like winning. Even now when we're going through a rebuilding process, I still don't like it when we lose. And I knew when we came into this, it's going to be tough and you've got to battle through it. I understand that, but I still don't like losing. That's just the way I am. I'll never accept losing. I've learned how to deal with it, but I'll never accept it.

Baseball's been my whole life, really. I've been around it since I could walk. Being able to play in the big leagues and move through the Phillies system in a pretty fast manner, it's something you don't take for granted. I've always respected the game and tried to stay humble. You can't get too high; you can get too down, on the East Coast particularly. You've gotta be able to handle all the adversity and the expectations that people put on you. On the East Coast, it's a live-and-die sport. I was always taught, just play the game hard, no matter what the score is, no matter what you're doing. If you're 0-for-4 or 4-for-4, play each game like it might be your last game. That's how I've approached it ever since I put on a uniform.

As far as memories, winning the 1980 World Series is the ultimate for me. That's your goal. We got in the playoffs a lot of years, but we always came up short. We played the Big Red Machine and the Dodgers. We had good teams and then finally to get over the hump and see the parade and all the people that came out, that's something that stays with you forever. All the individual stuff (All-Star games—I played in five of them—Gold Gloves, I hit .300), I can honestly tell you sitting here a lot of my buddies who played said, "Gosh, I wish I could've done that when I played."

I did everything I wanted to do. I played hard; I got the most out of my ability. No one thought I'd get 1,000 hits, never mind 2,000, because I was an out when I came up. But I worked at it, I persevered. I had a hitting coach, Billy DeMars, who probably worked with me more than anybody ever, and we learned how to hit. I just put in a lot of long hours, not just during the season, during the winter. I didn't take any days off; I might've taken two weeks after the season just to unwind, but I'd be right back at it again. Even after five All-Star Games, I approached spring training every year thinking I had to win a job. That was my mentality; I've got to win a job no matter what I did last year. People were waiting to take my job, so that's how I approached it. And I think it made me a better person playing the game that way.

I don't worry about whether my career was underestimated. When people bring it up to me, they tell me to look at Phil Rizzuto's numbers or Aparicio's numbers, and they're in the Hall of Fame. I don't look at it that way. I mean, if people say, "Man, he was pretty good," that's all I care about. It would be great to do that, but that was the farthest thing from my mind coming up. I just wanted to play in the big leagues. I'm just happy the way everything unfolded for me. I never had a smell of the draft. So to say you never got drafted and play 16 years in the big leagues . . .

Steve Palermo

*F*or the most part, anonymity is a good thing for umpires. They tend to get noticed only when they make what are perceived, by managers, players, or fans, as mistakes. On the other hand, there are some umpires whose performance sets them apart in a positive way. Steve Palermo was one of those umpires.

The grandson of four Italian immigrants, the Worcester, Massachusetts, native became a major-league umpire in 1977 at the age of twenty-six after a rapid ascent through the minor leagues. He was soon acknowledged as one the best in the game, gaining the respect of players, managers, and fellow umpires. Dan Bellino, a major-league umpire since 2011, said of Palermo, "Ask anybody that worked with him or worked in that era and they all say Steve Palermo would've been a Hall of Fame umpire. He was that good. Some guys were born to be umpires; Steve was one of them."

Palermo was part of the umpiring crew in the 1983 World Series, four American League Championship Series, and the 1986 All-Star Game. On July 4, 1983, he was the home plate umpire for Dave Righetti's no-hitter against the Red Sox at Yankee Stadium. He was also the third-base umpire who made the fair call on Bucky Dent's decisive home run in the 1978 AL East tiebreaker game between the Yankees and Red Sox at Fenway Park, a call that disappointed his father, a Red Sox fan.

On July 6, 1991, in the midst of his fifteenth season, his on-field career was cut short by a bullet wound he suffered while coming to the rescue of two women who were being beaten and robbed outside a restaurant in Dallas, Texas. Doctors told him he would never walk again, but Palermo rejected that prognosis and for almost five years went through the painful rehabilitation process that enabled him to walk with the aid of a cane. In 2000, he was named an umpire supervisor by Major League Baseball, a position he held until his death on May 14, 2017, at the age of sixty-seven after battling cancer.

Palermo provides insights into the world of umpiring and talks about the intricacies of dealing with players and managers, his role as a supervisor of major-league umpires, and how he dealt with his life-changing injury.

* * *

My grandfathers and grandmothers on both sides were born in Italy, in Foggia and Bari. With the last name Palermo, everybody takes it for granted that we're Sicilian. I remember one time Sal Bando, who is Sicilian, questioned a pitch, and I barked at him. He said, "That Sicilian temper!" I replied, "I'm not Sicilian." And he said, "Oh, excuse me, excuse me."

My mom and dad were first generation, born here. I grew up in Worcester, Massachusetts, for the first nine years and then we moved to Oxford, Massachusetts, because my dad was a school principal. Education kind of runs in our family; I have two sisters and a brother who taught. There was a strong bond because we grew up in a triple-decker. My aunt and uncle with their six kids and my grandfather and grandmother were on the first floor. Another aunt and uncle were on the second floor, and our family, with five kids at the time, were on the third floor. It was a lively house.

I played Little League, high school, American Legion, and college baseball. After I got out of Little League and I'm thirteen, I started umpiring Little League games, making two dollars a game. I really liked that atmosphere, and at that time Oxford was a hotbed for pretty good baseball players. I quit umpiring when I was sixteen and started working construction in the summer and did that through college trying to make some money for tuition.

When I was nineteen, I got a phone call from Stan Johnson, who ran the district Little League. He said, "Steve, I've run into a problem. I need an umpire for tomorrow; my guy canceled and I need a guy for the All-Star game. I was wondering if you could work." I said, "Gee, Mr. Johnson, I haven't worked in four years." And he said, "Oh, for you it's like riding a bike. Don't worry about it; you'll be fine."

I couldn't say no to him, so I did it. This was the summer of '70. Mr. Johnson came up to me during the game and said somebody wanted to talk to me after the game. I thought it was somebody's dad who wanted to punch me out. Come to find out, it was Barney Deary, a native of Massachusetts who ran Baseball Umpire Development, which was the minor-league arm of Major League Baseball. He was at the game on a lark because his nephew asked him to go. We sat down at a picnic table, and he said, "Have you ever thought about getting into professional umpiring?" I had never given it any thought and had no idea what it entailed. I said, "What do you do, work a couple of more high school games and college games and just go to Fenway Park?" I thought about it for a year and a half, and I told my dad, "I think I'd like to go to umpiring school."

I went in the winter of '72, came out of that class and was assigned to spring training in Tampa with the Cincinnati Reds. After that, I worked in St. Pete for three months when the new program for extended spring training started. I worked 60 games there, then was assigned to the New York-Penn

League, and then I went down to the Instructional League. All in all, I worked probably 220 games that year.

The next year I was invited back to the umpire school as a junior instructor. After that I never had another job because I was working ten months out of the year, teaching at the school late January into March, then right into spring training and all the way through to the Instructional League. So basically, I had December and part of January off, and then right back at it again. That's how it all started. I was the first and only one that Barney Deary ever found on the sandlots, in his own backyard. So it was kind of fortuitous for me and for him.

In '73 I was promoted to the Carolina League, where there were a lot of top-rated Class A players. I worked there for half a year and then was promoted to the Eastern League, Double A. That same year I went to the Instructional League again. Then, at the end of December, Barney called and said, "Steve, how would you like to go to the Dominican Republic to work in winter ball?"

Usually they sent Triple-A umpires down there, and I only had two years in the game. I didn't know it at the time, but the four Triple-A umpires that were down there had been threatened, and they all took off. Barney had called Rich Garcia, who was an excellent umpire and probably should be in the Hall of Fame. He had been in the Dominican the year before and was in Triple A and on the verge of going to the big leagues. Barney asked him who he would take down there with him, and he said, "Give me Eric Gregg and Stevie, and we'll go down there and clean it up. Then we'll work the playoffs and be home in time to teach at the umpire school." So we went down to the Dominican for about a month and a half. That was a hell of an experience.

I went back to the Eastern League for the full year of '74, then I went down to Puerto Rico. In '75 I got promoted to Triple-A American Association, and then went back to Puerto Rico for winter ball. At that time, you had to show them that you wanted to work and you'd go anywhere. If they sent you to hell, you looked forward to the trip.

Then I got a full schedule of big league spring training games in '76 because the American League was interested in me. I went back to Triple A in '76, and in '77 I went to spring training with the American League. Then, just before the season started, I was offered a contract. So in five years, from '72 to '77, I made it to the big leagues, when I was twenty-six years old.

I was just fortunate to be in the right place at the right time. You've got to be lucky as well as good because of the number of openings. When I got into the big leagues, there were fifty-two umpires, now we have seventy-six. When I was at Baseball Umpire Development, there were seventy of us, and there was a class of about 130, 140 guys at Al Somers's school, so you're looking at over 200 guys, and I think there were a total of twenty-one or twenty-two jobs in the minor leagues. Our 1972 class at Baseball Umpire Development is considered to be the greatest class of all time, not because I was in it, but because six of us came out of that class of only seventy guys. That's unheard of. You might have one, possibly two, maybe three guys, and that's a lot from one class, that eventually get to the big leagues, and we had six guys.

I had several mentors. Larry Napp, a former American League umpire, was a teacher at the umpire school and a great influence on me. He's Italian; he changed it from Napodano. And Al Barlick, who's in the Hall of Fame. Frank Pulli, another Italian and a former National League umpire, was a great influence, along with Richie Garcia. There were a ton of Italian American umpires prior to me getting there: [Al] Salerno, [Augie] Donatelli, Napp, [Frank] Dascoli, [Vic] Voltaggio, Pulli. John Hirschbeck is part Italian.

Nestor Chylak, another Hall of Fame umpire, was a huge influence on me. In the fall of 1976, before I was signed by the American League, Nestor called Dick Butler, the supervisor of umpires for the American League, and said, "Why don't you send Stevie to work the last couple of games at Fenway Park with my crew? You know he's coming to the big leagues, so why don't we let him get his feet wet." So Fenway Park was the first game I ever worked in the major leagues, and it was all because Nestor stuck his neck out.

I didn't know this story until 1991 when my dad visited me in the hospital after I was shot. In 1977 he had met us at the airport when our crew flew into Boston. He and Nestor drove to the hotel in one car, while the rest of our crew followed in another. My dad said that while they were in the car Nestor told him that he had never seen anyone with more talent on the baseball field than me. He said I had natural ability, I understood situations, I knew when to go off and when not to, and I had good field presence.

I said, "Really?" I was Nestor's whipping boy because I was the youngest one on the crew. If something went wrong, it was going to be my fault. But there was a reason for that. That's why I have such high regard for Nestor. I realized he wasn't picking on me; he was preparing me. And for that, I'm eternally grateful to him.

The job description of umpire is a lot greater than people realize. Obviously, you're making judgments on plays, but you also need to be a bit of a psychologist because you're dealing with all of these egos, whether it be the coaches, managers, or players. You've got to be a lawyer because you have to choose your words very carefully when you're explaining what took place on the field, how the rule is interpreted, and why you did what you did.

Obviously, you're a judge because you're making all of these decisions. And you're wearing the hat of law enforcement because you're keeping law and order out there.

So there are a great many things wrapped into being a major league umpire. It's not just what people think; that you throw a dime out there and just stand on it and don't move for three hours. There is a lot more that's entailed. Obviously, you're in control of the game. Umpires have never come into question as far as integrity. They stand above and beyond reproach as far as that's concerned. That's how it's been since the beginning of baseball. It just wouldn't be tolerated that you'd abuse an umpire, although there have been celebrated arguments going back to the days of Bill Klem. It's been going on forever. Umpiring was a noble profession.

There is nothing easy about umpiring. Some things are less difficult than others, but everything is difficult because every time you make a decision, 50 percent of the people you make the decision about aren't going to like it. And the other side is sitting there saying, "He's just doing his job." So you're not really getting a pat on the back for making a great call, and the other side is saying that was a terrible call. The vote is always split, 50–50. That's why you're out there, to always ensure that the playing field is level; allow the talent to decide the outcome of the game. The umpire just makes sure that the talent plays by the rules of the game.

The working conditions for umpires have changed tremendously. The air travel is so onerous now. You used to have more flights to get from one city to another. Now umpires have to take the first flight in the morning. So that means you may get off the field at one o'clock in the morning, if there's a rain delay or extra innings, and get back to the hotel at 2:00 or 2:30. You're up at 4:30 to catch a six o'clock flight. You have to be on that first flight because they want you in town by noon to one o'clock in the afternoon. Whereas we would have a flight at 8:00, 8:30, 9:00, and 9:45, say, and we could take any one of those flights and get there before noon. So it's a lot more difficult as far as that's concerned.

But now umpires have more time off. They get four weeks off in season, whereas we had none. My first year we worked, I think, nine extra games because we picked up other people's rainouts. Basically, in my first two years, '77 and '78, if you lived in a remote area where it wasn't close to a big-league city, you'd leave in April and get home at the All-Star break. Then you would leave two days later and get home in October. That's just how it was.

Bart Giamatti was very aware of what an umpire meant to the game. He took it seriously to try and improve the conditions. He was a great man.

Then his deputy, Fay Vincent, was also very aware and had a high concern for umpires.

For the most part, umpire crews got along. Yeah, there were a couple of personality conflicts with certain people, but overall guys just said, "This is the way it's going to be." It's kind of like you're married, and now you gotta make the best of it and figure out how it's going to work. When you think about it, during the baseball season you're with that crew for 184 days. You're only with your wife and kids for 181 days. You're married to them as much as you are to your kids and your wife. You just figure out a way to get along, because basically, you're that third team out on the field.

I think the technology now is very good. When I started, baseball was in its infancy as to what they could do with the cameras and everything, covering the game. Then they started saying we've got this thing called instant replay now. We can replay the play and slow it down a little bit. It's another given for the fans if you will. We thought it would be Big Brother looking over our shoulder and saying, "Aha, this guy messed up that play; that's it, he's done." And you'll just sit there and get nationally crucified. And as it turned out, people would approach us on the street and say, "Boy, you guys are awful good at what you do. I take a look at a play on TV and think he missed it. Then they run the replay and you see that he got it right." You know, these guys are awfully good at what they do.

There were a few managers and players that were difficult to deal with. I was in that era with Billy Martin, Earl Weaver, Ralph Houk, and Dick Williams. These were rough, tough old baseball guys, and they'd come out and challenge you. But the thing is, with most of them, all but Earl, if you stood by your convictions and let them know that you felt you were absolutely right and you worked hard, they left you alone. That's how you got your reputation.

Earl Weaver was a little bit more defiant. I jokingly made the statement that if God was dressed up in an umpire's uniform, Earl would still scream at him. He didn't care who it was. Then maybe later on in retrospect he'd come up to you and say, "You know that play yesterday? Let me tell you something; it was a lot closer than I thought it was." He may not say that you got it right, but in a roundabout way, he was.

My first two years, Billy Martin and I fought like cats and dogs. He'd say, "You're nothing but a hotheaded dago son of a bitch." And I'd say, "What do you think you are? You're half Italian."

We'd just go back and forth and we fought and fought. I'd say fair; he'd say foul. Finally, one day when he was managing Oakland and they'd been beat by the Yankees, we were going up the runway. As we were walking up the stairs it

Steve Palermo (left) arguing with Baltimore Orioles manager Earl Weaver.
AP Photo.

was quiet and somber; he never said anything after a loss. Then Billy turned to me and said, "Hey, 'Daigs,' you notice I didn't holler at you tonight?"

I said, "Yeah, Billy. What's the matter, you got a sore throat?"

He said, "No. I've come to the realization that you work harder than anybody else on the field, and neither me nor any of my players will argue with you."

So I respected him, and he respected me. He was great to me. But Billy couldn't stand losing. A little piece of him died every time he lost a game. It affected him that much.

It affects us too, you know. You don't want to make that bad call because it affects the perception of what we do. Of course, if we make a bad call it should be forgotten the next day. There were some players who didn't really abide by that philosophy at times. "You screwed up yesterday, and you screwed up again today," you'd hear from the dugout. That's it; they're gone. We don't play yesterday's game today. I learned that from Nestor. He had these sayings and that was one of them: "You don't play Tuesday's game on Wednesday."

You learn how to draw the line about ejecting somebody from instinct and experience. It's not imposing your will but letting them know that I'm strong in my convictions. I feel that this guy was out. I don't care what you say, but you'd better not say the magic word because that will be it.

I was known as a red ass when I got to the big leagues. I was working third base in this spring training game, Orioles and Yankees. Elrod Hendricks, the Orioles' catcher, knew me from winter ball in Puerto Rico. Billy Hunter was the Orioles third-base coach, and he said, "From what I understand, the rumor has it that you're a red ass. Is that true?" I looked at him, and I said, "Yes, it is." So he turned around and looked into the third-base dugout at Earl Weaver and just nodded his head yes. Elrod had said, "You see that guy at third base, Earl. He doesn't take any shit." Billy Hunter was basically confirming what Elrod had told Earl.

My current job as a supervisor is not quite the next best thing to being out there. There's nothing like being out on the field. But I do enjoy being able to teach and impart the little that I know to somebody young and help them avoid making mistakes that I made. Hopefully they understand what you're talking about. You have to be able to relate to them how you do certain things and why you do them. For example, I'll see a guy and he'll be standing in a certain position, and I'll ask him why he's standing there. What's the purpose of standing on that side of the base as opposed to standing on the other side? Is there a reason?

Those are the things I learned early on in my career. If I had a concern about something, in the middle of an inning I'd go over to Richie or Nestor and I'd say, "I felt uncomfortable as that play developed; I slid to my right and I really feel that I should've gone to my left." And they'd tell me, "Go with your instincts the next time because your instincts are right." We start supervising umpires in the minors when they get to Triple A because that's when we start bringing them to the fall league. Then if we feel like they're capable, we put them into some spring training games, then we'll feed them some games over the course of the season. They may get 10, 12, 15 games, depending on their maturity on the field and how they handle themselves. We've got three or four kids who are coming up, and they look like they're twelve. That's why I got tested a lot, because I had such a baby face when I first got to the big leagues. That's a detriment because they just don't believe you. Whereas if you see a guy out there that weighs 270 pounds and he's got a nineteen-inch neck, they'll say, "I don't think I want to fool with him."

We have five supervisors in the big leagues and we have seventy-two umps, so we split them up, and I might end up with four or five crews. We are scheduled to keep track of them predominantly, but we watch everybody. I happen to live in a big-league town, so when they come in here, I'm overseeing those guys that are in, even though they may not be my crew. You make evaluations on each and every one of them.

If there's an issue, you go in the locker room and talk about it. If it happens to be a getaway day, you may get them on the phone the following day when they arrive in another city. And you document all that. It's very detailed, what we do. With the crews that I have, if I've got sixteen umpires, I look at every one of the plays that each one of them had the previous night. All of that tape is sent to me, and I go through every call they made.

Joe Torre is the chief baseball officer of Major League Baseball, so we work in his department. He's terrific to work for. He's a good man, but I didn't like him when he was a manager. He was tough. He'd come out and he'd just scare you.

Baseball is an amazing game because you remember the play, you remember the pitch, you remember the situation. You know, you go to a game and watch Michael Jordan play, you come home and you go, "Wow, what a great player." But what do you remember of what he did? In baseball, you can say, "I was sitting with my dad, he was to my left and we both had a beer in our hands, and Ted Williams came up to hit, and the crowd was just going crazy. It was a 3–2 game, bottom of the ninth, there's a guy on first base, it was a 1-1 pitch. He hit it to dead left-center field. See that seat out there, right next to that pole? Well, that's where he hit it." You just remember everything.

The game is held in a timeless space and it's what you derive from it. You can make it as technical and as analytical as you want, or you can make it as light and enjoyable and carefree as you want. You see one person in the stands, he's laughing and having fun with his friends. Another guy is biting his fingernails, and the score is 7–1 and he's ahead. It's what it means to each individual in the context of that moment.

In 1978, I was the third-base umpire in the playoff game between the Red Sox and Yankees at Fenway Park. My dad played hooky from school that Monday and he and my mom got to Fenway about twelve o'clock for the 2:30 game. I took my dad to the locker room and he's like a kid in a candy store. I never realized how much he loved the game because all of my adult years I was gone. Of course, in the seventh inning, Bucky Dent hits the home run into the net. It was just to the right of the foul pole, and I point fair and signal home run.

After the game, my dad comes to the locker room, and he's quiet. We're all shaking hands; the season's over, that's it. We got in the car and we're heading back to Oxford. We're on the Mass. Turnpike, about fifteen minutes into the ride. There was no conversation in the car. I turned to my dad and said, "Pop, that was a hell of a game, wasn't it?" And he turned to me and he just looked at me and said, "You couldn't have called that ball foul?" I said, "What ball?" "Bucky's home run." I said, "Pop, the ball was ten feet to the right of the foul pole." "So what," he said. "You're in Boston; nobody would have said a word." So when people tell me about pressure, I say, "You have no idea what pressure is."

I very much enjoyed being an umpire. It was a great challenge to try and go out and be perfect every night. And then to improve on that perfection as time went on, just to get better and better. You're basically being asked to do the impossible, and that's being perfect.

We all have a story to tell. My injury is part of the story, unfortunately. The thing that I regret is that I didn't leave on my own terms; I was forced off. When tragedy strikes, everybody turns to the Bible and prayers; in the good times they're not asking for help because they think they're doing it on their own. In the bad times, it's done on your own too. It's how you handle adversity as much as the adversity itself. You learn along the way that you are as vulnerable as anyone else. You're not bulletproof, no pun intended. This thing that we call life is very, very fragile. It can disappear in an instant. I know that the colors in my world are a little bit more vivid than most people's colors. The reds are redder, the greens are greener. You appreciate a whole lot more the things that you've accomplished, the people you've met along the way. It's been a humbling experience in a lot of ways. But we'll keep fighting the good fight. You can either throw your hands up and say, "I give up," or you can pound your fist on the table and say, "I'm going to fight this thing until the end."

Dave Righetti

*F*or San Jose, California, native Dave Righetti, baseball has been part of his *life as long as he can remember. His father, Leo, was signed by the Yankees while a junior in high school and played professional ball for 13 years, including three (1953–55) as a shortstop with the San Francisco Seals in the Pacific Coast League.*

Drafted by the Rangers in 1977, Righetti was traded to the Yankees following the 1978 season. As a starter, he was the AL Rookie of the Year in 1981, then threw a no-hitter against the Red Sox on July 4, 1983. When future Hall of Fame closer Goose Gossage left the Yankees after the 1983 season for free agency, manager Yogi Berra gave the role to Righetti, who saved 31 games in his first year. In 1986, "Rags" established a major-league record of 46 saves (since broken) and won the first of his two Rolaids Relief Awards.

In seven years as the Yankees closer (1984–90), the two-time All Star saved 223 games, averaging just under 32 per season. In Yankees franchise history, only Mariano Rivera recorded more saves and appeared in more games. Righetti then spent three years with the San Francisco Giants before closing out his 16-year career with the A's, Blue Jays, and White Sox. From 2000 to 2017, he served as the pitching coach for the Giants, who won the World Series in 2010, 2012, and 2014. Widely considered one of the best in baseball, Righetti has coached pitchers who have won two Cy Young awards, thrown five no-hitters, and made 22 All-Star teams.

* * *

My grandfather came over from La Spezia, Italy, in the late 1800s. It was actually a little village up in the hills, the village of Righetti. And he actually married a Righetto who was born and raised in San Francisco. He was in San Francisco at the time of the earthquake, and I think because of the earthquake he started a company, called The Sunshine Scavenger Company. It was like a garbage company but I'm sure in those days it was more like cleaning up the city. Then in the late forties, early fifties, they moved the business to San Jose, and it became San Jose Tallow. My grandpa died when he was almost eighty, back in the early seventies, when I was eleven or twelve, so I didn't get to know him that much.

I came from a very rich history and I'm very proud of my heritage. Younger players today don't have as much sense of their background because they're farther away from the old country, unless they're from Boston, New York, Chicago. But I think the rest of the country, they get westernized a bit. The fishing towns up and down the West Coast, a lot of people who migrated to San Francisco, down to the San Luis Obispo area, places like that, you see a little bit more of it. But other than that, it's breaking up because you're probably marrying outside your background.

All my father's best friends were Italian, ex-ballplayers who played for the San Francisco Seals. My dad's best friends were Charlie Silvera, who caught backup for the Yankees for years, and Sal Taormina, who was probably his closest friend and roommate with the Seals. There were only two kinds of people who seemed to be around, the business people and a lot of baseball people. So to say what baseball meant, it's been our life. I've been making a paycheck since I was eighteen, so it's been my adult life.

My dad was drafted by the Seals in '44, when he was a junior in high school at Bellarmine. He actually left; he didn't finish high school. Bob Fagio was the coach, a very famous high school baseball coach on the West Coast. He was a bird-dog-like scout. Back in that time the Pacific Coast League was so glamorous, there were guys who were asked to go to the big leagues and didn't go. But they were all kind of caught in between because they thought the third big league was going to be on the West Coast. But once the Dodgers and Giants came out in '58, that was it; my dad retired, thinking that was the end of it.

Being with the Seals was kind of like being in the big leagues to those guys; they were being paid well, they were big stars. I remember my dad had a shot at Boston and he didn't go. My dad was a shortstop; he played from '44 and retired in '57. Jerry Coleman was his first roommate and Lefty Gomez was the manager. That was probably around the time Vic Raschi and those guys were playing, so he got a taste of that and played for some great managers: Lefty O'Doul, Rogers Hornsby, who he didn't like.

I didn't think about playing professionally when I was young. I don't look like it now, but when I entered high school, I was 5-foot-3 and 135 pounds. And I stayed that way for quite a while so I didn't do a hell of a lot. I sat on the bench my sophomore year as a basketball player and a baseball player. I grew a little bit my junior year and actually made the varsity. I played left field, hit about .240, but I made all the plays and I had a great arm. I was skinny and they called me "bacon legs." I could swim like a son of a gun, but I wasn't getting into those Speedos for nothing. Between my junior and senior years, I finally got to about 6-foot-1. I got a little stronger, so they let me pitch that summer in American Legion ball. I was getting older guys out, facing Carney Lansford and people like that who were a few years older than me.

I started getting confidence. I went back my senior year and had a pretty good year. I was wild, just learning how to control my fastball. A bunch of us decided to go to Junior College at San Jose City College. The coach was a roommate of my father in Triple A and a lefty, so I figured that would be a good place to go. My brother was there. So that November, within two months of pitching, the coach came up to me and said, "You're going to get drafted." And I said, "Oh, Christ," because I thought he meant the Army. It was the winter of '76 and there was still a draft going on. And he said, "No, dummy, its baseball." Back then there was a winter draft and they called it the second phase. Then the scouts started coming up to me and told me, "You're going in the first round." I just remember all these teams were trying to work me out. I didn't know if it was legal or not.

Bill Wight, the old left-handed reliever for the Yankees, was with Atlanta as a scout, and Atlanta was going to draft me number one and offer me $20,000. And, of course, I said no. I wanted to go to school because I didn't quite think I was ready. And I knew if I signed after the season was over I didn't have to go to spring training and I could immediately go to A ball. The other part of the caveat was that my brother was going to get drafted too. Texas told me they wouldn't draft me unless my brother signed. So they used me against my older brother. I would have signed with Atlanta but Ted Turner tampered with Gary Matthews, the free-agent with the Giants, and they fined him a first-round draft pick. It turned out to be me, so instead of going to Atlanta and being with Johnny Sain, the pitching coach, I signed basically so my brother could sign, and all I got was that $20,000. My brother ended up playing three or four years. He went to A ball and tore up his arches and his feet, stress fractures. They tried to make him a catcher; he was a third baseman, shortstop. He was a big, heavy-legged guy and he could swing the bat. But he broke down and went home to coach locally and work in the family business. He's still coaching to this day, so it's been a good thing. That's how it all got started.

I think my father thought we'd all be home in a few years like most of us were back then. He never said it out loud to me. He knew I had the guts for it and all that, but he didn't think I was strong enough to maintain a long career because I was built much like he was. I ended up filling out and finally getting up to about 200 pounds. There was no weightlifting, of course; we didn't have weight rooms. I definitely was stronger in my ass and my legs. I was lucky; I could pitch all day.

Then I was lucky enough to be traded to the Yankees. The Italian tradition was still there, and you felt some pressure too. But it was also great; it was an honor to live up to. Yogi was still there, Rick Cerone, the catcher, Lee Mazzilli,

Joe Pepitone. They drafted Italian ballplayers from the East so there were quite a few in the organization. After my first or second year they put you in the Columbus Day parade. That was pretty cool. You'd get invited to weddings, kids' graduations, a lot of stuff. It was fun. Once you start playing and you see Charlie Silvera from San Francisco scouting and Frankie Crosetti and all these guys come up to you and say, "Hey, I knew your father back in the fifties," and everything starts to make sense.

Many people remember the no-hitter I threw against the Red Sox in 1983. It's amazing, but that game comes up at least once or twice a week. But as I look back, two things come to mind. It's pretty simple. When I go to bed at night, whether I'm having trouble sleeping or not, two things dominate my sleep or pre-sleep. One is I try to get on a golf course and I play hole by hole. Sometimes I'll make it to the second hole and sometimes I'll go right through the whole eighteen and never fall asleep.

And the other one, believe it or not, I try to change history. My only shot at winning the World Series didn't go well, and I try to rewrite that in my head. I swear to you, it's at least three times a week I do that. Isn't that terrible? I should be thinking about the wins and the wonderful times. In Game Three of the 1981 World Series against Valenzuela and the Dodgers, we lost, 5–4, and I didn't pitch well. I came out in the third or fourth inning. It really came down to one pitch in the first inning. I was trying to pitch around Ron Cey with an open base and Rick Monday on deck. No easy batter, but I had a little advantage because he hadn't faced me yet. I made a bad pitch to Cey. The one pitch I controlled best was my fastball, but I pulled the darn thing over the heart of the plate and he took me deep. I had a natural movement away from righties, if you just relax and throw it. For whatever reason, I tried to straighten it out to make sure I kept it away and I actually cut it, I actually pulled on it, which you can do, and I think about it a lot.

Yogi made the call for me to go into the bullpen. The reason was pretty simple. The day before, Goose Gossage had left for free agency to go to San Diego. At that time it wasn't like it is now; they didn't have a kid prepped in the minors to become a closer. I think they asked Guidry first, but he said he wanted to keep starting. Back then, and even now, if you were a starter you made twice as much money. I wasn't in that kind of position. I was only in my third full year.

When Yogi called, I felt like I couldn't say no. Now from there I just heard tons of grumbling: "No, he shouldn't do it." I did it because I trusted Yogi. He was a brand-new manager because Billy Martin just got fired. When I got to spring training, it got worse because now the reporters got involved. Every day it was *the* story in spring training, to the point where I got tired of it, and I just said, "Hey, I'm doing whatever they want me to do. Am I happy about it? Hell, they're making me the closer of the New York Yankees."

To me, I thought it was an incredible compliment. But I felt uncomfortable because there were a lot of veteran relievers. I was a young guy, and now I'm supposed to be the man. Well, I had to earn it, right? So that was the gist of everything that happened, but it never stopped till the day I left the Yankees. Every year they tried to put me back in as a starting pitcher. That was always talked about. The fans didn't really accept me as a reliever and never thought it was a good idea.

I was supposed to be a closer and pitching less, but actually I threw a lot more. If you look at my first five years in the pen as a closer, I probably threw more innings than any American League [relief] pitcher. I averaged close to 100 innings a year those first five years. What saved me from 100 innings one year was I accidentally sliced open my finger in the bullpen one day on a water cooler, fooling around, talking. I sliced it right on the knuckle, right in the wrong spot on my left hand, so I couldn't go to the All-Star game. Steinbrenner was a little hot. That was the year the Tigers went out 35–5. He blamed it on me.

I'd say three quarters of my games were probably multiple innings. Back then a lot of relievers carried a lot of decisions. One year I had 19 decisions. You just expected to be ready from the sixth inning on. Back then they carried ten pitchers. Eleven was a big deal. They'd wear three of us out, pretty much every game. There were always two or three guys that were close to 100 innings on most staffs. That's just the way it was. Our starting pitching wasn't really very deep for the next few years, and I think that affected it. There was a period we couldn't get free agents that were prime. We'd get guys that were kind of beat up already and we just missed during that period of time because we had maybe the best offense you could put together. We had a hell of a ballclub for a lot of years. We won the most games in the eighties, but of course we didn't win a World Series.

Most managers weren't ex-pitchers, so they didn't like pitchers, especially those guys at that time. My father told me that when I was a young age. He'd say, "We're out there playing our ass off, and they're in there eating sunflower seeds." I can imagine if I was playing every day and I saw some pitcher with his hat off, his feet kicked up on the railing, I wouldn't like it either. So I always understood that. That's why being a reliever kind of appealed to my baseball background. I felt more like an everyday player.

Once I became a reliever I became a little streamlined as a pitcher. I didn't use all four pitches. I was worried about giving it up in the ninth inning with a changeup and that wasn't one of my main pitches. So when those great hitters could just think about me throwing a hard slider or a hard fastball, it actually became a lot tougher for me to pitch. When I was a starter, it was easier for me to face those kinds of guys. Manny Lee probably got the most hits off me, believe it or not. He didn't play all the time but it seemed like he got plenty of hits off me. The Cal Ripkens, the Eddie Murrays. Our division was one of the greatest in baseball from the late seventies all the way into the nineties. The Red Sox, Tigers, Blue Jays.

We didn't get a chance to enjoy Yogi long enough. In '84 we had a nice year; we ended up winning 90 games. We got off to a bad start in '85 and 15, 16 games into the season they fired Yogi. That was a big deal. Billy came back in and players were upset because Yogi never did anything that would make you want to feel like you wanted to do that. We all felt like we let him down. And that turned out to be a tough moment in Yankee history, to be honest. Yogi left the team and never came back for about twenty years. We didn't know it at the time; we thought we'd see him again but we didn't. That was a big deal. We ended up winning about 95 or 97 games that year, but that wasn't good enough.

I had Billy Martin four times as a manager, in four different periods. When I came up at the very end of the 1979 season, the first time I met Billy, the first words out of his mouth were, "Hey, Dago." And immediately you felt like you had a bond. Those things work two ways. You feel like a guy likes you and that's great, but if you let that guy down, it could be twice as hard on you. They're going to stick up for you, and if they do, you'd better be good. I ended up pitching for Billy for many years. I loved it. He gave me the ball; he showed me a lot of trust. He was the opposite of what I had heard, how tough he was on pitchers. He treated me and Ron Guidry and some of us like gold. I felt respected by him and that to me made it okay, because Billy believed he was the number one Yankee. He was Italian, he loved New York, loved the Yankees; he wasn't going to go anywhere else. Of course he did, but that was his dream job. So to have a kinship with him made you feel like you belonged.

He'd intimidate other teams. He'd do things to get noticed a little bit, but he did it on purpose. He'd wake players up that way. He'd take bench players and role players and make them feel like they were starters. There was always a small group of guys on the team, probably a couple of pitchers and a couple of players, who probably weren't his biggest fans, but they didn't do much playing. It was love/hate a lot with Billy; there was no middle ground. He'd wear out his welcome, but then he'd be welcomed back because he knew what he was doing. He could take a lot of heat off a team. Obviously, he could command a lot of attention. That's what those guys were all about back then. The division was filled with Sparky Anderson, Ralph Houk, Billy Martin, Earl Weaver. These people were stars in their own right, so it was a fun era.

Billy was very aggressive. Whatever the strength of the team was, if it was the bullpen, if it was the starters, he rode them. And if you look at his career you can see that in the stats. But I enjoyed him. I was close to him and his family. He took care of me in a sense; one, because I was Italian, and the other was that I was good, to be quite honest. He was really tough on guys that weren't at their best. He didn't know how to take those guys and make them better. Those are the guys he always lost on a ballclub. They thought they could just interchange those guys instead of making them better. You kind of lost those guys during the course of the season. But he still won, and he won a lot.

Gary Hughes was a scout with the Yankees back in the seventies. He called me up about a year after I'd been out and said, "Let's go to Candlestick and watch a game. Just come on up and hang out with me." I'm thinking, does he want me to scout or something? But it seemed like a nice thing to do, and I enjoyed being around Gary. We went to the game and the next day my phone rang. It was Brian Sabean, the new GM of the Giants. He said, "You want to go down to the instructional league and coach?" I said, "I don't know, Sabes, if I want to do something like that."

But I decided to go down, feel it out. There was one pitching coach there; instructional league was not as big as it is now. Bryan Hickerson, who was the pitching coach then, decided to leave. Next thing I know, I've never coached a day in my life, now I'm running instructional league. So I did a lot of listening, acted like I knew what I was doing, and used whatever instincts I had. Tried to get to know the guys. Next spring they offered me the roving job. And I thought that would be great since three of the teams were in California. So I got myself a big Suburban and did a lot of driving. I didn't fly to those places. I'd get in my car a day early and just drive easy. I enjoyed it; I dove in headfirst, and I was hooked.

That winter Sabean called me and said, "We're going to liquidate your job." They were going to take away the roving job to save money in the minor leagues. Then he said, "You're either out of a job, or you're going to the big leagues." Here I am, one year in the instructional league and they want me to be the big-league pitching coach. I wasn't in a position to turn it down, really.

Unfortunately, I didn't negotiate very well, and I was making the same thing I did as a rover. That changed after that, but that's how I got into coaching, and I've been doing it ever since.

I had Ron Perranoski as a mentor; he ran spring training with me. Every morning I would just sit with him and he'd map out an easy way to go through the camp. Don't be afraid to delegate authority, which is what I did. Every pitching coach I've ever had coming in to spring had total autonomy. Let them do their thing and trust them. Just let me know what the hell you tell the pitchers. Other than that, I want all the guys to know that we're on the same page so we know immediately if we're wrong. If we've got a bunch of guys telling the kids something, which one is he listening to, which one is he not listening to. You don't know that if everybody's on a different page. When everybody's together, even if we're wrong, we'll know immediately if we're wrong. Otherwise it takes you too long to figure out all these problems and all you're doing is losing games and losing the player. That's kind of my only philosophy.

I've learned from all of the coaches I had as a player. From guys that were totally hands-off, like the Art Fowlers of the world, that were as old school as you could possibly be, to Stan Williams, who was a power guy. Sammy Ellis, who coached for years and years in the Yankee system, probably taught me more about my delivery than anybody. I watched pitching coaches from all over the league and a lot of them are lefties, a lot of them are former Yankees, a lot of guys who are friends of mine and mentors, and you just listen to them. They're telling you by the way they coach. I got to know Chris Bosio really well when he lived in Sacramento. I just talked to him the other day about some stuff. We all text each other. There are ties all over the game. You love beating them, but you don't have a problem shaking their hand and wishing them well.

If you really don't pay attention to some things and keep it as simple as bats and balls, the bases are the same, the plate, the umpires. If you keep it like that, the game hasn't changed a bit. There's always been pockets of ebbs and flows in terms of run production and stuff, the balls are harder or softer, whatever; all that crap. No Astroturf now, which is a major change in the game. They can talk about everything else, but without the Astroturf, the game has changed dramatically. Speed became less important and it seems like swinging the bat and strength is first and foremost on everybody's mind.

The pitching has changed to where they actually care about pitchers now. Before they cared about the guys who were helping them win and that's about it. Put in another guy; that's just the way it was. Now they try to take care

Dave Righetti
© 2016 *San Francisco Giants.*

of every kid. If you go to any minor-league park, you can go to the lowest of the lowest teams and they've got food spreads in the kitchen, they've got nutritionists, they've got workout guys, they've got trainers.

These guys are much stronger. They don't even wind up anymore. I just watched Noah Syndergaard take a three-inch stepback, turn, lift his leg, and throw 99 mph, and he's a starter. I don't know how long he's going to do it, God bless him. I hope he does it forever. But it's amazing the less amount of momentum we use as pitchers now. Especially out of the stretch. We've got bigger men pitching than ever before and guys are trying to abbreviate their deliveries because they want to speed up the game. If a guy was a total basestealer, he got five to ten throw overs, and you just tired his ass out. Nobody booed; everybody knew it was just part of the game. They called you chicken, and this and that, but that was part of the strategy. But now an umpire would scream at you. You don't even see a manager [have his pitcher] throw over three times in a row now. It's amazing how everybody wants to get somewhere in a big darn hurry these days. That has really affected the pitcher.

The lowering of the mound—the fields aren't humpbacked any more so you're measured by a flat surface out there leading to the mound. Before you had a humpback, and the mound was on top of the humpback. That's why you've got all these sinkers and cutters. To me, the changeup dramatically changed the game in the last twenty years. The overhand curveball is a lost art. These hitters will go all day and never see a curveball. You just don't see guys throwing them. You just see pitchers bigger and stronger; these guys are monsters in terms of strength. And I think it's just too much for the tendons. But there's not a lot of shoulder injuries compared to the elbow. We tore out our shoulders for good.

I sure hope we go back to the windup. The problem is teaching a guy once he's gotten to the big leagues. That's almost too late, unless the guy is really loosey-goosey and a good athlete. You've got to do this since you were a young kid. Pitchers are likely to be gassed out by the time you get to the majors if they've pitched in college, a four-year program, plus minor leagues. They've thrown lots and lots of innings by the time they get here.

One thing that jumps into my mind is the lack of left-handed "touch" pitchers. Each team had at least two of them, maybe three or four if you count the bullpen guys. Mike Caldwell, Bobby McClure, Bruce Hurst, Tommy John; these guys flourished all over baseball. But people aren't used to seeing that; left-handed movement away from the bat, curveballs, sinkers. That part of the game. You don't see it, there's not enough of it.

I was lucky to see so many great pitchers. I saw Seaver. I played with Jim Kaat, Luis Tiant, Joe Niekro. The Dave Stewarts, the Eckersleys. The year I got to New York, Ron Guidry won 25 games. Goose Gossage, people like that. I was lucky to see Lee Smith, who I think is a Hall of Famer, Clemens when he came up, and Gooden at the same time. I was fortunate enough to be in the '86 All-Star Game when they faced each other in Roger's home state. It was my first All-Star Game, and it was the most electric game I've ever been a part of. Clemens and Gooden were just off the charts, and Valenzuela set the record with five strikeouts in a row. I was lucky to get in the game myself.

What motivates me now is to take care of my family. Get the kids through college so they can get off to a good start and we'll see where it leads. But the passion of the game is something that's built in. You don't have to look for it; it's there, the motivation to help somebody. When you walked in the door, Buster Posey asked me a question. This is Cueto's first game with us and we know he's faced Milwaukee quite a bit. Just pregame strategy. Something like that keeps you motivated as a coach because you know you're needed. I guess when we're not holding towels and hitting fungoes, we're people who these guys think can help.

Larry Lucchino

L *arry Lucchino is among the most influential executives in major-league history, but he himself describes his entry into the world of baseball as fortuitous. A star high school athlete in Pittsburgh, Lucchino was a reserve guard on the Princeton basketball team that Bill Bradley led to the 1965 Final Four. Then, with a law degree from Yale in hand, he went to work for famed attorney Edward Bennett Williams, who became the owner of the Baltimore Orioles in 1979. After impressing Williams with his legal work for the Orioles, Lucchino served as the franchise's vice president and then president from 1979 to 1993.*

Inspired by his memories of Forbes Field in Pittsburgh, Lucchino was the primary force behind the construction of Oriole Park at Camden Yards, a retro ballpark that bucked the long-standing trend of symmetrical, multipurpose baseball stadiums and inspired a return to traditional ballpark design throughout Major League Baseball.

Then, as president and CEO of the San Diego Padres between 1995 and 2001, Lucchino oversaw the building of Petco Park, which spurred the revitalization of downtown San Diego.

In 2001, Lucchino became president and CEO of the Red Sox as part of the ownership group that would end the "Curse of the Bambino" in 2004 by bringing a World Series title to Boston for the first time in eighty-six years, followed by two more in 2007 and 2013. Lucchino also directed the $200 million renovation of Fenway Park. In 2015, he became president/CEO emeritus of the Red Sox and the following year was inducted into the Red Sox Hall of Fame.

In addition to his four World Series rings (including one with the 1983 Orioles), he also has a Super Bowl ring from the 1983 Washington Redskins and a Final Four watch. But his most lasting legacy is his role as the visionary facilitator who brought back the charm of the fan-friendly urban ballpark while augmenting it with modern amenities.

* * *

I'm a thoroughbred, 100 percent Italian. My paternal grandparents, Frank and Margaret Lucchino, were from Nicastro, a small town near Cosenza. My maternal grandmother, Maria Rizzo, was from Motta Santa Lucia, also in Calabria. My grandfather, Joseph, died before I was born. My grandmother Rizzo came to the States alone, at the age of fourteen, with a note saying

Pittsburgh and the name of the family. Both grandfathers were city employees in Pittsburgh. My parents, Dominic Lucchino and Rose Rizzo, are both from Pittsburgh.

My father was one of six and my mother one of ten children, so there were always plenty of uncles, aunts, and cousins around. There was definitely a sense of Italian food, culture, and family values that permeated our home. My maternal grandmother lived with us and she spoke Italian with my mother. I regret that I didn't learn the language, but at that time I wanted to be an American.

My brother and I were the first to complete college and we remain close to our family. We grew up having big meals together and celebrating birthdays, and we still maintain that to some degree. My father passed away, but my mother is ninety-two. She watches every Red Sox game on television, and she keeps score of every game. She was a softball player when she was younger.

I'm a bit of a black sheep in that I went off to college and lived in other cities. My older brother, Frank, a judge, still lives in Pittsburgh. He's a more typical Italian American. I left a multiethnic community, surrounded by Italians, Germans, Croatians, and so on, and went to Princeton. As I was making that transition, I saw that I was different because of my name. I had an ethnic name as opposed to an old-line American name.

I liked New Haven because it had a very strong Italian culture and community. There I had one foot in town and one in gown, and I felt comfortable in both. I was a person in transition from an ethnic conclave to a broader American society. I'm sure I paid a psychological price early on. There's a herd instinct you fall into, and I think I lost some sense of ethnic identity. I began to recover it in New Haven.

Right after law school I went to Italy and visited family in my grandmother's hometown of Motta Santa Lucia and was welcomed with open arms. I stayed in a farmhouse built in the sixteenth or seventeenth century with frescoes on the wall. It was like a scene out of a movie. I sent a card to my parents letting them know I was in Motta and I was going to find an Italian girl to marry. My visit gave me a greater sense of identity. Italian Americans faced perils and difficulties, but America provided opportunities, in spite of the early difficulties. There's a price you pay for being a transitional American. The older and wiser I get, I recover a greater sense of my ethnic identity.

I grew up in Pittsburgh, which was of course a sports-crazy town. All I thought about was being a shortstop or a center fielder. I didn't think about anything related to ownership or management. It was quite fortuitous. I went to Yale Law School and after that I worked on the impeachment of

Richard Nixon. When Nixon resigned, I took my first job with a law firm in DC: Williams, Connolly, and Califano. It was a firm with an outstanding reputation. Edward Bennett Williams was the primary partner and he at that time was president and part owner of the Redskins. I started out as a general litigator, and Williams gave me an assignment to work on a small Red Sox case which had to be litigated. Because of that, I got to know him better and better. He was an Irishman from Hartford, so the kind of Irish/Italian compatibility—teasing, joking—came naturally to us. It gradually led to another case, and another, and before long he asked me to be the general counsel to the Redskins.

A year or two later he bought the Orioles, and instead of bringing in another guy, he said, "You can do that. You were an athlete; you can relate to these guys." So I did the Orioles and the Redskins together for many years. I kind of gravitated more toward baseball, but for about eight years I did both. Then he asked me to take his position as president of the team in 1988 after the team got off to an abysmal start. Several months later he died of colon cancer. A group of us, including Sarge Shriver, who was an old friend of the Williams family, bought the team from his estate.

Every sports opportunity I've had is because of a door Williams opened for me. I think part of that personal and professional compatibility that we had was because we were both ethnic kids from the other side of the tracks. He gave me the opportunity to build Camden Yards. When he was the owner of the Orioles, I suggested to him that we try to get a baseball-only ballpark instead of a combination ballpark, which was all the rage. I remember him saying to me, "Why don't you go out and suggest you don't want to just build one stadium, you want to build a baseball park and then a football stadium beside it. Mention it to the press, but keep my name out of it. They're going to crucify you for it."

So I did do that and surprisingly the media loved the idea, so we pursued this notion of a baseball park, and Ed was willing to make his commitment to Baltimore to sign a long-term lease because at that time were signing year-to-year leases in the old Memorial Stadium. So his commitment to Baltimore is what gave me the chance to help design and build Camden Yards. We didn't know the whole nation would embrace it quite as much as it did afterwards. I grew up in Pittsburgh and I saw the change from Forbes Field, which was built in 1909, and Fenway Park, which was built in 1912, and Ebbets Field. I loved the style and the feel, the tradition, the irregularity of them, and I wanted to do that in a baseball park. Those were three that were some inspiration for us as we were trying to build a traditional, old-fashioned ballpark with modern amenities.

We sold the Orioles at the end of the '93 year. In '94, I joined up with a man named John Moores, who was interested in buying the Padres and building a ballpark as well because he had seen the success of Camden Yards. He invited me to come out, and I became a 10 1/2 percent owner of the team at that point. Camden Yards was a sea change in the way people approached ballparks. Petco Park became one of the best embodiments of the urban ballparks that would be built in the city and would feel and taste and smell like the city in which they were placed and would have a profound economic revitalization impact on a portion of that town. I think Petco and San Diego stand out as places where the public investment and the public expectation for significant ancillary development was most obtained.

Then we came to Boston and rebuilt Fenway Park. We didn't exactly apply all the lessons we had learned about starting over with ballparks. We recognized that we had something of historic value here, and we spent the next ten to twelve years improving, preserving, expanding, and enhancing Fenway Park. One of my partners in San Diego was Tom Werner, who had been the previous owner of the Padres; we bought the team from him. When the Red Sox came up for sale he came to me and said, "A good friend of mine is working on buying the Red Sox. If we get the team, will you come out and join us?" I said, "Absolutely," and I proceeded to help form the group that acquired the team.

I brought to Boston many years of baseball experience and a natural antipathy for the Yankees, which was my good fortune because Boston and the Red Sox had their own natural antipathy toward the Yankees. Early on when the Yankees thwarted us in a move we were trying to make, I remember barking out to Murray Chass of the *New York Times*, "This is but another example of the Evil Empire extending its tentacles further into the world of baseball." I was lucky because it was a sentiment that resonated with Red Sox fans.

I didn't hate the Italians that played for the Yankees when I was growing up. I was searching in the sports pages for Italian American surnames to offer me some inspiration or to provide some sense of identification. So I did like some of those Yankee players when I was a kid, but when I became an adult, I put away the things of a child.

I got to know Joe DiMaggio in the early eighties. I did some legal work for him for about five years when Edward Bennett Williams was his attorney. He was reticent, almost curmudgeonly, but he had a big heart for Italian Americans. I think Joe grew into his role as a hero. I think there's some comparison to Jackie Robinson. I don't mean to demean the impact of Jackie—he had a broader impact on American society—but I do think Joe DiMaggio was a

Larry Lucchino
Boston Red Sox.

groundbreaker for Italian Americans. He showed it could be done gracefully and well, and he had a lifelong kinship with, and loyalty to, Italian Americans.

Obviously, 2004 stands out in my mind, particularly the reaction of the fans in winning it all. In our first press conference on December twenty-first, 2001, when we were selected to buy the team, I recited about three or four commitments of ownership. The last thing I said was, "This is not an obligation of ownership, but I will tell you that number five is that we will eradicate the curse of the Bambino." People laughed, but then of course in our third year we did just that. That was my Joe Namath moment. Two thousand and two was our first full season, in 2003 we had a great but heartbreaking finish, and in 2004 we won it all. You couldn't have put it together any better in constructing a Hollywood script.

We had a slogan around here that I instituted: "Any schlemiels can win once." So we had to be a group of schlemiels that could win more than once.

Two thousand seven was interesting because we had some challenges in the offseason and we had to put things together. Two thousand thirteen was very special too because of the bombing at the Boston Marathon and the role David Ortiz and the whole team played in the "Boston Strong" movement and the satisfaction we got in being a force for unification of the community in the face of that kind of ugliness. They were all good; you love all your children.

What also stands out in my mind is the year-to-year renovation and improvement of Fenway Park. It wasn't a single moment; it was an evolution. But I got enormous satisfaction from preserving Fenway Park and making it work again. There were six groups trying to buy the team. We were the only one predisposed to try and save Fenway. The others wanted to replace it. We had to take a little bit of time and some small steps to ensure that it could be saved and made into the kind of ballpark it needed to be in the twenty-first century to work for baseball.

It's hard to say what has given me the greatest satisfaction. There have been different varieties of ice cream in different places that have all tasted very pleasant. Certainly winning here in Boston is right at the top of the list, as hard as that was for eighty-six years. Building and preserving great ballparks is right at the top of the list. And using our baseball teams for charitable and philanthropic activities. The relationship between the Jimmy Fund and the Red Sox, how that got deeper and stronger when we were here. We created a foundation for the Padres, we created an Orioles foundation in Baltimore. That opportunity comes with baseball teams, and that was an enormous source of satisfaction.

1980–89

Mike Scioscia

*I*n his long major-league career Mike Scioscia has had success both as a player
*and as a manager. A native of Upper Darby, Pennsylvania, he was selected out
of high school by the Dodgers in the first round of the 1976 draft. He became the
Dodgers' regular catcher in 1981, his first full season, and except for 1983, when he
missed most of the season due to injury, he held that position over the next 12 seasons
and helped the team win two World Series titles. A .259 career hitter and two-time
All-Star, the 6-foot-2, 200-pound receiver holds the franchise record for most games
caught and was considered the best in the game at blocking runners off the plate.*

*After his playing career ended, Scioscia was the Dodgers' bench coach for two
years, then managed their Triple-A affiliate in Albuquerque for one year before being
named manager of the Anaheim Angels in 2000. A two-time Manager of the Year,
Scioscia has led the Angels to the 2002 World Series title, the first in franchise
history, and six AL West Division titles. His 1,570 wins through 2016 are third-
most all-time by a manager with one team. Mentored by Tommy Lasorda, the only
manager he played for, Scioscia became a mentor himself. Three of his coaches—Joe
Maddon, Bud Black, and Ron Roenicke—went on to become big-league managers.
Highly respected by his peers, he was one of four managers—along with Tony La
Russa, Joe Torre, and Jim Leyland—named by commissioner Bud Selig in 2010 to
a special committee of baseball veterans to review all on-field related issues.*

Scioscia also appeared as himself in two episodes of The Simpsons, *the
longest-running prime-time series in American television history: "Homer at the
Bat" (1992) and "MoneyBART" (2010).*

* * *

I absolutely identify myself as an Italian American. My four grandparents were
born in Italy; my parents were born in this country. My mom's family was
from Abruzzo; my dad's family from Naples. My grandfather was born right in
Naples. My dad worked in sales with a beer distributor, and my mom taught
school. I was brought up with the normal traditions: big Italian family, a lot
of cousins, aunts, and uncles, so that was quite an experience. Although my
parents spoke Italian, they didn't want to pass it on to us. My mom and dad
spoke Italian because it was the primary language of their parents, who came to
this country and tried to learn English. So their focus was to have my mom and
dad learn English and get assimilated to this country. So there was less Italian

spoken as my mom and dad grew up and more English. They spoke Italian, but by the time we were born no Italian was spoken. I wish my grandparents had passed that down to us, but the culture was to learn the language of where you're living.

I've met a lot of Italian Americans who work in baseball. Most of them are first generation; I was second generation. But there's no doubt about all of us embracing the culture of our ancestors and understanding it. And also understanding the reasons why they came to this country and understanding the privilege that we have to come to such a great place and have the opportunity that we have. You can't take that for granted. With anyone that migrates to the United States, there are usually common reasons. It comes down to opportunity, and I just know that I'd never take that for granted. My mom and dad talked about the opportunity they had as kids. My mom had a chance to go to college, and that would have never happened if my grandparents had never come from Italy. My dad had his own business, and it wouldn't have happened in Italy. They understood that at a young age. My grandparents always told the story that even though they loved Italy, there was a reason why they migrated here.

I had a chance to go to Italy, and it was quite an experience for me. I was a baseball coach in Milan and Bergamo, giving baseball clinics. The Italian Baseball Federation called and asked if I'd be interested in going because I was Italian. So I went over at the end of January and worked with the coaches. In Milan we got to see the Duomo, the Galleria, and La Scala, with all the history there. We had a great time.

There is a growing grassroots consciousness of baseball in Italy. The people that are interested in baseball have a passion for it. It's obviously not as widespread in popularity as soccer, but I think the groundswell of interest in baseball is pushing their program very rapidly. I think they've won the European championship a couple of times and within a decade should be able to compete with a lot of the Asian teams. Athletics are a big part of the Italian culture and kids grow up playing soccer. They develop athletic ability that would easily translate to baseball. They would be able to move into shortstop and center field. The raw talent is there; it's just a matter of directing it into baseball. Now the major leagues are as international as it's ever been, so now you're getting talent from the whole world.

I do have pride in being Italian because it's a great culture. Going to Italy really revitalized that feeling, to see the lifestyle, the way they interact. You go to dinner at eight o'clock at night, which is unheard of here, and you eat until 11:30. It's a big party every night. You always ate as a group and families ate together. You talked, from the grandparents on down, and it was just a form to communicate, where in our culture you eat because it's something to get through; that's all. I'll see you later, and you go on to do other things. My wife was with me and it was our anniversary, and we were going to go out, so we said let's make a reservation for 6:30. And the people laughed because nothing's open, that's too early. So we ended up eating at eight. In the corner was the owner, and he came over and spoke to us in his broken English. This was a packed restaurant, and he did this at every table. Our waiter said he does this every night. He goes around and talks to the people; his table is always open for friends to come and visit.

They don't live to work; they work to live. It was great to see the interaction, the hugging and kissing as a way to greet people. I think that really opened my eyes to some things. Their culture's been around a lot longer. We've only been around 200 years. There the cathedral, the Duomo, was built around 1310. People have had this lifestyle for not only a couple of centuries but for almost a millennium. There's something to say for that. I'm very proud that that's where my heritage came from, and I think you take some of that back with you.

I loved all sports as a kid. I grew up just outside Philadelphia and was always playing sports. It was a big part of our life. We loved following the Philadelphia sports teams. It was part of the culture. Whatever season it was, whatever team was playing, you were passionate about that sport. We'd play baseball through August, then we'd pick up a football, we'd pick up a basketball. There might be a little hockey mixed in. But that was what it was about. There was a strong athletic culture in the area I grew up in, and I was passionate about all sports.

It was a blessing that we were a pre-video-game generation. We would play some board games here and there, but for the most part we were outside. The snow didn't bother us. We were outside in the snow playing football; we were outside shooting baskets in the light rain. It didn't matter. It's just the way things were. You didn't sit in the house and watch TV. You did your homework; you worked hard if you had to get ready to take a test. You applied yourself in everything you did in school, including the academics. So along those lines there was no misunderstanding about the things that were important.

It was a different world. I grew up in, at best, a middle-class family. But you always felt safe. If there was crime around you, you never sensed it. We would leave our doors unlocked, and it wasn't like we were out in the country. We were right outside Philadelphia, so it was populated. We'd get up in the morning, and at nine o'clock we'd choose teams and play until four in the afternoon. We'd put a quarter in our pocket to get a soda or a candy bar at the five-and-ten, which was right next to the school where we used to play baseball. Your parents knew where you were, and they knew you'd be home, so it was never an issue. I think when you're in that environment, it gives you a great sense of discipline in your life. You had the freedom, but you also knew that there was responsibility that came with that freedom. I think it was just a great time to grow up.

I know about Italians in baseball from the stories you hear, like Joe Garagiola and Yogi Berra who grew up together in the Italian area of St. Louis called "The Hill." But I can't really say when I was a kid I was proud of Italian ballplayers. I was first-generation when TV exploded on the scene. I was born in '58, so by the time when TV was showing the *Game of the Week* and things like this, I was at a very impressionable age, so I had exposure to every baseball player. I never really made a conscious effort to say that guy's Italian. My dad certainly did.

As a kid, my idol was Johnny Bench because he was a catcher and I was a catcher. So I wasn't looking to see if a guy was Italian. I think it probably just reflects the melting pot of the United States. It's not like it was in my dad's generation where he, being first-generation, really identified. Where I grew up my friends were German, they were Irish. It wasn't an Italian ethnic neighborhood. There was more of a diverse culture, which I think is great. It adds a lot to your personality and understanding. Everything isn't in one way, whether it's Italian, whether it's Irish, Catholic, Jewish. So I think it's good in a sense.

I didn't think about becoming a manager until I was done playing. I was doing catching instruction in the minor leagues, and I was very happy doing that. I loved it. Within this game, that's my passion, the catcher position. But I got a chance to manage a little bit as far as running a game in the instructional league, then I went to the fall league. Then when I managed in Triple A in 1999, I felt like I'd like to give it a shot if I got an opportunity somewhere. Now I've been here for a while.

Tommy Lasorda was the only manager I played for. Watching him and playing for him you absorb so many things. Sometimes it's, "Gosh, I don't know about that viewpoint, but he really believes in it, so there must be some merit to it." Some things you learn, and you go, "Wow, that's really going to be important to what you need to put into a team, particularly the environment." So, yeah, I've been very blessed to be around guys, whether they took an active role or even a subtle role, that really understood the game at the grassroots level. That gives you a foundation to learn more about this game and keep growing with it. The biggest thing I've learned over the seventeen years doing this is that you need to hear ideas, you need to evolve. Sometimes it's a slow process and sometimes it hits really quick, and you get better. It's just a matter of absorbing information, and I was fortunate at a young age to be around some guys that were very willing to share it.

You get inspired from all different areas, and some of my biggest lessons came from guys who weren't managers in the big leagues. I learned so much about baseball from guys like Del Crandall, Johnny Roseboro, and Roy Campanella. Just being around those baseball minds instructed me about catching. But one thing about Roy Campanella is that I learned more about life talking to him. By the time I met him, he had been in a wheelchair for over twenty years and he never even spoke of it. It didn't slow him down from doing anything that he needed to do. He would talk about baseball and how it related to real life, and how if you really believe you can play you have to apply yourself and practice hard, and you become the player you can be. That's always stuck with me, even as you cross over into coaching and managing, to understand how important that mentoring is to young kids. It's extremely important.

The guys that talked to me had a great feel for the game, and I think that helped me to relax when I played. And that's what I try to infuse into our players, especially now. There's so much analytical data that is available that you have to be very conscious how you give it to a player. When I was getting into the major leagues, I was twenty-one and not a lot of experience of putting a game plan together and talking to a pitcher. This was drummed into me for four years. So when I got there I had an understanding of it, but also the support of guys saying you're going to figure this out so go out there and relax and play baseball, and I think that's important.

I think there are so many things that go into building a championship-caliber team. I think the biggest thing, and the thing I've given the most attention to, is building the environment of having guys feel like they can play the game aggressively and relax and let their talent come out on the field. That environment, I think, begins with the chemistry you have with the guys in the clubhouse. It continues with how you practice the game and the way you put the components together to try to win a ball game and hopefully reach the goal of a championship. I think that environment is very important, and my coaches and I pay a lot of attention to that. You really have to set those expectations to win, and your goal is to get to a World Series every year.

There is a lot to deal with, but once the game starts, you're still looking at that pitcher-catcher relationship. There are still other things on the field other

Mike Scioscia
AP Photo/Carlos Osorio.

guys will look at and that's extremely important because you want to control the defense during the game. As far as all the peripheral things outside of what you do in the dugout once the game starts, it's all important. But I think it's all about baseball, so whether you're talking baseball or teaching baseball, it's something we have a passion for, so it comes naturally to us.

I think some of the rule changes about catching will be beneficial. Probably 50 years from now they'll look at the way the game used to be played as being barbaric. When I grew up in Philadelphia, with every catcher I ever saw, it was a badge of honor to block the plate. You blocked the plate with the thought of helping your team save a run, so I think by a system of osmosis it just got into me; this is the way you make the play at the plate. And you bring it along through your professional career and into the major leagues. That's just what we grew up with. Obviously, we had different guidelines of how you can make the play when I played than are enacted now. But I think some of the changes are good and it will be an afterthought once the kids grow up with this.

The longer you're in this game, the more you understand how important the process is. You always dream it's going to lead to the opportunity to get to the World Series. That's the ultimate goal, that's what this game is all about. It's a team game, whether you're on the team playing or on the team as a manager with coaches. I think once the process is where it needs to be, hopefully the talent will get you to your goal. To be part of it has been a blessing.

I'm very blessed to do something I love, but baseball is not my life. Baseball is something I have a passion for; I love it. But when you talk about comparing baseball to your family, comparing baseball to your heritage, comparing baseball to your faith, it takes a back seat. Baseball has provided me with every opportunity to have a great life, but you have to have that foundation. That's something I've been blessed to be able to have and it makes all this worthwhile.

Ned Colletti

*C*hicago native Ned Colletti was a blue-collar guy who made it to the highest levels of Major League Baseball's front offices. After working as a sports reporter, in 1982 he began his major-league career in the Cubs media relations department before moving into baseball operations. In 1990 he won MLB's Robert O. Fishel Award for public relations excellence. He then spent 11 years (1994–2004) with the San Francisco Giants, first as director of baseball operations, then as the assistant general manager.

In 2006, Colletti moved on to the Giants' archenemy when he was named general manager of the Los Angeles Dodgers, a team that had posted a 71–91 record the previous season. In his first year as GM, the Dodgers posted a record of 88–74, went to the postseason as a wild card, and were named as Baseball America's *Organization of the Year*. In 2011, he reached 500 wins as a general manager in 953 games. The only GM in Dodgers history to reach that milestone in fewer games was Buzzie Bavasi, who in 1951 became the first Italian American to be named a major-league general manager. In Colletti's nine years as GM, the Dodgers went to the postseason five times, including three appearances in the NL Championship Series, and no National League GM had as many wins. Three of his major draft picks were pitcher Clayton Kershaw (a three-time Cy Young Award winner by 2014), shortstop Corey Seager (2016 Rookie of the Year), and Cody Bellinger (2017 Rookie of the Year). He also acquired Adrian Gonzalez in a trade and Zach Greinke via free agency. Colletti was replaced in 2014, following the Dodgers elimination in the NL Division Series, but remained in the Dodgers' front office as senior advisor to the president.

* * *

My grandparents, Luigi and Louise, came from outside Palermo, Sicily, at the turn of the last century. They came through New Orleans, then settled in Chicago and started to have a family in the late teens. My dad was number seven of eight. My grandmother didn't speak English very well at the time of her husband's death, so she had to learn the language much quicker and had to earn a living to raise a family of eight children. My uncles were, for the most part, great baseball fans, and my oldest uncle, Pasquale, was a huge Cubs fan. He went to Wrigley Field very often, and he passed on his love of baseball to my dad and my dad's youngest brother, Frank.

When my parents married in 1951, they didn't have money for a home or an apartment, so they moved into the garage of one of my uncles, about forty-five blocks due west of Wrigley Field. My dad was very handy and he put together three different rooms inside the garage with plumbing and heating. That's where I lived the first five years of my life. Then we moved to Franklin Park, an industrial town at the southeast corner of O'Hare Airport. My parents bought a four-room house for $8,500; it took everything my dad had to keep a roof over our heads.

I started to fall in love with baseball when I was five or six years old. My brother Doug was born when I was six. He's a banker in Chicago, and he's also been doing statistical spotting for the Chicago Bears for thirty-plus years. So our family ended up with almost seventy years in professional sports, baseball and football.

I went to my first baseball game on April 15, 1961; the Milwaukee Braves played at Wrigley Field. The game ended on a walk-off grand slam by Al Heist, and the Cubs won, 9–5. I still remember most of that game vividly. The next day I would turn seven years old. I became a fanatic. I listened to the Cubs every day; Vince Lloyd and Lou Boudreau. I watched on television; Jack Brickhouse on WGN. When I was fifteen, sixteen years old, I began to go to games at Wrigley by myself. I probably went to forty games a year. My dad would give me three dollars—on a day when things were tight he'd give me two—and that would suffice for the day.

That's when I began to look into the game on a serious note. I'd get there about ten o'clock, so you had about three hours before the game started. I'd sit in the front row of the left-field bleachers, as far over to center field as I could. You could see the life on the fastball, the break of a curveball or slider. You had the whole game in front of you and you could see how the infielders and outfielders played. I loved it.

I met Ron Santo. He used to come to Al and Joe's, an Italian delicatessen in Franklin Park where we bought our groceries. They knew I was a big fan and they'd call me once in a while at the house and say, "Santo just called from Wrigley; he's going to stop by tonight." So I'd ride my bike over and I had a chance to get to know Ron. Later, when Ron became a Cubs announcer, I had the chance to work alongside him. We struck up a great friendship that lasted until the day he died.

I played three sports: baseball, hockey, and soccer. I was always a good player. I understood the game and was a very knowledgeable player, but I knew I wasn't going to make a living doing it. I went to Triton College first, then I went to Northern Illinois University and got a degree in journalism in 1976. I got a job at a small suburban newspaper in Elmhurst, Illinois, covering high school sports. Then I went to the *Chicago Daily News*, which is now defunct but was a great writer's newspaper. Then I went downstate to Danville, Illinois, where I covered high schools and also the Big Ten. I covered Illinois, Indiana, and Purdue. This was when Woody Hayes coached Ohio State and Bo Schembechler coached Michigan, Lou Henson coached basketball at Illinois, and Bobby Knight was at Indiana.

In 1980, I had the opportunity to work at the *Philadelphia Journal,* where I covered the National Hockey League. Suddenly my life changed and challenges started to develop. In August 1980, I learn that my dad had lung cancer at forty-nine years old. At that point, my wife and I decide to start a family because my father isn't going to be around very long. We move out of our apartment and I buy a small duplex because I wanted my child to grow up in a home and not an apartment. In December I lose my job, and my dad had gotten a lot sicker, so I was not sure what I was going to do.

Luckily, I got a blessing from Bob Ibach, who had worked with me at the *Philadelphia Journal.* He knew my dad was sick, and he knew that the paper had folded, so he called and offered me a job with the Cubs. He said, "We have two jobs here; both are going to pay $13,000; one is a publications job, and the other is a media relations job. You can apply for either or both."

I spoke with my dad and he said, "If there is a way for you to come home, you should come home. But you can't come back to Chicago for $13,000. Your mortgage is going to eat up almost all of that money."

I called the Cubs and said, "I'd like you to give me $1,000 to move and $15,000 for a job, and I'll do both jobs." They said yes. So I moved back to Chicago and was living in my in-laws' basement, and I had a house in Philly that I had bought just weeks before. So it was a trying period of time, between my dad being very sick and dying, me being a new dad, losing a job, having to start a new job, and having to look out for my mom.

I started with the Cubs on January 3, 1982, and my dad died on April 27. One of my sorrows is that I never got to go to a game with my father while I was working with the Cubs. Because of my dad's work ethic, I never took a day of work for granted, and I never sloughed off. I made it known that I would take on any responsibility, and I would be an honorable employee, one with integrity. The Tuesday before Thanksgiving in 1984, Dallas Green walked by and said, "Ned, I want you to meet Frank Casey. He's an attorney with a big firm in Washington, and he's going to be doing our salary arbitration work. You care about the team, you know the game, so you can give him a little insight into our arbitration-eligible players."

We had one player, our first baseman, Leon Durham, who went to a hearing. We prevailed in the hearing and Dallas was very pleased. He started giving me more and more responsibility and other experiences: scouting, player development, negotiation of contracts. He really opened the door for a lot of things. Little by little I left media relations and publications and moved into the baseball operations area.

I stayed there for 13 years and left the Cubs in 1994 and went to the San Francisco Giants for two years as the director of baseball operations under Bob Quinn. Bob retired and Brian Sabean moved up to GM, and I became the assistant GM. My career really started to flourish. Brian Sabean is one of the greatest GMs of this era, one of the smartest people I've been around, and someone who is not territorial or insecure with his own skill set. So I had a lot of opportunities that most assistant GMs never have. I made trades, I did all the signings and all the negotiations. Brian and I and Dick Tidrow, the scouting director at the time, we kind of molded that team from a team that was in Candlestick Park and about to move to Tampa. We ended up staying there and thriving in San Francisco to the point that a new stadium opened in 2000 and they draw three million fans year after year.

We were on our own to build a culture and a good team. We suddenly went from a team that was losing 90 games a year to a team that started winning 90 games. We went to the postseason in 1997, my first year as assistant GM, and got beat by Florida on their way to a world championship. In 2002 we went to the World Series and got beat in seven games by Anaheim. This went on and on, and in 2005 I moved on to the Dodgers as general manager.

As a general manager, I always tried to look for players of character. Nobody's ever 100 percent successful, because you're dealing with the human element. I looked for people you could trust to do everything they could to win. No matter what they were making that day, $10 million or $10, they were going to give everything they had. Rating players on a one-to-ten scale, if there was a player with a ten ability and a three character and a player with a seven ability and a ten character, I'd take the seven and ten all the time.

I think I learned a lot about patience, about expectations, about people, and about myself. It was one of those jobs that lends itself to such a vast view of a sport that you love. But it's also a sport that has people involved, so you have a lot of different challenges managing people.

Part of our strength in San Francisco was the relationship I had with Brian Sabean and that both of us had with Dick Tidrow. When I went to LA I was void of that. It was a struggle for a while until the staff and I started to get on the same page. I had to make a couple of changes and promote some people that I believed in. But it was one of the toughest roles I had, transitioning and building a different culture. The Giants culture, which is still alive and rich today, has become one of the best in major league baseball, for twenty years now. I tried to recreate it in LA, and I was not really able to get it all the way there.

My greatest challenge was developing a culture I believed in. In a role like that you're really dependent on people, i.e., players. They are directly responsible for the won-loss record, but you're directly responsible for them. You can't just go to the warehouse and pick out a new outfielder or shortstop. You have to build, and you have to hope you're building it with the right types of people. We had a lot of work to do when I took over. We did not have a manager; we did not have a coaching staff. I had a staff that I really didn't know, and some were probably upset that somebody from the Giants had stepped into a role with the Dodgers.

The team I inherited was 71–91, the poorest record in the history of the LA franchise, so I was starting from a pretty low spot. I signed some players that I knew had the right character, like Kenny Lofton, Nomar Garciaparra, Rafael Furcal, Billy Mueller. And we won. The first year, in 2006, we went to the postseason. We came from 71–91 and won 88, and got beat by the Mets in the first round. Then in '08 and '09, we went to the LCS in back-to-back years, then went back to the playoffs again in '13 and '14.

I hired Joe Torre as manager in 2008 and worked with him for three years. It was great to work with Joe; he's a very, very smart guy. A Hall of Fame manager and a great player, an MVP. We had a great relationship. We went through some trying times because ownership was going through a rocky period at the time, but we stuck together. After three years Joe wanted to retire and work for the commissioner's office.

Then we hired Don Mattingly, and Don did a nice job as a first-year manager. We were going through all sorts of turmoil financially, so I wanted to hire somebody I believed in and trusted and who would work for an opening wage because it was the first time he ever managed. Donnie was one of the hardest working guys I know. All of the managers I worked with—Grady Little, Joe, and Donnie—all were class acts and great baseball men.

People view me as an old-school scout, but when I started working for the Cubs, I started doing analytics before anybody really had a computer to use. Jim Frey, who was our manager starting in 1984, had been a coach for Earl Weaver in Baltimore. He came to me and said, "I need to know how players hit with runners in scoring position, how they hit late in the game, how they hit against lefties and righties, home and road, and I need you to give me matchups."

So I spent the winter of '83–'84 going through box score after box store, all by hand, and we started using what would now be considered elementary analytics. The Tribune Company owned the Cubs, so as computers became more and more commonplace, we started to develop an analytics program, taken from the stuff I was doing by hand, along with many other things. So the advances I was able to make in my career were really due to analytics, hard work, and being somebody that Dallas could count on. But they were also due to my wanting to know what the numbers said. I'm never going to forget that there's a person inside that uniform, and you'd better know who that is. If the analytics tell me that a player is going to be good, I still need to know who they are. At the end of the day, it might be 51–49, scouting over analytics.

To anybody in a leadership position, information is key. You need analytics and you need scouting reports that tell you who this guy is. If I was thinking of signing a free agent player, I would talk to our media relations people, our trainer, and our traveling secretary. Those three groups know a player better than anybody. For a visiting player, I would go to the visiting clubhouse manager. He sees that player maybe nine times a year, but maybe

Ned Colletti
AP Photo/Alex Gallardo.

he's seen him for years. He sees what time he comes to the park, how he prepares, and how he treats people in the clubhouse. In the clubhouse, most people think nobody's watching, but the clubhouse guys I've worked with are always attuned to the human element and they would help me all the time.

There's no sport as all-consuming as baseball. No disrespect to any other sport, but you play 162 games in 183 days. You've got twenty-one days off and on those days you're traveling. It's a constant, from Valentine's Day until, if you're fortunate, Halloween. That's a long period of time to deal with your teammates, so you'd better know who they are, because if you don't, the chances of being successful are not strong.

There are guys who were really super impressive to me as performers. I was with Greg Maddux when he was drafted and during the first six years of his career, and I traded for him twice. He is a genius at his craft. He saw it different from everybody else and he could slow it down. I think the greatest athletes can slow the game down. It's almost like the difference between watching a movie and seeing it frame by frame. Right behind Greg was Zach Greinke— also a tremendous, tremendous feel for the game.

Then, on the hitting side, Barry Bonds was the ultimate player: speed, defense, power. He may not have known all the names of the National League pitchers, but he never forgot a release point, he never forgot what the pitcher was trying to do to him, what he was capable of doing. He was the best, and right behind him was Manny Ramirez. They worked tirelessly; they worked at the fine points of their craft.

One of the best baseball players I was ever around was Omar Vizquel, who we signed in San Francisco. Another guy who would use every facet of his ability to become successful. He was not a big man, but he was within a year or so of 3,000 hits. He played shortstop so flawlessly. Those are probably my five who stand out as exceptional minds and talents.

One of my absolute favorite people is Dave Righetti. He's one of the better pitching coaches in the game, but just a good guy. When I was growing up, my uncles and my cousins and my dad, they called me "Neddie." The only guy in thirty-five years of major league baseball who ever called me that was "Rags." He'd say, "Hey, Neddie, how you doing?" It's like the old Italian thing, you know. There's always that thread that ties you together; you talk about where you grew up, similar things you did as a kid, things like that.

I'm tremendously proud of being Italian American. A few years ago I was inducted into the National Italian American Sports Hall of Fame in Chicago. It was one of the greatest honors of my life. There was a dinner on Friday night that took place about a mile from where my dad grew up, and the induction ceremony the next night was about a mile from where I grew up. It was very, very special to me.

Baseball has provided me some of the greatest moments, as a fan and an observer of the game. It's given me great joy as a recreation, and it's provided a living for myself and my family. Where I come from, you're not expected to be in major league baseball; you're not expected to be the general manager of one of the most iconic franchises of the game. That I was able to do that, it will never be lost on me how blessed I've been. When I was growing up, I hoped that if I was fortunate enough to have kids that they'd be able to go to college. I have two adult kids who have master's degrees and have had great things happen in their lives and their careers. And I've been able to buy a place and not have to rent. So my simple goals were met because of hard work and opportunity. I had people like Dallas Green, Bob Ibach, Bob Quinn, Brian Sabean, Frank McCourt, and Stan Kasten give me an opportunity. Baseball is not something I ever take for granted. When the season ends I'm typically exhausted, mentally and physically, but a week later I can't wait for it to start again.

Matt Galante

*B*rooklyn native Matt Galante was a student at St. John's University when he was selected by the Yankees in the 1966 amateur draft. The 5-foot-6, 157-pound infielder played for eight years in the minor-league systems of the Yankees and Brewers. Between 1973 and 1984, he spent 12 seasons as a minor-league manager for the Brewers, Mets, and Astros. Except for 1997, when he had a front-office position, he was a Houston Astros coach from 1985 to 2001. In 1999, Galante served as acting manager of the Astros for 27 games while Larry Dierker was dealing with health issues. After coaching for the Mets from 2002 to 2004, he returned to the Astros' front office. In 2006 he managed Team Italy in the inaugural World Baseball Classic.

* * *

Both my parents were from Castellammare del Golfo in Sicily. My parents made me proud to be Italian American. Once they came from Italy and established themselves here, they became Italian Americans. When I was a kid in Brooklyn, ten, twelve years old, the neighborhood we lived in was Jewish, Italian, Irish, black, and no one cared if you were black or white, if you were a Jewish kid or an Italian kid, you just played together. You knew you had certain customs that you were observing and they weren't, and they had some that they were observing and you weren't, and it was fine.

In our house we always had Christmas customs that were Italian, and now we have the same traditional cooking that our mothers and grandmothers made and I think that's great. It's a great thing to have traditions. The kids look forward to it and the grandkids look forward to it. But each generation loses a little bit. Today there's less of a sense of ethnic identity. It starts with the parents. My parents came from Italy, so we get some of that tradition handed down. And then we get a little lax, so all the kids are more Americanized. We passed some of it down but maybe not enough of it. My daughter has three kids and she's probably going to hand less of it down. In a sense, you're probably going to end up losing it in time. It's sad.

I think it's important to maintain traditions because if you're willing to give up some of your traditions and some of the ways you were brought up, that's not a problem. But if those traditions are important to you, it's good to keep them, only because you're on the same page. I don't think I looked for an

Italian girl; it just happened. And my daughter wasn't looking for an Italian; it just happened. Of course if you're in a close-knit community with a lot of Italians there is a greater chance of it happening.

My parents made sure I went to college and they made sure I graduated, so I think they thought baseball wasn't a very good idea because it's tough to make a living doing this. But thirty years later we're still at it, so it's been good. My dad knew nothing about baseball when he came from Italy. And when he passed away, he was a manager; he could tell me every move we made in a game. He really learned the game by watching TV and going to the games.

I grew up in New York City and I watched Rizzuto play. I saw DiMaggio at the very end. I watched Berra pretty much his whole career. My parents were really into the Italian Americans who established themselves in baseball. We'd watch them on TV when we finally got TV. I remember it being a little round black-and-white, a nine-inch or five-inch, whatever they first came out with. And we'd go to Yankee Stadium, Ebbets Field. We saw Carl Furillo. We had great ones. I think guys like DiMaggio made the Italian American parents stand up and say, "Hey, this is pretty good. This is a good sport." Not only was he the superstar of that era, he might've been the first where that group of immigrants came to the United States and all of a sudden they've got a hero. If it was years later, it might've been a Berra, and Berra was a hero too. But DiMaggio was the first one of my era.

I'm proud of being Italian American; I'm proud of being in baseball. See, the guys I grew up with—Rizzuto, DiMaggio, Berra—those kind of guys, you had great Italian Americans in baseball. I don't think you have enough of them now. I think years ago we had plenty; now there's other things to do. More education nowadays. People want to be teachers or whatever.

I went to college at St. John's in New York. I got drafted my junior year by the Yankees, and I played professionally for about eight years and got traded to the Brewers. I played with their Triple-A club for a while. I managed in the Brewers organization for several years, then I went to the Mets for a couple of years, and now I've been with the Astros for 20 years. I don't remember hearing ethnic remarks in baseball, but I do remember hearing some in the service: "dago," "guinea." My drill sergeant would ask me every day if I knew what a dago was, and I'd tell him I didn't know. Every morning, "Do you know what a dago is?" And I'd say, "No, sir, drill sergeant." I wasn't going to give in. I think we're more relaxed now and it's better, way better.

When I got to Houston I wasn't aware they had a big Italian population. I kept saying there's no Italian restaurants around here. But there's a lot of Italians and a lot of Italian restaurants. I belong to an Italian American club in Houston; our organization probably has about 300 people. The Caminitis, the Biggios, and we had Incaviglia in the past, they do a lot in the Italian American community. They've raised money for us. We have an event where they hit home runs and we give $100 for each home run. We even included Bagwell, one of our better home run hitters, because we wanted to give out more money. We called him Bagwelli. They always come to the functions; they always give out the awards. They're a big part of it. We have a luncheon with about 300 people to give out the scholarships and the guys are always there to present the awards. They've been great. We've done a lot of good things; last year we gave out over $30,000 in scholarships to kids going to college. Over the past ten years we've probably given out $200,000 worth of scholarships to Italian Americans that pursue their education. I think that's part of why you don't see more in baseball.

Team Italy manager Matt Galante (right) with umpire Troy Fullwood, 2006 World Baseball Classic.
Ezio Ratti/FIBS.

Chris Bosio

*I*n 11 big-league seasons between 1986 and 1996, Sacramento native Chris Bosio, a 6-foot-3, 220-pound right-hander, posted a 94–93 record with a 3.96 ERA in 309 games. With the Milwaukee Brewers for the first seven years, he won 14 or more games three times, was named their Most Valuable Pitcher in 1989 when his 2.95 ERA was the sixth-best in the AL, and had a career-high 16 wins in 1992. He then went to the Seattle Mariners as a free agent in 1993 and soon made his mark there, pitching a no-hitter against the Red Sox on April 22, retiring 27 straight after walking the first two batters. Limited by injuries, in four seasons with Seattle he had a 27–31 record with a 4.43 ERA.

An intense, fierce competitor on the mound, Bosio developed into a disciplined and highly regarded pitching coach. In addition to various stints in the minors, he coached for Tampa Bay (2003) and Milwaukee (2009) before going to the Chicago Cubs in 2012. When the Cubs ended their 108-year World Series drought in 2016, Bosio was credited with developing or fine-tuning several of their pitchers, including Jake Arrieta, the 2015 Cy Young Award winner, and Kyle Hendricks, who had the lowest ERA in the majors in 2016.

Bosio reminisces about caring for his siblings when his mother was ill, his success as a young athlete, throwing a no-hitter while sick with the flu, and his philosophy of coaching.

* * *

My paternal grandfather, Louis Bosio, was born in Sicily. My mom was also of Italian descent. Her name was Scatena. My great-great-great-grandfather was Charles Schwab, as in the Schwab brokerage firm out of Jackson, California. That was my grandmother's maiden name. I did not inherit any money from the Schwab family, but my mom did inherit some property in San Francisco that is still in the family.

My mom and dad were born in San Francisco. They ran a liquor store and they ran a little numbers game out of there. My dad used to be the runner, picking up the little brown bag, saying they were for sandwiches, but you know what I mean. They were a very proud Catholic family. My mom was an unbelievably strong woman. She battled Hodgkin's disease for twenty-six years. It was one of the hardest things I've ever gone through in my life. It's something I'll never forget, watching your mom literally die before your eyes and having people tell you your mom's not going to make it another week.

My dad was a federal government worker. He spent his whole life working his tail off. We were by no means a wealthy family. My dad worked three jobs trying to pay the medical bills. My mom couldn't work; she was going through radiation and chemo. It was a really hard thing for me, being the oldest, trying to help out, and literally raising my brother and sister. I had to cook and clean; I learned how to do that at an early age. My childhood was awesome, but it was also difficult because you're trying to help out your family as much as you can. My job was to make sure my brother was getting to school and eating. My job when I got home was to clean and cook so my dad was ready to eat when he got home. Those other days when Mom was cooking were awesome because I could go out and play. I grew up fast. There was a lot of responsibility on me, but I wouldn't have changed a thing because I knew it was helping out my mom, and she did everything for us.

I think that's where I got not only my determination but my drive. I know I was fiery as a player, but as I've gotten older, I've learned calmness. I just remember my mom going through so much. I'm so lucky and so blessed to be a baseball player and now a coach. I think about all those tough situations my mom and dad went through. My brother died of lung cancer in my arms. It tests you when you're young, but you learn from it as you get older.

I was born in Sacramento, then lived in Carmichael, California. When my mom had Hodgkin's, we moved to Minnesota. Once we got there, my dad got me involved in some really good all-star teams. I made a couple of state championship teams and a tri-state championship. I also played football. I was a three-time Punt, Pass, and Kick champion in Minnesota. I was an AAU swimmer and a two-time state champ. I was a state champ in bowling before I was in high school. I was in ninth grade and we had just finished a tri-state tournament in Chicago, and my parents had already moved back to Sacramento because my dad got a promotion to the state capital. I stayed back for three weeks to see how far we could go in the tournament, then they flew me out after the tournament.

It was a wonderful, wonderful time and I hated my parents for moving us at that time, but it turned out to be a great move in that my dad moved into a city where he knew there was a good high school program. I played football, basketball, and baseball. But the guy that was most instrumental was my dad. It was hard because he was always working, but he always tried to show up for the games. My mom was sick so she couldn't come to a lot of games, but she showed up when she could. My parents had me in so many sports to try to give me some childhood because of what I was going through as a kid.

In my sophomore year in high school, we had just won a state championship in baseball and in football at Rancho Cordova High School. My dad did not want me to play football because I had a knee injury my sophomore year. He said, "You've got to make a choice." I was an outside linebacker and a quarterback because I could throw a ball sixty to sixty-five yards, like all pitchers in high school. My dad said, "Listen, you're going into your junior year and you're throwing 93 miles an hour. You're a baseball player." And he made me put my football stuff away and concentrate on baseball. That was my dad's decision and the best one I ever made.

I got drafted out of high school by Pittsburgh in 1981. I was going to be taken by Philadelphia, but I was pitching in a state championship game and in the fifth inning I hurt my arm. I slipped a little bit in the draft. That year I remember Jerry Weinstein from Sacramento City College saying, "You're throwing 93; I can make you throw 97 by next year." And he did. So I was drafted by Pittsburgh while in high school, then the next year, in 1982, I got drafted in the second round by the Milwaukee Brewers after a half year in junior college. I went to instructional league where I was a teammate of Dale Sveum and Dan Plesac. There were really good memories and really good players back then. That was the year the Brewers went to the World Series. We were the next wave of talent coming through, so it was special.

One of my most memorable moments as a player was when I was with the Brewers. It was Easter Sunday, 1987, when Rob Deer and Dale Sveum hit home runs over in old County Stadium to give us our twelfth straight win. I got a no-decision, but I was just one of the pitchers in the game. We had a 13-game winning streak that year: "Team Streak," "The Heart Attack Kids." That same year was Paul Molitor's [39-game] hitting streak. And there was Robin Yount's 3,000th hit in 1992. I started that game and was still pitching in the seventh inning when he got the hit. That season Cal Eldred and I won 20 games back to back. He had a 10-game winning streak, and I had a 10-game winning streak. I went 16–6 that year. Back then we completed games. I think I had 38, 39 complete games in my career; that's a lot. Nobody gets there anymore. I remember George Bamberger saying, "If I give you the ball, don't let anybody ever take it out of your hand. You'd better finish what you start." That was our mentality. We didn't have pitch counts back then. The hitters always let you know how you were doing.

Bamberger was one of my favorite managers because he gave me the shot. I remember when Rollie Fingers retired, Dan Plesac and I had a conference call with Harry Dalton and Bamberger. They said Rollie was retiring and you guys are going to come to spring training and battle it out for the closer's role. Danny and I had been starters our entire minor-league careers, and that year I was the strikeout champ in the Texas League after going 17–6 in Beloit. So we went to spring training and made it all the way down to the last cuts, and they started me in that last spring-training game. I remember giving up like five runs in the first inning. I was pissed because I knew I was getting sent out. They sent me down to Triple A to close. I was like, "Man, I don't know what's going on. I'm in the bullpen all spring, then you start me in this game, and now I'm going down to close. Bambi, I don't know what the hell's going on." He said, "Just keep your mouth shut and go down there and pitch."

I went down there and had 16 saves in two and a half months. Then they called me up. I walked into Bamberger's office and he turned around and grabbed the ball off the top of his briefcase on the shelf. He said, "Do you remember this ball? This is the ball I took from you in spring. You're starting tomorrow." I said, "Bambi, I've been closing the whole year in Triple A, now I'm going to start?" He said, "Listen, you big Italian bastard, I got you here didn't I? If I had started you down in the minor leagues, you probably were going to end up in Double A no matter what you did with all your strikeouts. We had a lot of good pitchers." And we did. The Brewers system was loaded with good pitchers.

Anyway, I started that game and had 4 2/3 no-hit innings in my first start. Then Russ Morman, the first baseman for the White Sox, hit a home run off me into the first row down the left field line in County Stadium. He wasn't even all the way around the bases and Bamberger was on the mound. I handed him the ball, and he said, "You just couldn't finish it, could you?" I looked at him like, *Are you kidding me? I don't know what this guy wants from me. Four days ago I was closing in Vancouver and now I'm starting in a big league game.* It wasn't like I was stretched out. I ended up throwing like 74 pitches, more pitches than I'd thrown for a year. Then between innings he said, "Get your ass out to the bullpen."

So I had to run out to the bullpen and Rick Cerone, "Spongy," looks at me and says, "What, you couldn't finish the game?" Then I found out that Bambi had called and said, "Hey, give Bosio some shit when he gets out there about not finishing the game." So I became a swing guy; I started and I relieved for the next couple of years. My second year, I had 20 starts and 20 relief appearances, then that third year they told me I was starting coming out of the gate and that's when my starting career really took off as a Brewer.

Chris Bosio
Milwaukee Brewers Baseball Club.

I began the practice of sliding my right foot across the rubber during my windup after talking to Molitor and Yount. I said, "What kind of pitchers are the hardest ones for you to face?" They said the guys that change their arm angle. They showed me in County Stadium the backdrop where my hand comes out of. Then they said, "Now, what happens if I move over here?" And I said, "Well, the release point moves." "That's what you should do," they said. "The better hitters will zone you." At County Stadium there were squares on the hitter's backdrop, so they'd figure out which square the ball is coming out of and instead of looking at the pitcher they'd look in that box for the ball. That's how they pick up the pitcher's angle, whether they're throwing fastball, curveball, or slider. So I started moving around on the rubber for some of the better hitters in the game: Wade Boggs, Don Mattingly, Ken Griffey. I practiced a lot. I really tried to perfect it because I knew what was at stake. It helped. Some of the swings I got by doing that, it was unbelievable.

The year I signed with Seattle was a really horrible, horrible offseason. My home got broken into by some transient guy who lived in my house for about ten days. There was a murder-suicide in our apartment in Phoenix. My dog got hit by a construction truck and was almost killed. On top of that, right toward the end of spring training my grandfather died. My grandfather was a big reason why I signed with Seattle because he wanted to watch me play baseball.

My first game with Seattle, I threw eight innings and lost, 2–0. My next game was in Detroit and I set a career high in strikeouts. Then I had to pitch on three days' rest against the Red Sox because Eric Hanson was sick. That morning I woke up with the flu, puking everywhere. They asked me if I could go, and I said, "I'll be fine." Normally I threw about 40 to 42 pitches in my warmup, but that day I threw about 20 and just threw the ball into the stands. My pitching coach, Sammy Ellis, said, "Is that it?" I said, "That's it, that's all I've got." He said, "Where you going?" And I said, "I'm going to go puke. Why, you wanna come with me?"

I walked the first two guys in the game, then I got Mike Greenwell to hit into a double play and I struck out Andre Dawson on three cutters. Next thing I know, I woke up in the eighth inning with a no-hitter. I was total tunnel vision, and I was still sick. But then I realized it, and every pitch was magnified by the crowd. I noticed people weren't sitting near me in the dugout. Last hitter I was facing Ernie Riles, a former teammate of mine. I knew Ernie was going to swing early because he always did, so I threw a little dead fish fastball. He hit a high chopper over my head and I remember looking up going, "Grandpa, you got that one?" I turned around and Omar Vizquel's hat goes flying off; he barehands the ball and throws to first base.

That wasn't the best game I pitched. In my career with the Brewers, I had a one-hitter, a two-hitter, a three-hitter. I mean, I pitched much better games than that no-hitter. I was pitching on three days' rest, it was a 96-pitch complete game. There were three big defensive plays in that game, but every no-hitter has a couple. Mine was no exception.

Pitching the first playoff game in Mariners history was quite an honor for me, being part of that 1995 club, saving baseball in Seattle. We've got trophies and plaques and crystal that ownership gave us in gratitude. That was a big thing; we were gone, we were leaving. But the people of Washington got that thing passed and now they've got a beautiful stadium that they'll be proud of probably the next hundred years.

I'd always been kind of a player-coach later in my career, helping guys out with grips, scouting reports. When I first got to Seattle, I brought a lot of the stuff over I had from Milwaukee. I knew then that I wanted to be a coach. I'd run a couple of baseball academies for several years, Bosio Baseball Academy in California. I had one in Rancho Cordova and another one in Shingle Springs. We ran an after-school program for kids and won an award from the state for best new business. It was very gratifying. I had that for about eight years. Then Lou Piniella got the job managing Tampa, and he called me up and asked me to be his pitching coach. Teaching was always in my blood. I don't think it really matters if you're teaching young kids or older guys. If you're a teacher, you're a teacher, period.

Being a coach depends on being a student of the game. I learned a lot from all the old Brewers: Molitor, Yount, Cecil Cooper, Ben Oglivie, Jim Gantner, Dan Plesac. These are all good friends of mine. We learned the game together, and a lot of the veterans said all you need to do is shut your mouth, look at the scoreboard, just listen and watch the game. The game will be a great, great friend of yours if you pay attention. I learned a lot from the position players. Obviously, I paid attention to my pitching comrades, but the position players we had, they're Hall of Famers. So I tried to get as much information from them as I could and learn as much about pitching from an offensive perspective, which helped me not only be a pitcher but a coach. I coach baseball, whether it's pitching or catching or outfield, everything, all aspects. And those guys helped me tremendously to be a good teacher.

When I watch a pitcher I look at everything. I start from the ground up. I watch how their lower half works, their feet, their hips, their upper body, their lead arm. People say, "Don't you watch the ball?" Well, in time. But there's so many other things going on before you get rid of the ball that could be a deterrent. I work off timing, visualization stuff. We work count-tendency stuff. I look for counts that hitters like to swing at, and we take advantage of those counts. If the guy's hitting .400 on first pitches, we won't throw him a strike on the first pitch. Take that count away from him. Manny Ramirez had a stat one year where 50 percent of his homers came on the first or second pitch. We deliberately threw balls first and second pitch, and he hit one home run off of us all year. The previous year he had hit 13. Stuff like that is huge, and that's the stuff I implement now.

I learned a lot from my own pitching coaches: Chuck Hartenstein, Larry Haney. One of the best guys I ever had was a guy in California named Rich Rose. He told me, "Just throw the ball as hard as you can for as long as you can." And I did. Back then I was throwing 93-97, and I didn't have any secondary pitches. That's why Pete Vuckovich took me under his wing and taught me how to spin the ball and be a pitcher, not just a thrower. I developed a slider I could throw at three different speeds. My fastball I could throw three different speeds. My changeup I could throw three different speeds. These are things I pass on to all the different pitchers I've had. Jake Arrieta is a perfect example. He's got three different speeds on everything he throws. All I'm doing is passing the torch to them and they're going to pass the torch to other guys. Change speeds on everything, have confidence, and be able to throw any pitch at any time and don't be afraid to do it. Once you have trust in somebody, it's a powerful thing.

Ken Caminiti

*A*n MVP Award recipient and three-time All-Star and Gold Glove winner, third baseman Ken Caminiti was the classic scrappy ballplayer who won the respect and admiration of fans and teammates by refusing to let injuries keep him out of the lineup. But the Hanford, California, native was not always so committed to the game. Frustrated with baseball while in college, he was ready to quit until his father convinced him to give it one more year. He did and performed well enough to be drafted by Houston in 1984 and break into their starting lineup in 1989. In eight years with the Astros, his offensive production was solid if not spectacular, but it was his glove and grit that made him stand out from other third basemen. In his years in Houston, Caminiti endeared himself to the local Italian American community, so much so that when he did not win the Gold Glove Award in 1994, they awarded him a replica.

Beginning in 1995, the year he was traded to the San Diego Padres, Caminiti won three straight Gold Glove Awards. In 1996 he led the Padres to a division title with career highs in homers (40), RBIs (130), batting average (.326), and slugging percentage (.621), culminating in his unanimous choice as the NL MVP. Over his 15-year career, Caminiti hit 239 home runs with 983 RBIs and a .272 average.

His legacy was tainted when, in 2002, one year after he retired, he became the first major leaguer to acknowledge publicly the use of steroids. He admitted that he had used them to cope with the pain of a torn rotator cuff during his MVP season, as well as occasionally in later years. Sadly, there were other demons that haunted Caminiti, who also struggled with addictions to alcohol and cocaine. On October 10, 2004, he was found dead at the age of forty-one in a New York City apartment; the cause of death was attributed to an overdose of cocaine and opiates. Hall of Famer Craig Biggio, a Houston teammate for seven years, told me, "We know he had some issues, but people need to remember him as a great guy, a great friend who would do anything for you."

* * *

I was born in Hanford, California, and raised in San Jose. I lived in Hanford for one year because my dad was in the service and stationed there. My dad's family is from Sicily. My mom, she has a little bit of Italian, but she's more German and Norwegian. I've never been to Italy, but my sister has. She said "Caminiti" in the phone book over there is like "Shannon." My best friend growing up was Christopher Camilli. His father was Dolph Camilli Jr., the son of Dolph Camilli, the ballplayer. I never met the grandfather.

I think of myself as Italian American, but not as part of a heritage of Italian American ballplayers. I'm very proud of my heritage, but I just play the game, you know? I think when I play, the Italian in me comes out to play: the hard work. I'm a student of the game. I have that drive. I think those are Italian characteristics: hard-nosed, play hard, clean but hard.

As a kid I didn't really follow the game. I was just out playing. I remember my dad telling me the World Series was on or we'd go to San Francisco to watch a baseball game. I was always agitated. I couldn't sit in the seat. I enjoyed being out in the parking lot with my dad throwing the frisbee or playing catch with the baseball, more those things than sitting watching a baseball game. I always wanted to be out playing.

My dad worked real hard to tame me down and bring me up right. He saw a lot of qualities in me that I didn't see. I probably wouldn't be where I am right now if it wasn't for my dad. He was the one that supported me; I just wanted to move on. My first year in college, I walked on, had a bad year and said, *No, I don't like this game.* I was really frustrated and thought, *This isn't my cup.*

He said, "No, no, I think you should give it one more year."

I gave it one more year and the doors started opening. I played on a winter league team and got a full scholarship to San Jose State University. From there, I was ninth in the nation in hitting and just went off. I started switch-hitting. Doors started opening and I was drafted in the third round the next year. My dad said, "If it wasn't for that one week of me pushing you, I don't know where you would have been."

My dad just didn't want me to be a catcher. My dad, who grew up in Chicago, was a catcher and he got drafted by the Chicago Cubs. When we go play in Wrigley, we drive by his old high school, Lane Tech, and it's in a really bad part of town. He turned it down, went into the army and then got married. I think that's why he's so stiff with me. He said, "You know what, you just never know what you can be until you're given an opportunity." So I think he takes his frustrations out on me.

I have three girls. They're being raised in a great neighborhood, and I'm part of the Italian American Foundation in Houston. The year I got traded they gave me the Gold Glove Award. I hadn't won it, but they said I deserved it. It was a replica of a Gold Glove. I had all my friends there, and I had tears in my eyes; it was such a great thing. I won three Gold Gloves, but the one the Italian Americans gave me was probably more special. There's a huge Italian

Ken Caminiti
AP Photo/Eric Draper.

American population in Houston. All those Italian restaurants, that's where I hang out. Italian food's my favorite.

Yogi's my man; I love Yogi. He was my hitting coach the first couple of years in the National League. I remember the Yogi-isms, how he used to talk. He was such a bighearted man too, to do so much for the game and be so giving of his knowledge. Yogi's not a real talkative guy, but when you know him, you can sit down and talk with him. He wasn't one of those guys you'd be scared to talk to. When you're in the clubhouse every day, he'll give you a piece of his mind. He's going to tell you what you need to hear, not just what you want to hear. When we were out in New York the first time this year we went to his new museum. Yogi took us out there, me and Biggio. We spent the day with his son, Dale. It's pretty sweet, really nice. It's unbelievable.

When we're in these locker rooms—black, white, Italian—that doesn't come into play. Mike Piazza's one of the few who will come up and say "Hey, paesan." I remember early on, he was one of the new guys in the league. He'd come up and say, "Hey, paesan, how you doing?"

I haven't heard any ethnic slurs; they just call me "Idiot." Or, "You suck!" That's a good one: "You suck!"

Craig Biggio

*F*ew *if any players in big-league history have achieved so much success at a variety of positions as Hall of Famer Craig Biggio. A seven-time All-Star as both a catcher and second baseman, he also spent two seasons as an outfielder. Biggio was also something of a rarity in the era of free agency, having spent his entire 20-year career with one team.*

A star running back at Kings Park High School on Long Island, Biggio chose to pursue baseball as his profession. Following his junior year at Seton Hall University, the 5-foot-11, 185-pound catcher was selected by the Astros in the first round of the 1987 draft. In 1989, he became the Astros starting catcher and won the NL Silver Slugger Award. Following the 1991 season, in which he made his first All-Star appearance, the Astros asked Biggio to move to second base. With the help of coach Matt Galante, he not only made the difficult transition but went on to win four Gold Glove awards at the position, as well as four Silver Slugger Awards.

On June 28, 2007, he became the twenty-seventh player in major league history to record 3,000 hits, and is the only player with more than 3,000 hits, 600 doubles, 250 home runs, and 400 stolen bases. He ranks fifth all-time in doubles and second in being hit by pitches. Biggio is also the only player other than Tris Speaker with 50 doubles and 50 stolen bases in the same season. In 2007, he received the Roberto Clemente Award as "the player who best exemplifies the game of baseball, sportsmanship, community involvement, and the individual's contribution to his team," and the following year the Astros retired his uniform number 7. Statues of Biggio and his longtime teammate, Jeff Bagwell, a 2017 Hall of Fame inductee, stand outside Minute Maid Park in Houston. In 2015, Biggio became the first Astro to be inducted into the Hall of Fame.

Here he discusses his transitions from catcher to second baseman to center fielder, Yogi Berra's superior knowledge of baseball, players he admired, and his disappointment with the lack of loyalty from both management and players.

* * *

I was born in Smithtown, New York, on Long Island, but I was raised in Kings Park. I'm not exactly sure where in Italy my dad's family is from. My grandfather was a typical short Italian man. He had rock hands, worked hard for a living with a cement company in New Jersey. My dad, he's six-four, a tall man. He's a retired air traffic controller. My grandmother is German, and my mother is

Irish, Swedish, Lithuanian; she's like a mutt. I kind of consider myself as an Italian because of the last name, but as I got older, I just learned how to go with the group you're with. If you're with the Italians, you're a big-time Italian. But I'm Irish too because of my mother's side. My wife is of Italian descent.

In high school I was a football player and I wrestled. I was actually a better football player than I was a baseball player. I was a running back and in high school I won the Hansen Award as the best football player in Suffolk County. But obviously things worked out for baseball instead. I started thinking about baseball as a profession when I went to the Cape Cod League after my sophomore year at Seton Hall, where I went on a partial baseball scholarship. I pretty much assessed my own talent and ability and said, *I have a chance to get drafted; I'm just as good as these other kids.* It's a great league with the cream of the crop, supposedly. Then I went back and played my junior year and got drafted.

Things happen for a reason. I don't know what it is. I had a full scholarship offer to Oklahoma State and turned that down. I could've gone to a lot of places for free to play football too. But for whatever reason, my destiny brought me to Seton Hall and that worked out great. I wanted to go away to college, but I didn't want to go real far. I liked the tradition and history that Seton Hall had and they always had a lot of guys get drafted. Mike Sheppard had over eighty guys that got drafted; that's a pretty big number. When you come out of there, you're ready for life because you're not babied. You had to wash your own uniform; it's just kind of the way life is.

I was pretty lucky and fortunate to be in the big leagues one year after I was drafted. To me, those were precious times. My first year was probably the worst year I ever had offensively, but to me it was one of the best years because I was around guys like Nolan Ryan, Buddy Bell, Billy Doran. I was twenty-two years old in the big leagues, so I did a lot of listening and asked questions. Those times were priceless.

Yogi was the bench coach for Hal Lanier and Art Howe, so I had Yogi for, I think it was about three or four years. The smartest baseball man I've ever been around. I know everybody gets on him for having all his Yogi-isms and this and that, and he does have them. But as far as knowledge of the game, you don't get all those World Series rings by not being very smart. He would say things and walk away and you'd go, *What's he talking about?* Then all of a sudden, there it goes, it transpires out on the field. A very, very smart man. He knew the X's and O's, or whatever you want to call them. But as far as the moves to be made and what the other manager is going to do, putting guys in situations where they are going to be successful, and that's the hardest thing to do, Yogi was Art Howe's best resource, I think. If you ever asked Art he'd probably tell you that he was the best bench coach he ever had.

The move from catcher to second base happened because I could run a little bit. I went to the All-Star Game the year before. Art Howe sits me down in the wintertime and says, "The club wants to take this direction about putting you at second base. It's going to be better for you and the club. What do you think about it?" So we had a long discussion about that and I said, "Let me go home and talk to my wife about it." I went home, and the rest is history. We zipped up the catcher's gear and said we're going to be the best possible second baseman that we can be and go out there and just try to do the best job we can. Obviously, I think things worked out real well.

The truth of the matter is that the motivational force behind it was that 90 percent of the people didn't think I could do it. I took that as positive energy and used it as a motivational force. Catching was pretty much where I liked to play, and I never played second before in my life, so it was a big, big step.

I had another Italian coach, Matt Galante. Without him, it never would have been as successful as it has been. We put in a lot of time. We'd get to the park early at spring training, go to a back field, and work. Then, when the day was over, we'd go to the back field again and work some more. That's the only way we got better, just putting in hours and hours trying to learn that position. Matty's a guy that did a lot of great things with a lot of infielders over the course of his career. Not just myself: Billy Doran, Craig Reynolds. He just knows infield.

I think I'm the only guy in the history of the game to ever start at catcher, start at second, start at center. That's a nice little feather. As an active player you don't get too caught up in stats and numbers; you just play the game and enjoy it and try to be the best you can. But the 50-50 thing, it didn't hit me at first, and then people said it's never been done before. Then you look at Speaker's numbers and you think, he was an unbelievable player. I was never a historian of the game, but you look at somebody who your name is there with and you look him up and you go, *Oh my God, this guy was an unbelievable player, one of the greatest of all time.* That's nice company to keep.

As a kid, I hated to sit there and watch the game. It was boring. My brother loved the Yankees, so obviously we watched the Yankees a little bit. Not many players moved around then, so you always knew who the Yankees lineup was: Willie Randolph, Thurman Munson, Lou Piniella, Oscar Gamble, Reggie Jackson. I mean, it never changed. A piece of the puzzle every now and then, but for the most part it was the same guys year in and year out. So as far as watching the game back then, I watched how they hit. Growing up on the

East Coast, stickball was always big, or Wiffle ball, and you'd always have to hit the way they hit. Then, after I got to the big leagues and got to know who the players were, I paid more attention to watching the game. Now, having almost twenty years in the game, you start doing a little more history when you have your name associated with other players.

Ken Caminiti was a great guy; he was a great friend. He would do anything for you. If he had five dollars left in his life and you asked him for it, he would give it to you and never ask anything for it. He had some issues, but for the most part people really need to remember him as a player and as a person because he was really a great person who would do anything for you. He was a gamer. Defensively, he was probably one of the best third basemen I ever had the opportunity to play with. He would save a pitching staff four or five runs a week. He would get to some balls that nobody would ever get to and throw guys out. He was an unbelievable defensive third baseman.

Bo Jackson was a guy that was pretty impressive for his size and speed and what he could do. He really sticks out. George Brett. Paul Molitor for having a short swing. Playing with Bagwell all these years, that's been something that's been special. There's a lot of guys. I think the great thing about our game is that everybody's unique in their own way. They have their own special little characteristic in whatever they do.

The game's a little disappointing now because there's no loyalty from management or players anymore. Being associated with one organization is something special. It's not just me. Bagwell's a part of that too, and it's something we take a lot of pride in because there's been a loyalty factor from the owner and management side of it. Both sides have given in over the years. I think from a fan's perspective, that's one of the biggest things our sport is lacking. Little kids can root for one of their heroes for a year or two, and then they're gone. In our case, to have your name associated with Robin Yount or Kirby Puckett or George Brett, people that have been there their whole career, in this day and age that is something that's great.

You never know what you're going to see on a baseball field. Sometimes you go to a game and you say, "I've never seen that before." We can go out and get shut out tonight, or we can score 20 runs. We don't know what's going to happen, and that's the great thing about it. It's the only sport that you don't control the offense. The guy throws a round ball and you hit it with a round stick in a direction that you hope they don't catch it. In football, you throw it; in basketball, you shoot it. You control that. In baseball, you don't.

Craig Biggio
National Baseball Hall of Fame and Museum.

Joe Girardi

A native of Peoria, Illinois, Joe Girardi was a three-time Academic All-American at Northwestern University and two-time All-Big 10 selection as a catcher. Following his graduation in 1986 with a degree in industrial engineering, the Chicago Cubs selected him in the fifth round of the draft. He went on to a 15-year career with the Cubs, Rockies, Yankees, and Cardinals, won three World Series rings with the Yankees in '96, '98, and '99, and was an All-Star in 2000. On July 18, 1999, in his final season with the Yankees, he caught David Cone's perfect game against Montreal at Yankee Stadium.

Following his retirement as a player, Girardi worked as a television commentator and as the Yankees bench coach before being hired to manage the Florida Marlins in 2006. He was selected as the NL Manager of the Year by the Baseball Writers Association of America after leading the team to a surprising 78–84 record, becoming only the third rookie manager to win the award. Nevertheless, he was fired after the season because of disagreements with ownership. Then, when he succeeded Joe Torre as manager of the Yankees in 2008, he requested uniform number 27, symbolic of his goal to lead the team to its twenty-seventh World Series title. He achieved that goal in 2009, followed by three consecutive postseason appearances. In his 10 seasons managing the Yankees (2008–17), they posted a record of 910–710, a .562 winning percentage. Both as a player and manager, Girardi applied the same discipline and work ethic that enabled him to earn an engineering degree and excel in baseball at Northwestern.

* * *

I wish we spoke Italian at home, but we didn't. But I consider myself an Italian American. My mom and dad's grandparents were immigrants. My dad's side came from Torino, and my mom's side came from Rome; a little mixture. My mom's maiden name was Perino, and her mother was Leone. I spent a lot of time with my dad's parents; they were twenty minutes away. They were born in the States and they lived in a little town outside Peoria. Like a lot of other Italian people, my grandfather was a mason. He taught my dad the trade, and my dad did it on the weekends to make extra money to feed all of us. My dad was a salesman and a restaurant owner; he did a bunch of things. I used to go with my father on the weekends and was the little boy that carried all the bricks and cement. It was great, though, because you learn the value of hard work. What I learned from my father's parents was what it takes to be successful, how it's about hard work and dedication, and that relationships are important in life.

My mom was the youngest of fifteen, and her father died when she was six or seven, and her mother, obviously, was very old. She died when I was about two, so I didn't really know my mother's mother and father. I learned a lot about perseverance from my mom. When I was thirteen, she was diagnosed with cancer and was given six months to live. She was a child psychologist and she never stopped working. She said she wanted to see her two sons graduate from medical school and my sister graduate from college because she missed her high school graduation when she had surgery. She lived for six years and passed on right after all three things happened.

I don't speak Italian. At the grade school I went to we had to take French, so I continued to take French because I had a head start, which was stupid. My wife, Kim, is Italian; her maiden name was Innocenzi. She and I went to Italy and didn't speak Italian. Obviously, we want to teach our daughter Italian, just so she knows her heritage. If she ever wants to spend time in Italy, it'll be much easier to communicate. I think you miss out on the true culture of Italy if you don't speak the language. We want to take a class in Italian; that's one of our goals. We hope to go over there and put on a clinic in Italy, so we hope that works out for us. I'm excited about this opportunity.

Being Italian American is important to me because it's who I am. It's where my family is from; it's where my wife's family is from. I think everyone should be proud of where your family is from. I feel very blessed to come from a home where both my parents worked very hard and were very diligent to make our lives better, and I think that comes from their upbringing. So I want to pass that on to my child.

When other Italian players come up to you, you joke a little bit. Before, there were a lot more Italians in the game. You don't see as many today. You change teams so much that you don't have the chance to make those bonds like they used to. I was with four teams in twelve years. Today, I think, the game has become more diverse. It's gotten a little bit out of New York.

Times have changed and education is stressed more for athletes today. College is more important. I was fortunate in that my parents pushed me and made me understand that school was first. My degree is in industrial engineering. I think what you do apply from that is the discipline and the concentration it takes to be successful in both. When you're trying to balance being a student athlete, you've got to pay attention because you don't have the time other students have.

Joe Girardi
National Baseball Hall of Fame and Museum.

As a manager, I've taken things from a lot of people, even coaches I had in high school and college. I think about Ron Wellman, who was my high school coach. I've taken a lot from Don Zimmer, Joe Torre, and Tony La Russa. When I think about Don Baylor, I think about toughness. I think about hard work and relationships with your players, getting the most out of your players. I thought Joe Torre was a master of that. You just pick a lot from people's brains when you're around them.

1990–99

Mike Piazza

*S*elected by the Los Angeles Dodgers in the sixty-second round of the 1988 draft, behind 1,389 other hopefuls, Michael Joseph Piazza seemed destined to be just another kid with an unfulfilled dream. Instead, the native of Norristown, Pennsylvania, went on to be widely acknowledged as the greatest offensive catcher in major-league history. In a 16-year career with the Dodgers, Marlins, Mets, Padres, and A's, he hit 427 home runs, including a record 396 as a catcher, and posted a career .308 average.

After initially struggling in the minor leagues, by 1992 he had become the Dodgers Minor League Player of the Year. In 1993, he became the Dodgers starting catcher, made the All-Star team, and was the unanimous choice as NL Rookie of the Year. A twelve-time All-Star, he was twice the runner-up in the Most Valuable Player voting, four times finishing in the top five, and won 10 consecutive Silver Slugger Awards.

Of his 427 home runs, none was more memorable than the one he hit at Shea Stadium on September 21, 2011. In the first professional sporting event in New York City after the September 11 terrorist attack, Piazza hit an eighth-inning, game-winning homer that not only gave the Mets a come-from-behind win over the Braves but provided a much-needed morale boost to a stunned city. When Shea Stadium closed in September 2008, that home run was chosen as the second-greatest moment in the stadium's history, and it is even mentioned on his Hall of Fame plaque in Cooperstown. On July 30, 2016, the Mets retired Piazza's number 31.

Piazza has long been involved with efforts to enhance the development of baseball in Italy. He was the marquee player for Italy in the inaugural World Baseball Classic in 2006, then served as a coach in the 2009 and 2013 Classics. In 2016, he further cemented his commitment to sports in Italy by acquiring a majority ownership share in the A.C. Reggiana 1919 soccer team.

While his record easily warranted admission to the Hall of Fame in his first year of eligibility in 2013, Piazza was not elected until his fourth time on the ballot. Unsubstantiated rumors of alleged use of performance-enhancing drugs, which Piazza denied, had tainted him with guilt by association, linking him with suspected and avowed steroid users whose names were also on the ballot. His induction in 2016 made him the lowest-drafted player ever to be enshrined in Cooperstown. In his acceptance speech, Piazza expressed his gratitude to his father, Vince, in Italian, saying: "Many thanks to the country of Italy for the gift of my father."

* * *

My dad grew up in Norristown, Pennsylvania, a suburb of Philadelphia. His parents were born in Italy and immigrated here in the teens. My grandfather, Rosario, was from Sciacca, Sicily, and my grandmother, Elisabetta, was from Naples. Back in those days it was very rare to marry someone from outside your region in Italy. My grandfather took a lot of criticism from his family for marrying a "foreigner." My father was a little bit scrutinized for marrying a Slovak, but that was about the time those stereotypes were being kind of lightened as far as having to marry an Italian. It's kind of nice, and that's obviously the melting pot of this country.

My dad said he would be called "dago" and "wop" when he was a kid, and all the Irish kids would want to fight him, and he would try so hard to assimilate himself to be an American. Then when he grew up and started losing that ethnic identity, he would strive to become more Italian. I remember, this Italian American group gave me the Brian Piccolo Award. At the banquet I was giving a little bit of history of my family and I said I'm only half Italian, my mother is Slovak. There was this deafening silence over the crowd, and my dad said, "Why did you tell them that?" I said, "It's your fault; you married a Slovak."

Back when I was a kid I would get razzed for my name; people would call me "Pizza." I think that in the last thirty or so years in this country, ethnic identity has sort of dissipated because males are carrying on the name, but they are marrying Irish and German girls, things like that. Plus families are moving more so you become more American. In one way it's good, and in another, it's not so good because you are losing track of your heritage.

We grew up in the United States and we love this country, but we're very proud of our ancestry, the fact that Italy is a country of historical tradition. There are differences between the regions in Italy; the country was only incorporated in 1870. They were a bunch of city states. That's what I find fascinating and that's what I like to read about. My first trip to Italy was in 2002 for Major League Baseball. I went to Rome for a few days and enjoyed it very much; that whet my appetite and I've been back several times since. I went to Sicily, Rome, Florence, Parma, Milan. People were really sweet and nice. I've always looked for that sort of bridge between the Italians who stayed and the people who migrated here in the late 1800s, the farm workers and the laborers.

I wouldn't have missed the World Baseball Classic for the world. It's important to reconnect with your roots. I think you have to be realistic about baseball in Italy. I think once you get one or two in the big leagues it would kindle some interest over there. I don't know if they'll ever be a powerhouse like the Dominican Republic because a lot of those kids are playing out of sheer desperation. Because of the media now being worldwide, I have friends who have been to Italy who have said I have a very big following with fans over there because baseball is becoming a lot more popular. Obviously, it's always going to be second to soccer, but baseball is becoming a lot more popular.

My dad was a left-handed second baseman, so he obviously knew his career was not going to take off. He played a little semipro ball, then he played for a lot of teams in the army; he was in Korea and Germany. He had aspirations to play professionally, but he had to work to support his family. My father came out of the army with a couple hundred dollars discharge pay and built a new-car dealership organization. I could have easily gone into that, but I wanted to play baseball and forge my own identity.

I grew up watching the Phillies in the late seventies, early eighties. They had a really good team and I enjoyed watching them. That's when I fell in love with the game. I liked Mike Schmidt; he was an All-Star third baseman and a great hitter with a lot of power. I picked up a lot of his mannerisms. He was a great ballplayer. I also liked to watch Lou Brock and Johnny Bench.

My dad bought me a batting cage when I was eleven and a pitching machine. At times I didn't want to go out there, and he kind of forced me to go out and practice at least a little bit. He knew that I had talent, and looking back now I have to thank my dad for being very stern and making me practice. And even if I had never made it in baseball, it taught me responsibility and discipline, how to apply myself to something.

Joe DiMaggio was very much an influence on my father, but on the same note, my father was very much enthralled by Ted Williams. He always debated whether Joe would have more home runs playing in Fenway and whether Ted would have hit more home runs in Yankee Stadium. When I was growing up my dad was taken in with Joe DiMaggio's legacy, and it wasn't even so much baseball. He had this off the field legacy with Marilyn Monroe and being in New York. And back then, too, your private life wasn't scrutinized as much and people kind of romanticized about the off-field exploits of the players. Today, you have to really watch yourself because there are a lot of people that are trying to exploit your private life. You can get in trouble if you're not careful. The eras are so different. Back then, the media wasn't out to exploit athletes and they probably had just as many problems as they do today off the field. It's not a complaint on my part; you just have to deal with it.

I met Joe many times. The first time I met him he told me he was very proud of my accomplishments and to just carry on and play hard. At times he's very introverted, understandably so. He's probably pestered a lot. But he has an aura about him that I don't think will ever be achieved again.

I'm honored when people associate me with him, as sort of a descendant of the DiMaggio era. That's something I'm very proud of. Being of Italian descent and knowing how people, especially other Italian Americans, respond to my career is very flattering. Obviously, there are a lot of predecessors who have a great tradition and have contributed a lot to baseball. With what Joe DiMaggio stood for as far as being Italian, I think it was good and bad because he set such a precedent it is almost impossible to measure up to as far as popularity and talent and legacy, being the Yankee Clipper and winning all those championships. I think Italian Americans are ever searching for the next Joe DiMaggio, and I think it's almost impossible to live up to those expectations. I've met many prominent Italian Americans and a lot of them try to put me somewhat in that category, but I'm just kind of besieged by humility. I can't try to place myself there. I can only say I'm very much inspired by Joe DiMaggio, and if people put me in that category it's very flattering.

The key is, when people doubt your ability you have to welcome that. You have to use that. I never really wanted to prove anybody wrong. I wanted to do it because I really felt I could compete in the major leagues. I felt like I had the ability and I didn't let anybody discourage me. It's easy when you have the higher-ups or expert scouts telling you should go back to school and coaches telling you you should not pursue your major-league dream. But I was fortunate. I appreciated Tommy Lasorda. I did do a lot of the work, but he helped me and gave me an opportunity. He went to bat for me when I finally proved I could be a major-league player and gave me the opportunity to be the everyday catcher in 1993. Following in the footsteps of Mike Scioscia, another Italian American catcher, was difficult because he was a very popular player with the Dodgers. So I felt some pressure, but I just tried to be myself and not worry about those expectations.

People think Tommy's my godfather, but he's not. My father and Tommy were very good friends, both from Norristown. When Tommy went off to play baseball and my father went into the army, they always kept in touch. The story got misconstrued and I wasn't into setting the record straight. It didn't matter to me, but it started perpetuating that I was Tommy's godson. In actuality, my youngest brother Tommy was named in honor of Tommy Lasorda. He was born in 1981 after the Dodgers won the World Series and Tommy said, "I want to be Tommy's godfather." Actually, my mother's brother, Bud, is my real godfather.

In 1997, I hit .362 and finished third in the batting title behind Tony Gwynn and Larry Walker. I really wanted to be the first catcher since Ernie

Lombardi to win the batting title. I never figured hitting .362 as a catcher I'd finish third. In a way, I'm a little disappointed, but in a way, I'm not because I know I was beat by the best. It was just something that wasn't meant to be. I always look at what I have instead of what I don't have. I had a really good chance in the mid-'90s when I think I was as good as any hitter in the game. In '97 I had the Triple Crown in the second half with 40 home runs and 124 RBIs and finished second in the MVP voting.

As for my defense, I think there have been very few catchers, or very few players, who have had the kind of scrutiny I've had. The glory of defensive catching is purely throwing. If you catch a good ballgame or if you block a ball or if you catch a popup, those things don't get the glory. But if you throw a guy out from your knees, everybody's like "Wow!" I'll be the first to admit I haven't been the most prolific thrower, but I don't think I've been the worst thrower ever. I just think the fact that I hit so well put more scrutiny on my defense. It's affected me in some ways. Sometimes throughout my career I've been a little bit self-conscious of it. I've tried to work on it; it isn't as if I haven't applied myself.

Mike Piazza
AP Photo/Nam Y. Huh.

When I was asked to play first base, I wanted to be a good soldier and a good teammate. Obviously, it was out of my control. I did it to the best of my ability but after having been non-mobile behind the plate for 12 years and then being asked to be mobile, it was a little difficult. But I worked hard at it. It was frustrating. You feel like you're learning at a big-league level, which is very difficult because the expectations are high. I made the most of it.

I just want to relay to people you don't always have to be the most highly regarded athlete or highly regarded student. You can still make your way through discipline, determination, and faith: faith in God, faith in your family. I had a great support system. You don't have to be the most highly exalted person in your field. You can forge your own way through discipline and hard work. You might have to work harder than the next guy, you may have physical obstacles, and sometimes you have to work twice as hard, and I enjoy doing it. I find pleasure in that because the discipline and the work make you appreciate it more. It keeps you more grounded and makes you more able to deal with anything that comes your way.

Jerry Colangelo

A native of Chicago Heights, Illinois, Jerry Colangelo starred in baseball and basketball in high school before earning All-Big Ten honors as captain of the University of Illinois basketball team.

Named general manager of the expansion Phoenix Suns in 1968 at the age of twenty-eight, he remained involved with the NBA franchise until 2012 in various roles, including head coach, managing general partner, and CEO. A four-time NBA Executive of the Year, he was inducted into the Basketball Hall of Fame in 2004. In 2005, Colangelo was named to head the US men's national basketball program. Under his leadership, the USA won the Olympic gold medal in 2008, 2012, and 2016.

In 1998, three years after a group of investors headed by Colangelo as managing general partner were awarded a major-league expansion franchise, the Arizona Diamondbacks made their debut, with Joe Garagiola Jr. as their general manager. Then, in 2001, they became the youngest franchise to win a World Series by beating the Yankees in seven games.

Also in 1998, Colangelo headed a fund drive to build the new home of the National Italian American Sports Hall of Fame in Chicago's Little Italy. The new facility, named The Jerry Colangelo Center, was dedicated in 2000.

His son, Bryan, a two-time recipient of the NBA Executive of the Year Award, has served as general manager of the Suns, the Toronto Raptors, and the Philadelphia 76ers.

In his office in the America West Arena in Phoenix, where we spoke, Colangelo had what he called his "roots corner." Among other things, it displayed the accordion he played as a youngster and a photo of the small house where he grew up, which his grandfather built from railroad boxcar remnants.

* * *

My grandparents came over from the old country. My grandfather worked for the city, he was a janitor working in the jail; he had a number of jobs. He died when I was fifteen. I was a pitcher myself and had offers to sign, but my arm went out. Jim Bouton pitched behind me in high school. On the day my grandfather died, I had a game I was supposed to pitch. I debated what to do and I asked the family what they wanted me to do. They said he'd want me to pitch. I remember I pitched a no-hitter, and in the last inning I'm just crying the whole time because I wanted to do it for him. The only house I ever lived in was the house my grandfather built out of remnants of a couple of railroad boxcars and some extra lumber. Of course, it's taken a lot of different looks since that time. We lived upstairs and the square footage was the size of my office.

Our neighborhood was mostly Italian, with some Polish, but on specific streets. Legend says the area was called "Hungry Hill" because people were hungry, but that's a hard one to prove. It was a blue-collar, lunch-pail neighborhood. I tell the story that I knew *Roots* before *Roots* became popular. Everyone in the neighborhood took care of one another. I have great memories of that childhood growing up in a poor neighborhood, but no one really cared. We were just thankful for whatever it was that we had.

A friend of mine sent this accordion to me after I purchased the Phoenix Suns. He said, "Put it somewhere where you don't forget." This had a meaning to me because as a kid I used to play all the old Italian songs for my grandfather: "Santa Lucia," "Oj, Marie." I used to take accordion lessons from a guy from the old neighborhood. When I was about eleven or twelve, he was really on my case about basketball, baseball, and the accordion. One day, in broken English, he said, "Now what's it going to be, the accordion or basketball and baseball?" I said, "I'll see ya, Frank." And that was it.

This is important to me because with all the things that have happened in my life, it's important to keep your feet where they need to be, and I'm always this close. This past year they renamed my street for me. I love the street I grew up on. They renamed the gym. I know that vicariously the people who are still around live through my experiences, they enjoy the success. I don't forget that, and I don't forget them. So I go back.

I was always proud of my heritage, even as a youngster when I was starting to get a bit of notoriety because of sports. There was a fellow who was kind of the neighborhood counselor. He was an old-timer, an immigrant who really spoke broken English. He must've been about sixty-five and I was twelve when he said, "You know, you're going to have to change your name." And I said, "Why?" He said, "Because they're going to hold you back because of your name. You may have to shorten it or change it and become Americanized." I said, "No, I'll never do that. I'm too proud of my name and my heritage."

I still tell that story about him because it had that kind of impact on me. The other thing is, in my world of competing in sports, for some reason I was never intimidated by someone who had more materially. I knew where we lived, on one side of the tracks, and where more affluent people lived on the other side of the tracks. But it never made any difference to me. It wasn't as if I felt wanting. That's the way it was. I accepted it.

Had I not been blessed with some physical ability in sports, I never would have had the chance to go to college. It was through those opportunities that I had a chance to go from there. Many of the people I was raised with went to the mills like their fathers and grandparents before them. Many of them are still there. The neighborhood is dilapidated. They've all kind of scattered, but many of them still live in the area and they all get together for doings. So in many ways I'm kind of a link for them to the past. They had a parade last Fourth of July where I took my whole family. They had floats made and it was a big deal for me to see some people I hadn't seen in a long time. When I go back I see a lot of the same people, my friends that go back many years. I wouldn't trade that upbringing for anything.

As I kind of moved up and got involved with the Chicago Bulls franchise at twenty-six, I met people like Lamar Hunt and Harold Meyer of the Oscar Meyer Company, people I never would have met in the normal walk of life. But I felt as comfortable with them as I did in the neighborhood. I think, without knowing it, I was being prepared for all of that by being street-educated in the old neighborhood. Just the feel for things and people and values; all of the things you don't see much of today. I think for those of us who came up in that kind of environment, we were blessed to have had that kind of a family situation, to have learned the things we did about the important things in life: family, friends, loyalty, and hard work. I think, in my case, that prepared me as I've gone up the ladder.

To finance the National Italian American Sports Hall of Fame's new home, we raised, I think, a million seven or a million eight in $100,000 increments from each major league: NHL, NFL, MLB, NBA, from the four commissioners. What was very rewarding to me were some of the calls I made to people like [Rick] Pitino, [John] Calipari, P. J. Carlesimo. They said, "Jerry, if you're committed to this, we're in." [They contributed] $100,000 each. And Vince Naimoli and Jerry Reinsdorf did it. I'm missing some obvious names, but it was very rewarding to get that response.

In September 1998, Joe DiMaggio was in Chicago for the groundbreaking ceremony and it was really a very touching time for me. As a kid growing up in an Italian American neighborhood, I knew very soon that he was a hero in our neighborhood. I had met him once, maybe fifteen, eighteen years ago, but it was just, "How are you, nice to meet you." I've always had great respect for how he's maintained himself over the years, the dignity that he's carried himself with and so forth.

I'm in the lobby of the hotel in the morning and I see Joe. I went up and I said, "Joe, Jerry Colangelo." He said, "I know who you are. I've followed your

Jerry Colangelo
AP Photo/Mike Fiala.

career and I'm proud of you." For the next couple of days we were together all the time, for lunches, dinners, different activities, and he was always right next to me, saying, "Stay by me, I want you next to me." So in my mind there was kind of a bonding that took place over two days that had such a tremendous impact on me. As I think back on that, it was one of the highlights of my life.

Most of the Italian immigrants came over and settled in Italian communities, no different than some of the other ethnic groups, because they were looking for security, and they found it in their own little neighborhoods. They kind of rallied behind those who were doing something good in the entertainment world, in the sports field, obviously. They were immediately heroes because they were carrying the banner. It was kind of the world against us. People took pride in Joe DiMaggio's achievements; it gave them hope, in their own families, that if it could happen for Joe, it could happen for any of us.

It was an interesting time for him to surface, going to New York and being with the Yankees, which was *the* team at the time. I mean, he could have been lost a little bit. So God had a plan for him, and it was for him to be with the New York Yankees in that era and for him to have that kind of impact, which has lasted decades. How many people have that kind of impact? It's amazing. Baseball offered an opportunity for people of all kinds of descent. If they showed they had the physical ability, they had a chance. And some of the Italian Americans really did achieve, in baseball in particular. And Joe DiMaggio epitomizes that. He's the number one guy; no question about it.

I always knew my roots, and I've never left them. In fact, it's probably gotten stronger as time has gone on. I'm on the board of the National Italian American Foundation. I've taken on this responsibility with the Italian American Sports Hall of Fame. On a local basis, we had a statue of Columbus erected, tried to put on some events here in Phoenix just to bring people together. It's more difficult to hang on as time marches by. I think it's important for people to understand that being born here, we're Americans, but we shouldn't lose sight of the fact that we are of Italian heritage. And we should be proud of that. We should be very proud of those who have been able to achieve in this world, many against great obstacles.

Joe Garagiola Jr.

*L*ike his childhood friend and neighbor, Yogi Berra, Joe Garagiola Sr. grew up to be a major-league catcher. After five-plus years with his hometown St. Louis Cardinals (1946–51), he spent the last three-plus years of his career with three other teams before going on to an award-winning career as a popular radio and television personality. He received the Ford C. Frick Award in 1991 for excellence in broadcasting and the Hall of Fame's Buck O'Neil Lifetime Achievement Award in 2014.

His son, Joe Jr., followed a different path to the major leagues. After earning a law degree from Georgetown, he worked as general counsel to George Steinbrenner's Yankees, spent seventeen years as an agent, then became a partner in a Phoenix law firm. It was in that capacity that he was instrumental in securing an expansion franchise in 1995. Once the franchise was granted, Jerry Colangelo, the managing general partner, hired Garagiola to be the first general manager of the Arizona Diamondbacks, a position he held until August 2005.

In his tenure as GM, Garagiola led the team to three division championships, including the pennant and World Series title in 2001, only four years after the team's debut. In 2005, he was named Major League Baseball's senior vice president of baseball operations, and in 2011, senior vice president of standards and on-field operations. He also served as general manager for Team USA in the 2013 World Baseball Classic.

* * *

I'm very proud of my heritage. My dad's parents were immigrants from a little town called Inveruno, which is just outside of Milan. My grandparents only spoke Italian. When I was a kid growing up in St. Louis we saw them quite a bit. We'd stop by, usually on the way to the ballpark. Unfortunately, I never learned to speak it. We grew up in south St. Louis, maybe about a half hour from where they lived. They lived in the same house the whole time they were there.

I hark back to the notion that my grandfather, my dad's father, what courage he had. Here was a guy who didn't speak English living in this town in Italy where the family probably lived for 100 generations and some friends of his write him a letter and say, "Hey, it's better over here in America." Somehow he makes his way from Inveruno to Milan to wherever the boat left from. He takes the boat to New York, gets on the train, rides one thousand miles into the heart of this country where he can barely speak the language. What courage to do that. He worked in a brick factory. He'd go to work every day, and that was it.

Two generations later, here am I. If you don't think about that, there's something wrong with you. That's what I think about in terms of what being an Italian American means and how fortunate I am to be able to stand on his shoulders, and obviously my dad's. My dad married, as the term goes, an "Americana." That was a little bit of a problem for his folks. He couldn't find a nice Italian girl. In fact, he and Yogi both married non-Italians.

When I was in college at Notre Dame, I had a summer job with the Yankees as an intern and kind of got the bug at that point. I went on to go to Georgetown Law School. After four years at Notre Dame, I felt I owed the Jesuits a shot at me. When I got out of law school in 1975, there was a position with the Yankees as an in-house lawyer. So I went back there and stayed until 1977 when I went on my own and became an agent. I was an agent for about seventeen years, which encompassed the time I moved from New York to Arizona, which was in 1982. When I got out here, I got involved in a lot of baseball-related things, initially having to do with the Cactus League.

I was part of the whole process that led to building new facilities in the Cactus League and was also involved in the first unsuccessful effort to bring major league baseball to the Valley of the Sun, which was the Rockies-Marlins expansion in 1992. I then got involved with Jerry Colangelo and was able to excite his interest in pursuing baseball and wound up, from about 1993 on, working almost exclusively on that, even though I was in a law firm then. When the franchise was awarded in 1995, Jerry asked me if I wanted to leave my law firm, representing players, and become full-time with the team. It didn't take me very long to answer the question.

There are a few executives in the majors now: Sal Bando, Ned Colletti, Larry Lucchino. It's one of those things you don't think about, but when you do you realize it's not a long list, so it's kind of nice to be on it.

Yogi Berra moved to the East Coast once he made it with the Yankees, so I didn't see much of him. Later on, when we moved to New York, which was about the time I was starting high school, the families would see each other more frequently. But certainly I knew who Yogi was. I knew who DiMaggio was. I knew who Ernie Lombardi was, Lazzeri. Frank Crosetti I got to know a little bit later on, when he was a Yankee coach. I knew who Rizzuto was, obviously. A lot of those guys I got to know later on when I was with the Yankees. I became a good friend of Phil's, as a matter of fact. What a sweetheart. He's just the nicest guy, a wonderful man.

Joe Garagiola Jr.
AP Photo/Roy Dabner.

I think Joe DiMaggio epitomized in many respects those great Yankee teams he played on. The way he conducted his life, he was a role model at a time when, unfortunately, many Italians were achieving fame in ways people weren't terribly proud of. So here was DiMaggio, an Italian American, whose name was in the paper every day for doing positive, heroic things. I think it's hard for somebody of my generation to fully appreciate that, but I know from talking to people that he was as important as anything else. Here was a guy that Italian Americans could justifiably be proud of. He was a guy that rose above all the jokes and the ethnic stereotypes; he just transcended all of that and that's his place in history.

Any time people preserve ethnic stereotyping it's offensive, but it's not something you dwell on. Every day you go out and live your life in a positive way, and hopefully, you erode a little bit of that so that in a couple of generations it is relegated to the dustbin of history.

Frank Catalanotto

*F*rank Catalanotto was a high school senior in Smithtown, New York, by the time he drew the attention of pro scouts who had come to watch some of his teammates. He impressed them enough to be selected by the Tigers in the tenth round of the 1992 draft. Following six years of development in the minors, he went on to play for five teams in a 14-year big-league career between 1997 and 2010.

The 6-foot, 170-pound left-handed hitter was versatile, playing first, second, third, and the outfield. His best year came in 2001 when he hit a career-high .330 for the Texas Rangers (fifth best in the AL) and was engaged in a late-season contest for the batting title with rookie Ichiro Suzuki until a slump in the final week dropped him out of contention. Over the course of his career, he compiled an impressive average of .291.

Catalanotto has also been committed to Team Italy's involvement in the World Baseball Classic. After playing in the first two events (2006 and 2009), he coached in 2013 and 2017, and has twice gone to Italy as a special instructor at Grosseto and Nettuno. He is also a co-founder of the Italian American Baseball Foundation, whose goal is to support baseball in Italy.

Describing himself as "one of the last of the old-school mentality," Catalanotto talks about the ways the game changed during his career, which coincided with the so-called steroid era.

* * *

From what I've learned, my dad's side of the family is from Santa Margherita di Belice, close to Palermo. My great-grandfather came over when he was five or six years old and they moved to Brooklyn. I'm a little fuzzier on my mom's side. My brother told me that our great-great-great-grandfather was featured in the movie *The Leopard*, with Burt Lancaster. His name in the film is Don Ciccio. Apparently he was a friend of Prince Salina, the main character in the film, and came to the US to find a location for the prince in case he had to flee from Garibaldi. His name was Francesco, and the name has been passed down to my great-grandfather, my grandfather, my father, and then to myself. When I was a kid we always used to go into Brooklyn to see my great-grandfather, and I remember my great-grandparents from my mother's side as well. They lived on Long Island. They all spoke Italian. Trust me, having a conversation with them was difficult because their English wasn't very good.

I did have a sense of being Italian American as a kid, but not as much as I would've liked to. However, now, with the World Baseball Classic and the Italian national team and going over to Italy, I'm learning more about it and I wish when I was younger I had known more about my heritage. But it is nice to now kind of figure everything out and have conversations with my dad. It's really very fascinating.

I've only gone to Italy one time, about three years ago. I went over there to help coach the Italian national team. It was pretty neat because the coach of the World Baseball Classic team, Marco Mazzieri, brought me to his hometown. I got to go to Rome and Florence and all those great places, but I also got to see Italy like an Italian that lives in the small towns.

I've played baseball as long as I can remember. As a little boy, when my dad would come home every night we would go in the backyard and throw, and he would pitch to me. I really grew a love for the game at such a young age. After we'd be outside playing, we'd go inside to eat dinner and then my dad would put on the Yankee game. Unlike kids today, I remember being fascinated by the game for two and a half or three hours. I really, really enjoyed it. It seems like nowadays, with all the social media and video, kids can't sit and really watch a game anymore. Those were some of the times in my childhood I really cherished. I'm so happy that my dad introduced me to the game at such a young age.

I started playing T-ball when I was about five years old, then moved up through Little League, travel baseball, and high school baseball. Honestly, it wasn't until my senior year of high school that I thought about playing professionally. I was a good player, but I wasn't necessarily the best player on my team, especially not on my high school team. We had three guys on my team that were highly scouted by college and major-league scouts. It wasn't until my senior year that I really started progressing. I benefitted by those scouts being there looking at these other guys. I played well and kind of turned their heads, and when the draft came in June my senior year in 1992, some of the scouts came up to me and said, "We were looking at these other guys, but we think you're a player that should get drafted." Once I heard that, I thought, *Wow, I really have a chance to play professional baseball.* Even though it was a dream of mine since I was a tiny boy, I don't know that I necessarily believed that dream until I was eighteen years old and these scouts were looking at me.

I was offered a full scholarship to Seton Hall, so it was a tough decision because schooling was very important to me and my family, and I was drafted in the tenth round by the Tigers. The draft was in early June and it took me over a month to make my decision. My mom and dad were very instrumental in helping me make that decision. They said that whatever my decision was, they would stand by it. I kept weighing the pros and cons and trying to figure out what happens if I go to school and I get hurt; then I wouldn't have a chance to possibly live out that childhood dream. It came down to the Tigers putting a clause in my contract saying that if I wind up quitting baseball after a year or two, they'll give me some money toward schooling; I believe it was $25,000. So that helped me make my decision and I went ahead and signed.

There were times when I got discouraged, especially after my first year in the minor leagues. I had never used the wood bat before, and it makes a huge difference when you go from metal to wood. Here I was an eighteen-year-old kid, very weak, and to pick up that heavy wood bat and swing it, it was difficult. So I didn't do well when I played, I missed my family and friends terribly, and the way of life wasn't what I was used to. I had my mom and dad that always did everything for me; now all of a sudden I was out on my own. It was a culture shock. I remember coming home after that season and saying to my dad, "I think I made the wrong decision. My friends are at college having a great time, and I'm miserable."

My dad told me, "Hey, Frank, you can't give up on this, you can't quit. Give it another try. Go back for another season and see if you get used to the lifestyle and start to enjoy playing baseball again."

And that's what happened. I went back and had a good season. That's when I met Larry Parrish. He was my coach and for whatever reason, he took a liking to me and took me under his wing. He kind of made me his project. He made sure I was in the batting cage early every single day. He not only taught me the mechanics of my swing, most importantly he taught me the mental part of the game. He taught me to be prepared, how to watch a pitcher and be able to pick up the little tendencies he might have to get an edge. I felt like had I not met him I probably would never have made it to the major leagues. So I give him a lot of credit.

I was maybe a little bit crazy with the way I would prepare. I wrote down everything that I learned, everything that I saw, and I felt like I had to be a student of the game to do all the little things correctly because I wasn't 6-foot-4, 250 pounds and didn't run like a deer. I didn't have some of the talents that the superstar players have. I feel that becoming a student of the game helped me get there, and the fact I was able to play multiple positions made me a little more valuable and allowed me to stay in the big leagues for as long as I did.

I think once you get there, you have guys coming up behind you that are dying to get to the big leagues, so you're always kind of looking over your shoulder until you maybe sign a big contract and you have that comfort level.

It was tough getting there, but I think staying there for the first five years was equally or even harder than getting there.

I kind of knew I had made it in 2001 when I hit .330 and finished fifth in batting. I was not just an extra player on the team, I was a guy who was playing every day and my name was in the paper every day. That was Ichiro's first year and the Japanese media was all over the place. Every time we played them there would be like fifty Japanese media at my locker and the attention I was getting was amazing. Even if we weren't playing Seattle I would still have Japanese media at my locker the last two weeks of the season. Not being a superstar player, sometimes you don't get that attention, but especially the last month or two weeks I got a lot of attention and it was pretty neat.

The last three games I went 0-for-12, and Ichiro was something like 8 or 9 for his last 15. He got hot and I got very cold. Before those games it was pretty close; it was only about a four- or five-point difference. It was disappointing, but I didn't have any regrets. I was happy that I was in that position.

Playing in the majors exceeded my expectations. To be treated the way we were, from the hotel rooms, the flights. I never knew that these guys didn't have to fly with everyone else. We would just pull up to the airplane, get on the plane, and the next thing you know we're taking off, not waiting in security lines and stuff like that. The food that they put out for us. The way that you are perceived by the fans. As a kid I loved going to Yankee Stadium, and my favorite player was Don Mattingly. I was able to get an autograph from him and I always said to myself, *If I ever get that opportunity I'll be there for the fans and sign autographs.* And that's what I did. It really was amazing how I was treated by the fans and by the organizations. So it definitely exceeded my expectations, and I'm so happy that I was able to get that opportunity.

I don't have any regrets. The one thing, and it's nothing I could've changed, over my 14-year career I never played on a team that went to the playoffs. I remember at the end of my career there was a stat that came up during the playoffs, and I was in the top five of major-league players that had played that long and never made it to the playoffs. When I was with the Toronto Blue Jays, a team that won 90 or more games a season, we were playing the Red Sox and the Yankees 19 times each, and those two teams were on fire. Everyone I've talked to who's been in the playoffs says it's just amazing, just a whole different level. So I wish it would've been the case, but it just wasn't meant to be.

It was hard to give it up. It was 14 years in the major leagues and five years in the minors, and it was something that I did for my whole life. Now it was going to be taken away and I wasn't going to be playing anymore. I remember when I was released by the Mets in 2010. I wasn't upset that I got released. It was just that I knew in my mind and in my heart that that was it. I knew that mentally and physically I had had it, so to know that the game was done for me, I had a few tears in my eyes and it was tough. It was something that I knew was coming, but even though I was prepared for it I didn't know how hard it would be.

The game did change when I was playing. I feel like I'm one of the last of the old-school mentality. It seems like after I got there we had kids getting drafted and signing $10 million contracts before they even play one professional game. I didn't think that was right. When I got there I kept my mouth shut and I did what I was told to do. The kids didn't respect the veterans, and I felt that was a little bit of a problem. To me it was disappointing because I was always taught to respect the veterans and basically do what you're told. There should be a time when you are the rookie and you have to carry the beer on the bus. I saw that change right before my eyes, and I didn't like that.

As far as the game itself, obviously when I played it was what we now call the steroid era. I saw firsthand that there were guys on my teams that were doing steroids. So I felt like that changed the game on the field. It changed the numbers these guys were putting up. You had guys that were bigger, stronger, faster, and were recovering better after these games. For those who weren't steroid guys, it was a little unfair. I'm happy to see that Major League Baseball is doing everything they can to get steroids out of the game and get it back to what it used to be.

With regard to the Hall of Fame, I've got a different type of stance on this. I did play in that era and if we don't let these guys in, it's basically kind of forgetting that era. I saw it happen with my own eyes; I saw these guys put up those numbers. So I'm not saying necessarily that these numbers are valid. However, I feel like we need to recognize the guys that put up these numbers because if we don't, if we just pick and choose—I think this guy did steroids, this guy didn't—then we're going to have guys in there that did do steroids and guys that should be in there and didn't do steroids.

I know this will never happen, but my thought process is you would have a hall or a wing at the Hall of Fame that has a title on it that says these were players that played in the steroid era, or from 1990 to 2010, or whatever it is, and put the guys in who put up the numbers to be Hall of Famers. In that way the public can decide. I just think it's too difficult for people to say I think he did steroids because he had acne on his back or because he got very muscular. You don't know that that's the case. If there are guys in there already who did do steroids, it would be terrible to keep guys out like Barry Bonds or Roger

Clemens who had great numbers, but now the voters and fans don't like them because they know they did steroids and lied about it.

I understand there's not an easy solution to this, but it becomes very subjective. I remember Barry Bonds coming into our ballpark in Texas and our pitching coach saying to the pitchers, "We're not going to let Barry Bonds beat us tonight, so don't throw him a strike." So four at-bats in a row he got walked on four pitches. The fifth at-bat was the ninth inning and the pitcher throws ball one, ball two, ball three. And the next pitch that he threw, he missed his spot and it was outside, but it was a spot that Bonds was able to put the bat on the ball and, sure enough, he hit a game-winning home run. And I'm thinking, *You've got to be kidding me.* This guy knows that we're to pitch around him the whole time, and you'd think that after four at-bats he's probably just putting his bat on his shoulder and thinking they're going to walk me again. But the one pitch he was able to hit he put it out of the ballpark. I'm sure he was aided by steroids, but I don't think we can forget some of the numbers that he put up.

In 2005, I got a phone call from the Players Association asking me if I was interested in playing in the World Baseball Classic because Team Italy was looking for some players. I said, "Absolutely." They asked me if my parents were born in Italy, and I said, "No." And they asked if my grandparents were born in Italy, and I said, "No." Then they said, "All right, do you like pizza?"

They told me that if I could prove that my great-great-grandparents were born in Italy that would be enough because they were trying to get some major-league guys on the team. I was very happy I was able to play on the team. It got me more interested in my heritage and I started looking into things, talking to my parents and my grandparents. That's how it started, and my experience with the Italian baseball team has been awesome. I really love working with these guys. These kids over there in Italy, they want to get better and they really do love the game. Both myself and Mike Piazza are trying to do our best to help baseball in Italy by doing some camps and clinics. I know Mike is very instrumental in doing things over in Italy. We've always told each other, whatever we can do to help out, that would be great.

What stands out most about the first Classic in 2006 is when Mike and I were sitting on the bench talking about hitting. All of a sudden one of the Italian players came over, then another guy, and another guy. The next thing you know, we had a group of people around us and they were just trying to learn from what we were saying. Then we were interacting with them and telling them this is what you should look for in this situation or the pitcher is tipping his pitches. These guys were kind of locked in on us, so I was pretty

Frank Catalanotto
Ezio Ratti/FIBS.

impressed with that. Then I went back in 2009 when it was in Toronto, where I had played, and in 2013 I coached in that one.

I had never played in a game where it was about pride in your country, your heritage. Now it was a whole different ballgame. This is more about showing people we've got some good players in Italy as well. Over the course of the years beginning in 2006, there are definitely players from Italy that are getting better. I always tell the guys in the Italian Baseball Federation what a good job they're doing because I think baseball is getting better in Italy. Obviously, Italy is not known for baseball, but I do feel like they're doing a great job with the youth. And also at their Academy in Italy, because these players are noticeably better as I see them at each World Baseball Classic.

So it's really been a great experience. To get that opportunity was awesome, and I really embraced it. The father of my former teammate, Vernon Wells, is a painter and he paints a lot of baseball pieces. So I have a huge painting that he did of me in my Italy uniform. I have it downstairs in my man cave, so I'm reminded of it all the time.

Although I don't want to be identified as just a baseball player, it has been such a huge part of my life and my family's life. Baseball has brought me and my family members closer because they have traveled with me, not only all over the country but also to other countries. I've been able to live out a dream, I was able to make a lot of money playing baseball, and baseball is always going to be so special in my life. Obviously, I want to be the best dad I can be and the best husband and son, but I will always remember my time playing baseball, not only at the major-league level but also with Team Italy in the World Baseball Classic. I was very fortunate to be able to live out a childhood dream and baseball will always be a big part of my life.

2000—09

Barry Zito

*A*fter being coached incessantly from an early age by his father, Joe (who learned about pitching from books), Barry Zito was selected by Oakland out of the University of Southern California in the first round of the 1999 draft. By midseason the following year, the 6-foot-2, 205-pound lefty with a paralysis-inducing curveball was in the A's starting rotation. After compiling a record of 24–12 through the 2001 season, he had a career year in 2002, going 23–5 with a 2.75 ERA and winning the Cy Young Award at the age of twenty-four. After four more solid seasons with Oakland, he signed a seven-year, $126 million contract with the Giants as a free agent, becoming the highest-paid pitcher in baseball history. He posted losing records in his first four seasons with the Giants, was sidelined by injury for most of 2011, then bounced back with a 15–8 record in 2012. That postseason he won the opening game of the World Series, setting the stage for the Giants' four-game sweep.

After sitting out the 2014 season, Zito returned to the franchise that drafted him, signing a minor-league contract with the A's. So here was a thirty-seven-year-old former Cy Young winner going back to the obscurity and grind of a minor-league season, pitching for Oakland's Triple-A affiliate in Nashville. Called up by the A's in mid-September, he appeared in three games, then announced his retirement. In his 15-year career, the three-time All-Star compiled a record of 165–143 with a 4.04 ERA.

Zito, who was born in Las Vegas but raised mainly in California, was almost as well-known for his offbeat, zen-like personality as he was for his pitching. He was a surfer with long hair (occasionally dyed red or blue), practiced yoga and transcendental meditation, and played the guitar in the clubhouse. Though he grew up in a musical environment—his father was a conductor and arranger for Nat King Cole, and his mother sang in a group that toured with Cole—it wasn't until his minor-league days that Zito began playing the guitar as a way to relax. He became more serious about songwriting during his season in Nashville and released his first EP in January 2017.

* * *

My father's mother and father were born in Calabria. My father's father, Giuseppe, was a five-star general in the Italian army, alongside Mussolini. He won the Medal of Honor, the highest award. And my father's sister was the godchild of Mussolini; that's how close they were. My grandfather died when my dad was four, in 1932. He survived a lot of wars and actually died by choking on a fish bone. Recently, we just went back and, as a gift to my dad, we took his father's medals and all his different things we could find and put them in a scrapbook.

I didn't really grow up with a sense of Italian heritage, but I definitely take a lot of pride in the fact that I'm Italian. The Italians have probably contributed more to the world than anyone else in terms of art, architecture, music, food, and wine. I was born in Vegas and we moved to San Diego when I was six. I mean, I knew I was Italian for sure, but we never spoke it around the house or anything like that. My mother's German and English, but she learned all the Italian recipes from my dad's mother.

My dad was born in New York, in the Bronx, then he grew up on a farm in upstate New York. He spoke Italian until he was thirteen or something like that. He only went to school up to the eighth grade, but he started educating himself, literally going into libraries and reading books on contract law and stuff like that. On the musical side, he was self-taught, playing piano, probably in his teens, and ended up conducting and arranging for Nat King Cole for fifteen years. He managed many groups and different entertainment acts and took care of the business side of a lot of that stuff.

My dad met my mom when she was a singer for a group called the Merry Young Souls. They traveled with Nat; it was four women and a couple of guys. My dad was the conductor; he was thirty-three and she was eighteen. She dropped out of UCLA to tour with Nat.

When we moved to San Diego, I played T-ball and I ran out to the pitcher's mound. I mean, I didn't really know about baseball growing up because we were in Vegas and there were no teams there. My dad found that I had a natural knack. I started throwing my curveball at seven. He saw that and he wanted to cultivate it. So we just started working in the backyard every day for years. At that point he was retired because there was no entertainment industry in San Diego. My mom was a minister, and my dad didn't work.

He had no background in baseball. He just kind of knew the ingredients of a champion, as he put it, and he knew the signs of failure. He had helped a lot of acts reach a high level of success, so he just applied that to baseball. He bought a bunch of instructional books. He'd go over them the night before, unbeknownst to me, and then the next day we'd go over them together. To me, he knew the whole book, but really he was just reading it the night before. He was like a professional dad. He really dominated that responsibility like no one I've ever seen.

He would always tell me, "You're going to be great; you're going to be a major-league pitcher." I believed him. He said, "If you want to achieve these things, you've just got to keep working. When you're eighteen, you can decide for yourself whether you want to keep going. But until then we're going to do this." At eighteen I got a scholarship, so it was a no-brainer.

It was probably my freshman year in college when I realized I wanted to do this for a career. I went to UC-Santa Barbara and was throwing hard and wanted go right into the draft, so I dropped out the next year and went to junior college to get in the draft. I actually didn't sign that year. I was a third-rounder by the Texas Rangers, but came back the next year at USC and went in the first round.

I've been blessed with a rubber arm, or whatever it is. A lot of kids get hurt throwing curveballs too soon, so I don't know how to explain that. I never patterned myself after anyone. I never looked up to the major-league guys; I always just felt like I wanted to be my own whatever. Some of the most challenging hitters I faced were Derek Jeter, Manny Ramirez, Ichiro.

I have other interests outside the game. Music, obviously, is ingrained, but ironically, I never picked the guitar up until I was twenty-one. I always liked music, but it didn't really speak to me growing up. My sister graduated from the Berklee School of Music in Boston, and she's an amazing musician as well. For me, I just picked up a guitar in 2000, coming into my first big league spring training, because I knew I was going to need something to take my mind off the hype and the craziness. So I've been playing for seven years and it's more fulfilling than anything. To be able to write a song or come up with your own music and put words to it and sing; it's pretty fun, you know.

I've been getting into a lot of jazz the last few years. I always go to my dad; he knows music theory beyond anything. He used to write for the Buffalo Symphony and he would write for 105 people. So he had to know the intonation and the range of every instrument so he could write for it.

I like photography too, mainly for documentation purposes of what I experience. I know that math is kind of on the other side of the creative thing, brain-wise, but I think music is all a mathematical language. Photography is math too; you're screwing with your shutter speeds, your aperture, ISOs. Even composition-wise, if you look at different angles and degrees, color, temperature; it's all math.

I also apply that analytical bent to baseball, way too much. When you see something from twenty-five angles, you always see the potential, good and bad. I think some people just have this kind of blind determination sometimes and they don't take a minute to stop and smell the roses. I think sometimes

Barry Zito
© 2016 *San Francisco Giants.*

that can be good in a sports environment because it's such a pure competition. I think the analytical side can hurt guys sometimes until they learn how to harness it in a positive way. I'm always dealing with that.

I don't look at tape and study hitters quite as much. I've always been most successful when I just focus on what I do. I mean, I'll go to pitchers' meetings and hear about this or that, but when you get caught up in what hitters are doing or thinking or anticipating, you start to lose sight of yourself. So I've never been a huge advocate of that. Guys like Curt Schilling, he can tell you how many 1-1 changeups he's thrown. It works for him. But for me, I think I'm too analytical, so I like to swing it back. Yoga is good for the stillness and calm, but I don't actively pursue seminars or anything like that. I think it's more just a quieting of the mind, which can be called a lot of things. Self-trust is the biggest thing. There's a guy named Christian Nestell Bovee who said, "Self-distrust is the reason for most of our failures."

At times your thoughts get out of order and you start focusing on the wrong things, as with anything in life. But for me, baseball is a good indicator of where my mind is at all times. If everything's in line and working the way it should, you go out and you have easy games, effortless success. At other times you fight yourself and you get in your own way. You start to complicate things and it seems so much harder than it actually is. But it's all learning.

I don't think I'm eccentric. I just think I'm a thinker, a regular person, maybe a little more aware of things in general. I don't know the depths of anyone else's mind except my own, and I don't even know that.

Jason Grilli

*J*ason Grilli has been remarkably resilient throughout his long major-league career. A top pitching prospect and the fourth overall draft pick at the age of twenty, the 6-foot-5, 235-pound right-hander seemed destined for a stellar career. But baseball can be cruel at times. A series of injuries intervened, forcing him to reinvent himself again and again. In his fifth year he was converted from a starter to a reliever, and over the course of his first 15 years he was traded five times, released twice, and was a free agent six times. Yet for all that, thanks to his tenacity and adaptability, he managed not only to survive but ultimately thrive at a relatively advanced age. Grilli's explanation for his dogged perseverance was simple: "I love the game."

The son of Steve Grilli, a pitcher who spent parts of four seasons in the majors in the mid-1970s, Jason was drafted by the Giants in 1997 following his junior year at Seton Hall University. Following a trade to the Florida Marlins, he pitched in seven major league games between 2000 and 2001 before Tommy John surgery forced him to miss the entire 2002 season.

In 2006, the same year he was converted to a reliever by the Tigers, he pitched for Italy in the inaugural World Baseball Classic, then returned to pitch in 2009 and 2013, making him the only active major leaguer to play in the first three Classics. It was also in 2013 that Grilli, now with the Pirates, became a closer for the first time, was named to the All-Star team, earned 33 saves at the age of thirty-six, and was on the cover of Sports Illustrated. The following year an injury cost him the closer's role, but in 2015 the thirty-eight-year-old reliever bounced back to notch 24 saves in the first half of the season for the Braves before a ruptured Achilles tendon put him out for the rest of the year. In 2016, he was traded to the Blue Jays, who sent him to the Rangers, his tenth team, in 2017. In 16 postseason games through 2017, he had allowed no runs in twelve innings.

* * *

I'm 75 percent Italian, one quarter Irish. My mom's mother was Irish, and she always claimed that was the best part of me. Three of my grandparents are 100 percent Italian. My great-grandparents are the ones who came over to Ellis Island. My one grandmother's side was from Naples, and I know there are some Grillis in a town outside of Rome called Ferentino. The Grilli last name comes from the word for crickets. The Grillis in Italy were farmers, and they warded off some locusts and crickets from their crops. That's where I think the name came from, or so I hear; that's the family lore.

I had the fortunate opportunity to go to Italy back in 1996. In my sophomore year in college at Seton Hall, I found out I had a chance to play for Team USA in the Olympic Games. Then I got a call from the coach, Mike Sheppard, that Team Italy wanted me to play in the Olympics. "I got this crazy phone call telling me that if you can prove your Italian heritage and become an Italian citizen, you can play for Italy," he said.

I realized it was a once-in-a-lifetime opportunity and I understood what it meant to get into my heritage. So I went to New York City with my parents to get all these stamped documents to prove my Italian heritage and I got my citizenship.

I got to go over to Italy and I was supposed to play for Team Florence in the Italian league, but that all fell through because the Italian players were pissed because they brought over some American players. Here I am an American proud to be Italian and I'm getting boycotted and these guys want to strike, saying I don't have Italian blood. So they wound up sending us home because they were threatened that the strike was actually going to happen.

I was a small town kid from Baldwinsville, New York, getting sent off pretty well by the people in Central New York. There was a lot of Italian pride. I can't say it was all a negative experience, because I got to see the motherland and put my feet on the soil where my ancestors came from. I've really come to appreciate that desire my ancestors had to come over here and pursue the American dream. It's just by chance that I'm living it. I've been able to experience great things here because my great-grandparents came over on that ship in hopes of better things. And I became an Italian citizen, so I can pass that on to my kids.

Coming back benefitted me in the long run because I got to go to the Cape Cod League, which is a pretty good summer league and you're playing against guys from all these Division I schools. So I had a great summer there, did very well, and I think that's what really put me on the map to be a top prospect by my junior year.

After I got drafted, it came full circle because I met up with one of the Italian players who was threatening to strike: Claudio Liverziani. He got drafted by the Mariners, and I got drafted by the Giants, and we went to the Instructional League. So when I faced him in an Instructional League game, he comes up to the plate and I drill him. I said, "Welcome to my turf."

When I was asked to play for Italy in the World Baseball Classic in 2006, I thought it was great. That was when I was trying to make the Tigers team and they were training in Lakeland, so I was training on the same grounds as the Tigers. It was a perfect match because I made the team that year and I got to go to the World Series. So by playing for Italy, I got ready and I was in a competitive mode right out of the gate. It heightened things for me and got me locked-in.

The chance to play in the World Baseball Classic once again gave me the chance to do something affiliated with baseball, the game I love. The first go-around was great. We even had Tommy Lasorda give us an unbelievable speech. And after what had happened in Italy, it gave me a chance to mend the ties by being able to represent Italy. Some of the same guys were playing for Team Italy, even Claudio Liverziani. I said to him, "Hey man, I'm so sorry. That's in the past."

I think the 2009 WBC was the most fun for me. With guys coming back from the first one, it was kind of a reunion. And it was in Toronto, a place that I love and where there was a good Italian following. And how could you forget coming so close in 2013 with a guy like Anthony Rizzo. It really kind of exploded because nobody expected us to do so well. You want to grow up to be like your dad, and my dad just happened to be a ballplayer and I learned a lot from him. He never pushed me, but he was always around, whether he was announcing at the Triple-A ballpark, coming to my Little League games, or being my pitching coach. It's always been a great relationship; he's one of my best friends. I think a lot of it comes from the fact that we pride ourselves on strong family ties.

I started thinking about playing professionally in high school. I had scouts checking me out my senior year, and I was drafted by the Yankees coming out of high school. I was with the Marlins when I made my first major-league appearance. I was in Triple-A Calgary at the time, which made no sense for the Triple-A team to be so far away. I had to fly eight hours and got no sleep at all. I didn't know who I'd be pitching against. I looked at the schedule, and it was the Braves, and I thought, "Holy crap, my big-league debut's against the Braves." And I wasn't pitching well at the time. I had almost a 7.5 ERA; I was getting tanked up there in the PCL. I guess a couple of guys got injured and I just happened to be available. But I did my thing and I got the win against the Braves that day.

It was just a magical experience because I so longed for that and everybody remembers what it took to get there. It was a proud moment to share with my family. It was a big victory; it made me feel so confident to know that I could beat those guys. Then, to boot, I had a stress fracture in my arm which I didn't know at the time. I had to have surgery after my big-league debut, so there was a long time lapse between my debut and being a mainstay in the big leagues.

When I went to the Tigers in 2006, they told me there weren't any more starting spots that year and I didn't want to go down to Triple A and be an insurance policy. I said, "I'm a big-league pitcher. I think you know that, and I'd like to think I can help you in the bullpen some way. Just give me the opportunity." They picked me and I was on the team that year, but it was a long, bumpy road to where I'm at now.

I've played on twelve different teams in all this time and I've met so many people who have helped me along the way. Todd Oakes, who was my pitching coach in Double A, he was one guy I really value. He had leukemia and he passed, but he was a great mentor. When you're twenty years old and you're sent to Shreveport, Louisiana, don't know anybody and it's your first pro ball experience, there are certain people that you know just care more, even beyond making sure that you're executing all your pitches. With the Giants organization, Mark Gardner and Joe Nathan took me under their wing. Todd Jones with the Tigers took care of me and made sure I was staying in line.

You know, every pitcher wants to be dominant. My heroes were guys like Clemens and Ryan; these guys are the aces, so you wanted to be one of those guys. But I dealt with some injuries along the way. I was thinking that in the pros I'm not going to strike out eighteen every night. If I was going to be a successful starter, I knew I had to go deep into the game. I struck out a lot of people with the breaking ball. I was also a sinkerball pitcher, throwing a two-seamer.

As a middle reliever, I prided myself on inherited runners. You're bringing me in with runners on first and third and no outs, so if I throw a sinker and it's hit to the shortstop for a double play, I've done my job. Then, when meeting with Clint Hurdle when I got traded to the Rockies, he asked what I wanted out of my career. I told him, "I think I can pitch at the back end of the bullpen. I want to do something more significant. I've been pitching with inherited runners, so if I can do that, you think it's going to be a bigger challenge doing it later in the game? What can I do with a clean inning? I'm facing the same guys, so that's what I want. I know I can do the job."

So when I finally got to be a set-up man for [Joel] Hanrahan in Pittsburgh, it was like, *This is what I've been waiting for.* I relished the job, more so even than starting. As a starter, my first inning was usually my worst because I had so much adrenaline. I needed to get tired to be an effective starter. I think I'm more built to be a reliever because I love the adrenaline rush and it's all or nothing. I love it.

I think I'm still evolving as a pitcher. I've always tried to find another little edge. Whether it was an injury or something wasn't working, I went from

Jason Grilli
Pittsburgh Pirates.

curveball pitching to slider, and I went into the bullpen, incorporating slide steps, certain arm positions that I feel can be deceptive when I'm not throwing hard that day. I think that's what's kept me in the game. I'm not saying I figured the game out, but I figured out me by making those adjustments. You figure it out or you starve.

Over the course of time I've been asked to do different things. One time they wanted me to sweep the floor, so I swept the floor. Another time it was wash the windows, so I'd wash the windows. I can only do what you're asking me to do. You don't always get what you want. You've got to fight for it, especially in sports. I had to kick and claw. You need to figure out what the hell you have to do to get there and keep battling until you get there. That's how strong the belief is that I've maintained. Call it narcissistic, call it confidence.

But looking back, it makes you appreciate a lot of things. I guess you've got to love what you do, right? There's no better feeling than the rush you get when you get to experience that competitive edge that can't be fulfilled for me by much else. I just love the game. I've loved and respected it as long as I can remember. It's hard to let go of the wheel when you know you've still got something left in the tank. People have written me off a few times with this and that, especially my Achilles tear.

I'm not over-embellishing anything, nor do I want to. This is just my journey. I'd like to be able to tell my kids I've never given up. Don't give up until you've had enough. When you get to experience something that you love and dream about doing, there is a time you've had enough, as opposed to quitting. I could have quit a long time ago. Everybody will tell you it's hard to get there, and it's harder to stay. Baseball is a love and hate thing. It's so long, it's very hard, it's very frustrating. It can be humbling, and it can be so exhilarating. I've been fortunate to experience so much in baseball, despite all the injuries, the four surgeries, being away from family, trades. All these crazy experiences, I think you just try to appreciate what it all means in the end. A lot of people would give anything for the opportunity.

I'm very humble that I get to do what I do. I like to think that I work as hard if not harder than a lot of people. Everybody at that level, when you get to the top, is very, very, very good. There's not a formula; we're not robots out there. There's a reason why steroids happened, because guys are that good. Everybody's always looking for that edge. I've lived through an era where it was hard to make that decision. I could've taken it many times to help me heal from the injuries I've had.

I called my dad one day and said, "I'm thinking about taking it." Having my dad in the game, I always had some somebody to bounce it off of. My dad loved and respected the game and advised me not to do it. He said, "You've made it this far on your own merit; why stop now?" Maybe that's why I'm in the game now. My dad made me love and appreciate the game and know how hard it was, but I think the hard is what makes it addictive. If it was easy, everybody would do it.

There's so many good memories: the playoffs, of course, and the World Series, albeit a loss. That's the highest of the highs. To me, that's what you play for. Just to know how sore you are and you go out there and empty the tank. It's such an intense world. Then, the laughs and the camaraderie, that's what everybody says you will miss the most. You watch a game on TV and you say, "God, I did that once." Some of the friendships I've made, the good guys you get to meet from different backgrounds. Just batting practice, laughing with your buddies. There is more to it than just the game, more to it than just one memory. I don't think you can appreciate it until you stop.

It's been a very volatile experience: the highs and the lows, good and bad, joys and pain. But I wouldn't trade the experience for anything. It's like the curtain of Oz; you have this assumption that it's all going to be these amazing things. But like every occupation, it has its good and its bad. The toughest part, I think, is the strain on the family. It's a big sacrifice, to be away from the family weeks at a time with your wife holding things together. Being Italian, you go back to the roots of what family means. Baseball has brought my family together.

When I'm retired, I have some aspirations. One is to be an awesome dad and husband, a family man like my Italian roots have taught me. Baseball has consumed so much of my focus, and any ballplayer will tell you it's hard to balance the three months time before you have to go through that schedule again. I've loved it all, but I've had to put a lot on hold. My family has been more than patient with me. It's been very one-sided, but joyfully, everybody has been grateful for the journey they've been on with me. And it's not over yet. None of us are ready to let go.

Chris Capuano

A star pitcher-outfielder, as well as valedictorian, at Cathedral High School in Springfield, Massachusetts, Chris Capuano was drafted out of high school by the Pirates but chose to go to Duke University on a baseball scholarship. Following his junior year, he was signed by the Diamondbacks, but before beginning his professional career he completed his degree in Economics at Duke, where he was elected to Phi Beta Kappa. The discipline and tenacity that enabled him to be a successful student-athlete at Duke helped him to endure and survive several obstacles in his big-league career, including two Tommy John reconstructive elbow surgeries and assorted other injuries.

Following a trade to Milwaukee, the 6-foot-2, 225-pound left-hander had his breakout season in 2005. His 18 wins were the most by a Brewers pitcher since 1987, and only three have ever won more in a single season. He continued to win in 2006, posting a 10–4 record by midseason, and was named to the All-Star team, but a second-half slump saw him finish with an 11–12 record. After getting off to a 5–0 start in 2007, he struggled before undergoing his second Tommy John surgery, which forced him to miss the 2008 and 2009 seasons. He returned to the Brewers in 2010, mainly as a reliever, then spent the next five seasons pitching for the Mets, Dodgers, Red Sox, and Yankees, alternating between starting and relieving roles. In 2016, he returned once more to Milwaukee, where his season was cut short at the All-Star break by an elbow injury.

In spite of his many setbacks, Capuano never gave up on returning to the mound. His determination and work ethic enabled him to spend part or all of 12 seasons in the majors, compiling a record of 77–92 with a 4.38 ERA. Throughout his career he also served as his team's representative to the Major League Baseball Players Association.

Here he discusses the mechanics and the art of pitching, the physical and mental aspects of coming back from Tommy John surgery, and the adjustments a pitcher has to make as the years pass.

* * *

My parents, Frank and Cathy, have lived in Springfield, Massachusetts, their entire lives. My mom is Irish. My dad's parents came from Italy, a place called Monte Sant'Angelo in the province of Foggia. My dad, the youngest, comes from a family of thirteen, a big, crazy Italian family which makes for interesting reunions.

I played soccer, basketball, and baseball all through high school. I was a pitcher-outfielder in high school, and my last two years I realized I might have a chance to play in college and maybe after that. My senior year we went 19–0; my record was 8–0. Roger Clemens was a big idol of mine. I also looked up to Tom Glavine and Andy Pettitte. Those were the three guys I kind of emulated.

I was drafted by Pittsburgh in the forty-fifth round out of high school. At that time I was accepted at Yale, but Duke offered me a full-tuition baseball scholarship. I played three years at Duke and was drafted by Arizona in the eighth round after my junior year. Two days before classes started I met with the scouts from Arizona at Duke and signed the deal, which let me go back and finish my senior year. I wouldn't play for the Duke team, obviously.

My first year in professional ball, in South Bend, Indiana, with the low-A team of the Diamondbacks, I had a pitching coach, Royal Clayton. I won my first game and thought I pitched pretty well, but he said, "That was pretty good, but we've got some stuff to work on." At that time he really helped me develop my changeup, which has been a really good pitch for me. Even though I was having success at that level, he wanted to make sure that I was prepared to have success as I went up to the higher levels.

When you get to the big leagues, you have to be comfortable throwing any pitch in any count. Unless you've got overpowering stuff, you have to learn to be confident so that a hitter can't sit on pitches. I really learned more in that first year of professional baseball than I had learned pretty much my whole college career. That's the debate of whether you should sign out of high school or college. If you're a high enough pick, the education you get in professional ball is so much more advanced and faster.

The elbow injury in 2002 really came out of nowhere. I'd never broken a bone or missed a start for any reason. I went to Tucson and I was pretty close to getting called up. On May 4, we were playing the Colorado Sky Sox. I was throwing a shutout, everything was going great. Then in the eighth inning I threw a fastball on the inside corner for a strikeout, but right when I let that pitch go I felt a pop in my elbow, almost like a rubber band had been pulled back and snapped back together. Pain just shot down my arm.

Your heart starts beating fast, panic starts setting in. I got the ball back and told myself I want to finish the game. I threw the next fastball; my fastball had been around 92, and this one was around 80. I threw a couple of changeups, then I called the manager out and told him something's not right. And that was it. At first they were confident it might just be a strain. I got up the next day and it was real stiff. I went out to play catch; one throw from 60 feet went straight into the ground. I was off to Dr. Andrews the next week and had surgery May 17.

There were three or four days when you go through kind of feeling sorry for yourself; why did this have to happen? It was very scary. With the surgery there is a high success rate these days. A lot of guys come back from it, but still, there's that percentage of guys that don't come back. All the doubts rush in. Then you get over that initial stage and say, *OK, this is where I'm at.*

I was basically rehabbing for the next ten months. After the first couple of weeks they stretch your arm out and you try to get a range of motion back and do a lot of icing. Then you start doing little exercises with five-pound weights and rubber bands. Then gradually you start lifting weights again. Four months out is when you start a throwing program. You start out just lobbing the ball, literally on your knees. Over the next few months you gradually build up the distance and the intensity. Sure enough, it started to feel better in four or five months. But that was a scary time.

I made my first start eleven months after the initial injury. It was a little frustrating because I was used to having a fastball around 92, and my fastball was around 84. I had to learn how to use my changeup a lot and learn how to pitch. John Denny, our pitching coach, worked with me a lot. I think it was the biggest learning experience for me in the long run because my velocity came back to almost where it was. And now I have that good changeup. I learned that pitching isn't about overpowering guys; it's changing speeds and location. The object isn't to strike everyone out; you want them to put the ball in play weakly or hit your pitch. As a pitcher you always have to pitch to your strengths. So I have to mix what I know about the hitter's weakness with my strengths.

I got an interesting phone call from Coach K [Mike Krzyzewski] at Duke soon after I got called up to the big leagues, a year to the day after I had the surgery, May 4, 2003. I'll never forget it. He talked to me for twenty minutes. He has this reputation for being a great motivator, and he really was. I told him it was a little frustrating not having my best stuff, and he told me the important thing was to focus on winning with what you have. And that's great advice for baseball, especially being a pitcher. There are very few games when you have everything working perfectly with all your best stuff, but you still have to go out there and win.

Being traded after the 2003 season was another shock because I was very loyal to the organization I came up with. I really liked playing in Arizona; they were a class organization with great facilities and people. I wasn't really disappointed. I was just scared because all of a sudden you start thinking about finding a new place to live and meeting all new people. But then I looked at the situation and realized Milwaukee was going to be the perfect place for me. I was just trying to break in and establish myself, and I knew that in Milwaukee if I earned it I'd get a fair shot to be a starter.

In 2005, my first full season when I was healthy all year, I made all my starts and won 18 games. It was good validation for a young player as you finally realize, *OK, I'm here; now let's see what you can do.* As a player you don't think about the big numbers, whether it's getting 20 wins or 220 innings. You just go out there and compete every day. It's not really until the offseason when I sit around and assess how things went, but at the end of that season there was certainly a sense of accomplishment. The All-Star Game in 2006 was really special, certainly one of the highlights of my career.

With Tommy John surgery, typically recovery is anywhere from ten to sixteen months. It ended up taking me closer to sixteen or eighteen months to get back from the second one in 2008. It was six years later, and I was twenty-nine instead of twenty-three. But it's always worth it. I don't think there's anything any one of us would rather do than come out here and do this for a living. I had to accept the fact that maybe it wasn't going to come back and

Chris Capuano
Milwaukee Brewers Baseball Club.

I had to be OK with that. I thought, *I've had a pretty good career up to now, I have my degree and a lot of options after baseball.* Once I accepted that, I felt a real weight lift off me and things actually became a lot easier. I was able to come back and appreciate it a lot more.

I've had some great coaches. My first pitching coach in Milwaukee, Mike Maddux, was really good about teaching the mental side of pitching, how to break down attack plans against different hitters. After him, I had Rick Peterson when I was coming back from my second Tommy John. Rick was very big into the biomechanical analysis and did a lot of video breakdown and motion analysis to try to help you get your delivery to be as efficient as possible. He also had some ideas on Eastern philosophy. He had spent some time in Japan and some of that I actually enjoyed and I've continued to use it: meditation, the visualization of hitting a target, just very different ideas that I hadn't heard before.

Rick Honeycutt in LA was a very good left-handed pitcher and a very good pitching coach. I took a lot of things about working with my delivery from Rick. And also getting to play catch with Clayton Kershaw for two years when I was there. He basically gets to the same position out of his windup that he gets to with his stretch. He has the high front side, which provides a lot of deception, and then comes straight over the top. I've taken a little bit from everybody and the result is the experience I have now.

Typically, a pitching coach at the major-league level will be mainly focused on rhythm and timing issues, making sure everything is on time in the delivery. Pretty much in every rotational sport, whether it's golf, swinging the bat, or pitching, there's a certain sequence of things that has to happen in order to maximize power from the ground up through your hand and into the ball. So you're looking for good rhythm and timing and just making sure that everything is happening on time.

Physiology affects how a pitcher throws. That's why you can't take a pitching delivery and just try to clone someone and say do this and you'll have success. Everybody's body is built a little differently; the way your hips and pelvis work, the way your shoulder and joints work. Everybody has to try to maximize their own potential in their delivery, and it definitely varies based on body size and type.

The way the ball is leaving a pitcher's hand will dictate a lot. When you hear someone say, "The ball is coming out of his hand really well," that means it's just a pure throw, a true throw, if you will. Anybody who's played any sport has experienced when the timing is right and everything comes out right; that feeling is what keeps us coming back. So a pure throw is one where you feel yourself push right through the baseball the way you're supposed to. It comes out on the trajectory that you imagined, and typically there is some late action. The ball is going straight for about fifty feet or so, and it's that last ten feet when the hitter starts to react that the ball moves or explodes.

Making the transition from a starter to a reliever was frustrating in that I had a really hard time learning how to become a reliever and learning how to tackle that schedule at the big-league level. As a starter you have your five-day routine, and I've done that my whole life and was very confident in navigating that. In the bullpen it's different. You're ready to pitch every day and you can't go out there and give up a run in the first and still go seven or eight innings allowing one or two runs and keeping your team in the game. There's no leeway there; you've got to be on it from pitch one. Also, how do you stay strong when you're potentially going to be in the game pitching every day? That's been the biggest adjustment for me. But the camaraderie in the bullpen, it's like a team within a team. That's something I really enjoy.

It usually takes me about an hour to an hour and a half of warming my body up in the weight room. I spend a little time in the hot tub at first just getting my body warm. Then there's a whole bunch of exercises I do just to make sure the muscles are activated. We're trying to make sure that our hamstrings are firing properly and our rotator cuff and shoulder muscles are all properly turned on and primed before we throw. When you play catch as relievers, some days you stretch it out more, some days it's light catch, you practice breaking balls, you're working on your stuff. That's really your time to practice because you can't throw a full bullpen session like you would as a starter because you have to be available that night. That's where it gets tough because you might be pitching back-to-back days or you might not pitch for a week.

I think the way I pitch hasn't changed very much, but the way I train and the way I think about my mechanics has changed a lot as my body has changed to enable me to go out there and make pitches in the same way. You have to make adjustments because physically your body changes from your early twenties to your late thirties. I think you just try to be a little more efficient in your training and in your throwing because you can cover up some mechanical flaws when you're really young and strong, but over the long haul those things are going to wear you down and you need to learn to be more efficient.

I'm still awed by the fact that I faced two 300-game winners—Clemens and Greg Maddux—in my first full year in the majors. But it's great; it gives you a lot of adrenaline and you get really pumped up to go out there and play against them. And getting a hit off Clemens, that was one of my favorite moments. All of us pitchers think we're the best hitters in the world, so being able to get a hit off him is something I'm sure I'll look back on when I'm older.

I didn't actually realize I was pitching against him until I was hitting. I was in the batter's box looking out and there's Roger Clemens staring over the mitt at me. He was pretty imposing. He had gotten a jam-shot single off me the inning before and then I ended up picking him off first base. So Roger wasn't happy at that point and when I stepped in the box he's looking at me like some rookie punk, and sure enough the first pitch was high and tight. He grunted out there after he threw that pitch, and I was ready to jump out of the box at that point. My second time up he threw one down the middle; I took a swing at it and hit it up the middle for a base hit.

The first time I pitched in the postseason was in 2013 with the Dodgers against the Atlanta Braves. I think it was in the middle of the third or fourth inning and I came in the game. I could feel my heart pounding and I looked down and I could see it actually moving underneath my jersey. I think I was throwing 92, 93 that day, which is really hard for me. I ended up throwing like three innings and I got a win.

That was the most amped-up I think I've ever been on a baseball field, pitching in that playoff atmosphere. And I think I really understood what guys meant when they said they got that second wind when the playoffs came around. It's a long season and in September your body's tired, but as soon as you switch over to October you have this new life, this new energy, and you feel like you could keep going forever. So that was really memorable to be able to experience that.

Maybe early on I faced some stereotypes in the locker room as a Phi Beta Kappa, but ultimately, we're all the same in here. The only thing where I was treated a little differently, especially when I first got to the big leagues, a lot of veterans said, "You're going to be going to the union meetings and you're going to be our rep." They wanted to get me involved in the business side of baseball, our union side. I've been a rep every year since I started going in 2003.

Book smarts are great and doing well in school is great, but I've learned to respect the genius that I've seen in a lot of my fellow major leaguers. The guys who make it to the top level, these are smart individuals. They've had a lot of life experience. They have to be pretty well-developed to navigate all the ups and downs and to get to the top of the game. I respect the genius that a lot of these guys have in their craft. It is humbling sometimes.

Clayton Kershaw is probably the greatest pitcher I've ever seen in my current era. He really is the total package in terms of just the kind of person he is; he's very humble, just a good human being. His work ethic is second to none. He's very disciplined and regimented with his schedule and work. His ability to elevate his game when the situation gets tough is one of the things that impresses me most. He'll be going along in cruise control and as soon as he gets a runner on second base, it's like he turns up the heat and all of a sudden he gets better when the situation gets tougher.

Zach Greinke is another one who the last few years has really been on top of his game, and he's someone who is just a pure athlete, whether it's basketball or ping-pong or golf or baseball. He has unbelievable body control and hand-eye coordination. Just to watch him throw practice bullpens is mesmerizing because of how perfect his mechanics are. He can go through stretches where he's just in total control of the baseball. We always joke that when someone is in that good a zone, it's like they're playing a video game; it's like they're controlling it with the controller.

Baseball for me has been great because there is a simplicity to it that you don't often find in everyday life. Whatever struggles you're going through in your personal life, when you come to the park, no matter where it is, on a playground or a big-league stadium, it's still 60 feet, 6 inches from home plate to the pitcher's mound, the basepaths are still ninety feet, three strikes you're out. The rules don't change, so to be able to do something where you can see your hard work directly pay off that day I think is one of the things I feel really lucky to be able to do.

I've never spent a lot of time looking back on my career and thinking of the big picture. I guess if I did, I'll always say I think I could've done a little better, I wish I could've pitched better in this situation. It's easy to do that, but the biggest thing that I want to be able to do is just be able to be at peace when I'm done, knowing that I worked hard every day, I always tried to take care of myself, I always did the best in every situation I was put in with the information I had available.

You just want to leave it all out there, as the old cliché goes. But if I thought about how I want to be remembered, mostly someone who gave physically and mentally everything they had, someone who was a good teammate and a good person to be around, a positive influence to be around. And hopefully through some of my involvement in the union, someone who tried to ensure that the rights and benefits that we have as players continue and continue to get better for the guys who come after, so that the guys twenty, thirty, forty years from now, hopefully, enjoy a meaningful stake in this game the way we do.

Joey Votto

*I*n his first 11 seasons (2007–17), Joey Votto's statistics placed him among the elite hitters in the history of major league baseball. According to the March 27, 2017 issue of Sports Illustrated, his career "slash line" of .313/.425/.536 (batting average, on-base percentage, slugging percentage) had been equaled or surpassed by only five players: Babe Ruth, Ted Williams, Lou Gehrig, Jimmie Foxx, and Rogers Hornsby. What makes his record even more impressive is that Votto is a native of Toronto, Canada, not exactly a cradle of big-league stars.

Drafted out of high school by Cincinnati in the second round in 2002, the 6-foot-2, 220-pound left-handed hitter became the Reds starting first baseman in 2008. As of 2017, he was a five-time All-Star, a Gold Glove winner in 2011, and the National League's MVP in 2010, finishing in the top seven three other times. A patient hitter, he led the NL in on-base percentage six times and in walks five times. He also played for Team Canada in the 2005 Baseball World Cup and the 2013 World Baseball Classic. He is a six-time winner of the Tip O'Neill Award, given by the Canadian Baseball Hall of Fame to the player judged to have excelled in individual achievement and team contribution while adhering to baseball's highest ideals.

A devoted student of the art of hitting, from his early days Votto studied the techniques of past greats in order to improve his game. His primary role model was Ted Williams, whose book, The Science of Hitting, he virtually memorized. Notwithstanding his impressive offensive output, there were those who criticized Votto at times, as others once criticized Williams, for refusing to swing at pitches outside the strike zone, even with runners in scoring position.

Here Votto discusses the fine points of hitting, the challenge of sustaining excellence over time, the "rabbits" he chases, and the changing nature of baseball, maintaining that it is his obligation, and that of all major leaguers, to progress and evolve so as to make the game better.

* * *

My first love was basketball. I started playing baseball when I was six or seven, and I joined a league when I was eight or nine. I took to it, but basketball was my preferred sport for most of my pre-professional years. I played baseball in high school, but the season is very modest in Toronto. We played six or seven games, maybe as many as ten, depending on the weather. I also played in a local league, but in terms of playing a lot of travel ball, I didn't do that throughout my high school years. I played one year on a travel team, but never extensively. I didn't play on any national teams or anything like that.

The environment in Canada was relatively modest compared to the Latin American countries and American baseball. There were a few very good players, but for the most part, in my neighborhood there certainly weren't a lot of examples of players that ended up being really good major league players. There were a few, but they were from another part of the country. When I was fourteen, fifteen, sixteen, I felt like I had a legitimate chance to play professionally, so I pursued it and it ended up paying off. Some scouts came around my senior year in high school, but there weren't many. At that time I was a catcher, and playing a little bit in left and at third. When I started playing professional ball, they decided that I probably wasn't going to be good enough at catching or third base; it was more a demotion, a step backward, I suppose. It ended up working out well. It took me a long time to learn the position and get better at playing first.

I don't know if there was ever a time that I had legitimate doubts that I would make it to the majors. I had times in the minor leagues where I was intensely frustrated, where I was confused and wasn't able to understand why I wasn't playing as well as I should have. However, I don't remember a time where I thought I'm not going to make it. I was mostly just frustrated and trying to navigate the challenges I was being presented, if that makes sense.

Leon Roberts, who was our hitting coordinator, and Freddie Benavides, our first-base coach who was formerly the minor league director as well as the infield instructor, both were very supportive and very helpful to me, but also stayed on me throughout my minor-league career. There's always something to improve on. I work with Freddie daily, and it's been sixteen years that we've been working together. I just know that I have to be better.

My interest in Ted Williams began when I was a younger player. I'd always had a fascination with the greats and I tried to understand what made them different and special, and how they honed their craft. I had a pretty intense interest in that and I ended up copying a lot of the characteristics that I had read about. I read Ted Williams's book on hitting and I carried it around for years. Even to this day there is a lot of value to it. I have a good bit of it memorized, so traveling with it now is less necessary.

I know Williams was criticized for not swinging at pitches that were a little off the plate. Having a conversation about people's opinions is not something I get terribly excited about. It feels like I'd be chasing my tail. There are going to be people who are for or against just about everybody. There are examples of that all throughout sports. I think the higher you go up, the louder the opposition can be. I find that if you train yourself long enough that it's almost like, I don't want to say impossible, but it becomes a very uncomfortable, out of the ordinary, feeling of expanding your strengths. It's a fish out of water sort of thing. I just couldn't imagine a guy like Williams behaving like that because it didn't fit within his style of playing. It would be like him hitting right-handed; it didn't make sense. You create a habit over the years and decades that you play. Eventually the habit becomes ingrained and instinctual, and you can't do anything about it except be yourself.

I think the most inspiring thing for me was to hear when he failed, when he struggled and why he struggled, and how he overcame that. He was clearly an all-time great and maybe in the conversation for best hitter of all time. However, he wasn't without his own struggles. I admired that a lot and I learned from that, and I think that gives hope to just about anybody that struggles. There's no doubt that he was highly gifted: strength, power, quickness. He had to have had just about everything, but I think he must've had pretty good practice habits developed by his natural perfectionist personality. Lots of guys work hard, but I think he would've been great no matter what.

I don't want to elaborate too much on pitching, but in his book he described facing some of the all-time great pitchers and he said he had some success. And that makes sense to me because oftentimes pitchers with reputations for being all-time greats, everybody thinks that a great hitter would still fall in line with the general population. But that's not entirely how I find it works. It's about matchups. Sometimes there are guys who are a little less known and they've got a very quirky style, and oftentimes I find those guys to be a bit more challenging than, say, the elite pitchers in the game. I think sometimes there can be some shrinking when hitters face great pitchers, though, speaking from a hitter's perspective, I'd like to think that all hitters raise their level.

Every situation is different and I think that's part of the responsibility as a hitter. If a pitcher has a particular style that leads to more swings and misses, or more fly balls, more ground balls, or if he's always going to keep throwing breaking balls, you always have to adjust and be willing to change your game. I think that's the most important thing a hitter can develop, the ability to have a different club for every single lie, a different swing for every single situation, every single pitch style. I think that's when you know you can handle just about everybody in the game.

A good example is, before Ted Williams passed away, they asked him about facing Randy Johnson. The story goes that he closed his eyes and said, "I've already thought about it; hit a base hit up the middle." That tells me that he can envision facing him, he can see what the ball looks like coming in, he knows he has a limited set of options facing a guy like Randy Johnson. He knows he doesn't want to get burned on a slider, he knows he has to be aware of the ball in his face. He's saying to me, "That's what a good swing against him looks like."

That tells me that a guy who is known as a line-drive-hitting pull hitter is saying, "I've got to use a different swing." I've tried to develop options against every single guy, no matter if he's a lower tier pitcher or Clayton Kershaw. You have to have an answer for everybody. A big priority for me is a two-strike swing. Being a really competent two-strike hitter is the biggest priority for me over the last few years.

I do think that at some point someone will hit .400 again. It would be awfully shortsighted of me to think that something that's been done in the past will never happen again. No one would've thought that a player would hit over 61 home runs, then someone hit 73. I think there's certainly a possibility that a player can hit .400.

When I got to the big leagues, I thought it was much easier than I anticipated. But the last two years, maybe three years of my minor-league career, I played pretty angry. I was not happy that I was still in the minor leagues. I thought I was ready when I was about twenty-one or twenty-two. Fortunately, I got to refine some of my offensive and base-running skills, but I wasn't happy. So when I came up, I played angry and I played with a chip on my shoulder. I played to prove that I should've been here a long time ago. So I didn't find it difficult at all. I had success immediately. I think that was a byproduct of being ready in the minor leagues. I may not have found it difficult, but that doesn't mean I was getting the most out of myself. A player can manage to play at this level, but that doesn't necessarily mean they're getting the most out of themselves. And the travel can be a challenge, for sure.

I think the biggest appeal about being a major-league player is that I enjoy the challenge. It always changes; it always asks the most out of you each day. Because the game is played at such a high level, I find that if you don't give it your all and you don't focus on the details, you can go from the top tier to the bottom tier very quickly. There's such a fine line between all the different groups of players and teams that effort and discipline and consistency end up being cumulative and the differences become apparent very quickly. If you take a cross-section of anybody over six months, they're going to have their good days and bad days no matter what job they have. It's definitely challenging. Every year is different, but I think ultimately it's always, always challenging. It's always going to push you to your limit.

Joey Votto
The Cincinnati Reds.

Certainly there's a mental component to baseball, but I'm more of the mind-set that it's probably physical. The best players in the game are typically the best athletes. You look at the young players now and I'm not sure many people could debate that Trout is not one of the best athletes, or Harper, or Giancarlo Stanton. These are all very good athletes, so that's a variable, certainly. Eventually, as you get older, discipline, consistency, knowing yourself, and not being satisfied; those are important factors.

The game has changed quite a bit since I've been up here. It seems to me like the players are faster, smarter, things are done more efficiently, defenses are aligned more efficiently, and it's a younger league. Scouting reports are more efficient; it's not just a conversation, it's backed up with data. Because of the data that's available, you're able to make sense of people's trends and turn that into scouting reports and be able to counter your opposition. I think most players find the sweet spot for what's helpful and what isn't helpful.

Expectations change on a consistent basis. One year expectations are matched, then in the following year there's a new set. Things change. I do set expectations for myself, but they're mostly related around effort. It's very, very difficult to accomplish, but the players I admire the most are the ones who play every day on a consistent basis, through all the rigors of a six-month season.

That's something that I set as a goal for the season. If I'm consistent with my intensity and my work, then that's where the satisfaction comes from.

I will say, whether too low or too high, a dangerous thing is to buy into your own hype, whether good or bad, whether people are saying you're not worth something, or you're the next great thing. I really try to disconnect from commentary, disconnect from perception, and focus on the essentials of my job. I find that that has a tendency to yield the best results. The tough part is, I want to satisfy myself, but the dogs run better when they chase the rabbit. Ted's not a good guy to look at, but I always look at Mickey Mantle, I look at Willie Mays, Hank Aaron. I look at their careers and their game logs. I pay attention to guys that I have great admiration for, and I feel I would have to be reaching to get to their markers. I use those guys as my rabbits. It's good to be challenged outside of your own standards.

To this point in my life, baseball has always felt natural, meaning I feel like I'm being challenged and doing something that I like to do. Just that in and of itself is plenty. I've enjoyed meeting people and traveling and learning new things and learning about myself and experiencing growth in different ways. Ultimately, I'm grateful to be able to do this for a living.

It's very important for me that I've remained with the same club my whole career. You see all kinds of teams go through rough spells, no matter the market. Nobody's immune to it. I'm looking forward to consistent winning baseball here and being in this uniform. You know the old saying, don't cheer for the player, cheer for the laundry? I find myself beginning to cheer for laundry. I think about teams I cheer for in professional sports, and I don't think I have one anymore except for the Reds.

It's difficult during the season to really let go and have a good time. It's more of a satisfaction thing. I think that I feel satisfied when I do a good job, when I put in maximum effort, when I'm focused, when I find my sweet spot in terms of the routine of the job. I do feel good about that, but in terms of just pure joy on the field, I don't often feel that. I feel like there is a balancing act between having a good time and doing your job to the utmost. The reason why I look up to a guy like Ted Williams and why I admire and am challenged by a guy like Carl Yastrzemski is because they got the most out of themselves. I feel like it's an obligation, in a way, to following generations to push the boundaries, to make the game better. I feel like the game evolves and gets better, and that's better for the fans, better for the players. This is a better version of the sport than what it was when I first entered the league, and I don't envision that stopping. So I need to do the same. I need to progress and evolve as a player.

Dan Bellino

*I*llinois native Dan Bellino was in his second year at the John Marshall Law School when he decided to become a professional umpire. Given the long odds of making it to the major leagues, this would seem to have been a curious career change, especially since he admits that he didn't know how difficult the process would be. In fact, his original plan was to be a Division I basketball referee as well as an attorney. In spite of the obvious obstacles, he persevered, receiving his law degree, completing umpire school, and passing the bar exam, as well as working at several part-time jobs while umpiring in the minor leagues.

After working eight years in six different minor leagues as well as the Hawaii Winter League, the Arizona Fall League, and the Puerto Rico Winter League, he beat the odds and was hired as a full-time major-league umpire in 2011, one of only three of 150 in his umpire school class to make it. He was selected to work in the 2014 and 2015 American League Division Series.

* * *

My great-great-grandfather on my mother's side was German, but everybody else in my family—the Bellinos, the DiLeos, the Moricis, the Digiglios—we're all Italian. On my mother's side it was the great-great-grandparents that came to the States; on my father's side it was great-grandparents. On my mother's side we're from Palermo, and on my dad's side we're Tuscan. I absolutely grew up with a sense of being Italian. My grandmother on my dad's side spoke fluent Italian. I wish to this day that she had taught it to us, but she only yelled at us in Italian.

I played a lot of sports as a kid, but basketball was the sport that I enjoyed more than anything. I enjoyed being a catcher, but as you know, the higher levels you, go the more difficult it is. I didn't play baseball outside of high school, but I did play basketball throughout high school, and then I became the manager of the Northern Illinois University basketball team. One of my duties as the manager was to let the basketball officials in and I gave them their paychecks after the game, so I got to know the officials. That was my first introduction to officiating at a high level.

After Northern Illinois I went straight to law school. My goal was I wanted to be a Division I basketball official and be a lawyer. That was the blueprint I had. I'd be an attorney in the Chicago area and I'd referee Division I basketball. I just really enjoyed officiating. It was my part-time job through law school. The highest level I got to was Division II.

The turn to baseball was a strange decision. I was working for a federal judge, Judge [Charles] Kocoras, and at the time he was the chief judge for the Northern District of Illinois. He had four clerks and I was one of them, part-time. The other part-time clerk that I worked with was Rudy Minasian, and his father worked for the Texas Rangers. When I'd leave work I'd say I was going to referee basketball, and Rudy was the one who said, "Did you ever think of going to umpire school? If you like officiating, you should go to umpire school."

I was twenty-two years old. I said, "What are you talking about, umpire school?" I didn't think it was a real thing, but I started looking into it. One of my best friends in law school was named Amy. We started talking about umpiring and one day she bought tickets and took me to a Cubs game. We were right behind the first base dugout, and I'll never forget it, she said, "Look at those umpires and tell me, can you do that job?"

I said, "I absolutely can do that job."

And she said, "I think you absolutely need to go to umpire school."

Then I sat down with my parents and told them what I wanted to do. They said they would support whatever I did as long as I finished law school and passed the bar. That was the spring of my second year of law school. Since umpire school is only in January, once I made the decision I went to the Dean and said I needed to be done with law school by January. He told me that if I wanted to graduate early, I needed to take two or three classes in summer school and an accelerated trial advocacy class over Christmas break. So I did that, graduated a semester early, went to umpire school, then flew home in the middle of umpire school to get my diploma. There were a lot of balls in the air, but it was pretty cool.

I went to the Wendelstedt Umpire School. I didn't realize there were four levels of A ball and I didn't realize that guys would be in the minor leagues for ten-plus years. I was kind of floored by that and the amount of money they made. It was pretty challenging to me because I had student loans. That was the toughest part of umpire school. I met one of my best friends, if not my best friend to this day, at umpire school, Vic Carapazza. He and I climbed the ranks together, and we're now both full-time major league umpires.

From our class there were three of us that made it to the majors out of 150. I did get discouraged along the way. There were eight years where there were a lot of people wondering what the heck I was doing. When I was in the minor leagues I worked part-time for a funeral home, I refereed basketball, I substitute taught. I had these jobs until I passed the bar.

My first year in the minor leagues was 2003 in the New York-Penn League. I hadn't had time yet to take the bar exam, I was making very little money, supervisors don't know you that well when you first get started, and I was trying to downplay the fact that I went to law school. I didn't want people to think I wasn't serious. That first year, out of forty-five umpires I was ranked like number thirty-one. It turned out one of the reasons I was ranked low was because my league president had an issue with the man I was partnered with and I was kind of lumped in with him. They didn't really know me, so that first year I was ranked low. I considered retiring then and focusing on law because I was at the lowest level of the minors, they're ranking me thirty-first, and the odds of making it to the big leagues are so slim.

But then I got a call from Harry Wendelstedt asking me to be an instructor at his school, which was a big honor. That kind of puts your star on the map. I would say the majority of major league umpires were asked to be instructors at some point. So I made the decision to give it another year and give it all I've got. But I still needed to pass the bar. In 2006, when the minor league umpires went on strike, I used that as an opportunity to take the prep course. So while the umpires were on strike, I studied and passed the bar. Some people have strike babies; I passed the bar.

I worked my first major league game in 2008. I worked one game, at Wrigley Field, in an emergency situation. I was at home in Crystal Lake, Illinois, when they called at 5:15 p.m. and said, "We need you right now. How long would it take you to get to Wrigley Field?" I said, "How much time do I have?" He said, "Game time is 7:05." I said, "I'll be there."

So in rush hour, which is typically a two and a half-hour drive, I was driving on the shoulder of the road, on the expressway, and I made it there with about fifteen minutes to spare. By the time I got there, it was a rush to get out on the field. I worked third base. I couldn't tell you if the game was two hours or four hours. To me it was Game Seven of the World Series.

So that was a big break. Getting the first call is one of the toughest things to get. Once I got that under my belt, in 2009 they gave me, I think, thirty-two games. I'd go to a crew for about three games, then I'd go back to the minors. It was sporadic, which was pretty common back then. They wanted you to get your feet wet, then go back to the minor leagues and catch your breath. In 2010 I was up the entire year, basically. I worked with Joe West for five months. I had a great year with Joe, then I was hired full-time during spring training of 2011.

The progression for umpires is a lot different than it is for players. When you get to Triple A you have milestones you have to achieve. One of the milestones is, you work your first year in Triple A, then at the end of the season they select you for the Arizona Fall League. They only select twelve umpires for the fall league. Of the twelve, six are going back for their second year, and six are new. So that's a big assignment to get, a big milestone.

Once you start working the Arizona Fall League, your goal is to be assigned major-league spring training. That's a big deal because it's your first taste of making much better money than you make in the minor leagues. Once you work your first major league spring training, then you hope that they add you to the roster, which means that they assign you a number for your sleeve. That's a big deal. Back in the day, the National or American League would purchase a contract for the umpire; they would own the rights to him. When they give you a number, that's the equivalent of owning the rights. You are officially on the roster and eligible to fill in.

My first number was 93. Then, when Jerry Crawford, an umpire I very much looked up to retired in 2010 and I was added to the staff in 2011, I called him and asked his permission to put in for his number. I told him, "You wore it for thirty years; I promise I'll wear it for the next thirty." So they switched me to number 2 in the 2012 season, and I'll wear it until I retire.

My mentors were Steve Palermo, Jerry Crawford, Joe West, Tommy Hallion, Phil Cuzzi, Harry Wendelstedt—just some wonderful people. Steve Palermo had a very short career on the field, but you ask anybody that worked with him or worked in that era, and they all say Steve Palermo would've been a Hall of Fame umpire. He was that good. Some guys were born to be umpires; Steve was one of them. I got to work with Jerry Crawford for two weeks before he retired. Just an incredible human being and incredible umpire. These are guys that taught me early on that this is a lifestyle. You're part of baseball; this is pretty special.

When I came up as a fill-in, my first interaction with Joe Torre was when he was the manager of the Dodgers. It just so happened that when Joe took a job in the commissioner's office at the end of 2010, he took over the umpiring department, so I was hired full-time by Joe Torre. I'd like to think that from the experience he had with me on the field he understood that I worked very hard, did my best, and carried myself in such a way that I would never embarrass Major League Baseball. It's pretty awesome for me to say that Joe Torre, a Hall of Fame manager, hired me to be an umpire right after he was a manager. In fact, he said to me, "One of the first things I did when I took the job was hire you."

Dan Bellino
AP Photo/Carlos Osorio.

There weren't what I would categorize as surprises when I got to the major leagues. I pride myself on trying to avoid being surprised. I ask a lot of questions, I try to prepare. For me the biggest incentive was security for my family because I come from an Italian family and I wanted to have a big family. I've got four kids. To me, it was the benefits, the insurance, the pension. You're part of something pretty awesome; Major League Baseball is an incredible family to be a part of.

After a while does it become a job? Well, sure. The best way I can put it is this; we make a very good living and are very blessed. Umpiring is the easy part. They don't pay us to umpire. We love umpiring. They pay me to leave my family. They pay me to miss birthdays, to miss milestones within my family. To me, that's the sacrifice we make. But the umpiring, the game itself, the challenge of going out there and doing a good job, I love every aspect of that.

When you're new, players and managers push the envelope. They want to see how much you'll take. They're kind of gauging you; does this guy have a quick temper, is this guy afraid to yell back, does he yell back quickly? Players and managers are competing. They're under a lot of pressure, and it's our job to be that calming influence, to be that neutral voice, to enforce the rules.

I would say that probably the first five years of your career you're establishing your reputation. After about five years people get to know you. And once they get to know you, they understand that you care about your mistakes, that you care about doing a good job, you care about representing the game, and your integrity will not be compromised. I'm very matter-of-fact about doing my business. I want to go out there, work as hard as I can, leave it on the field.

There's two things that have changed the way I umpire. Number one, I was always told to umpire as though my kids were sitting in the front row watching me. I don't ever want them to be embarrassed by me. The second thing is that players nowadays are making a tremendous living and are under huge scrutiny, and managers are under incredible pressure, and we are the only people in their lives that tell them no. You have to appreciate the fact that these guys are surrounded by people that tell them yes to everything, so I expect them at times to not like to be told no. I expect them to be upset. It's just human nature.

I don't think that ordinary fans have any appreciation for the amount of scrutiny that we and the commissioner's office put on us. Every pitch that we call is tracked and graded, every play that we call is tracked and graded. You call a ball fair or foul, they clip it and it is sent to us. We are given a midseason and end-of-the-season evaluation. So we are graded at such a high level that the most disappointing thing to me is when you hear announcers say, "That's a makeup call," or "He made that call because he must have dinner reservations." That's never true because if I make a mistake it gets graded against me and at the end of the year my mistakes are tallied. The theory of a makeup call, that doesn't happen; if I miss one call then do a makeup call, I'm missing two calls and compounding the problem.

We're human beings, so we're not infallible. We make mistakes, but for the most part, we are really good people. We carry ourselves in such a way that we don't expect to be the show; we don't expect to be the story. We're privileged to be part of the game, and at the end of the day, if we've done a good job, we're happy. Some days are more challenging than others and some games are very intense. When they're over, it's a relief. You got through a tough game, you did a good job and you're proud. To me, making my parents proud is paramount. And for all the people that helped me get to this position, those are the people that I continue to try to get better for because I don't ever want anyone to say they made a mistake in helping me.

Instant replay is a different animal because it's somewhat new. I can tell you that since I was in the major leagues only for about five years without instant replay, I feel as though it has its advantages and its disadvantages. The days of having an umpire's career defined by one missed call, that's the one true advantage. There is a litany of umpires that have been defined by one call, whether it be that Jim Joyce perfect-game call, Don Denkinger's World Series call, the Rich Garcia Yankees-Baltimore call in right field. They're all calls that, unfortunately, in a thirty-year career you're remembered for one call, and that's not right. Instant replay righted that wrong.

The downside of instant replay obviously is that it takes away some of the excitement. You'll have a close play at the plate and you call the guy safe or out, the crowd would erupt. Now it's like a delayed eruption. Okay, let's watch the replay, which isn't necessarily a bad thing because I can't have it both ways. I can't tell you that I don't want to be defined by a missed call and not have the ability to fix it. But it also takes away the art of arguing. It has eliminated the excitement of the manager arguing. I really enjoyed the arguments, I enjoyed the dialogue. It was fun at times. I'm not going to tell you I won every argument I was in. I mean, my call was my call, but there were times when a manager would get me. I'd think, "Man, he's right." You hold your ground, but if I had the ability to go back, I might change my answer. But this is the call I made and I'm sticking with it.

The downside of baseball becoming such a big business is that these players are paid so much money and they want their product on the field. So when you go back and look at the ejections, we've all ejected somebody maybe too soon, other times too late or not at all. I understand the logic. If you've got a superstar and it's the second inning of the game and you call him out on a close play, and he says something that's objectionable, and you eject him, I understand that's a pretty valuable asset that is not on the field for that team. I don't ever want to have somebody say that the White Sox would've won that game if Bellino had not ejected Abreu. I want to be impartial; I want to be fair but firm.

I don't ever look at ejecting as being an easy conclusion to make. My goal is to try to keep them in the game. But if they focus on you and take it personally, they cross the line. They could say, "That call was terrible. That was bullshit," versus, "You suck." It's clear as day; argue the call, argue my judgment, but don't say, "You were lazy," or, "You didn't care." I won't put up with personal abuse. I will definitely defend my call and give you the opportunity to voice your displeasure but don't question my integrity, and I won't question yours because I realize you're competing.

To take it one step further, and this was taught to me by all my mentors; if I stand on the field and somebody was to verbally berate me personally and

I just stood there and took it, it's not that person's respect that I just lost. It's the other forty-nine players that saw it, it's the managers, the coaches, it's my colleagues. Those are the people that lose more respect for me.

[Former White Sox manager] Robin Ventura loved to come out and say, "Dan, I think you got this play right, but everybody in the stadium wants to see me cause a fuss. So I'm going to point over at second base, then I'm going to point at first base, then I'm going to point at you because everybody here needs to think that I'm upset with you." That happens a lot more than people know. So it may look like we got yelled at and didn't do much.

When I retire I want to spend time with my family. With all the sacrifices I make as a father, I want to be twofold better as a grandfather. We sacrifice a lot to do our jobs, but what people need to understand is that traveling the country, staying in hotels, and being part of this great game of baseball is a privilege. For me, I don't think that will ever change. I don't think I'll ever get to the point where I don't view it as a privilege or appreciate the good fortune that I've had to be in this position. If that day were to come, that would be the sign that it's time to retire and go home. The crazy thing about umpires is that when they retire, it's usually because their bodies have taken a beating: too many head blows, the knees, the back, the neck. I want to be able to leave with good quality of life.

Rick Porcello

*P*itching prodigies are rare in big league baseball, with good reason. Given the rigors of the game at that level, even the most promising prospects usually require a few years of apprenticeship in the minors. This is especially true for pitchers, who tend to mature more slowly than position players. Rick Porcello was an exception to the rule.

After being acclaimed High School Player of the Year by USA Today, Porcello was selected by the Tigers in the first round of the 2007 draft. The following year he pitched well enough for the Tigers High-A affiliate in Lakeland, Florida, to be invited to spring training camp in 2009. Then, with only 24 professional games under his belt, the twenty-year-old right-hander was chosen by manager Jim Leyland to be part of the Tigers' starting rotation. After posting a 14–9 record, he was selected to start in a one-game playoff for the AL Central Division championship and finished third in the AL Rookie of the Year vote.

By his own admission, the next three years were a struggle as he faced adversity for the first time and worked to figure out who he was as a pitcher. Nevertheless, in his six seasons with Detroit he compiled a record of 76–63, with a then-career-high of 15 wins in 2014. Traded to the Red Sox in 2015, he led the staff in strikeouts but struggled to a 9–15 record in his debut season. He then rebounded in spectacular fashion in 2016, winning the Cy Young Award with a league-leading 22 wins against 4 losses and a 3.15 ERA, as well as the AL Comeback Player of the Year Award. What did he learn from the ups and downs of life in the big leagues? "You're never a finished product."

Porcello's maternal grandfather was Sam Dente, an infielder who was signed by the Red Sox in 1941 and logged nine years in the major leagues with five teams between 1947 and 1955. A slogan that caught on when he was with the Washington Senators went, "We'll win plenty with Dente." As was usually the case with the Senators, they didn't.

* * *

Both my parents are Italian. My dad's family is from Avellino and my mother's family is from two towns over, but I don't know the name of the town. My great-grandparents came over from Italy and they spoke fluent Italian. The only grandparent I spent any time around as a child was my grandmother on my father's side. My grandparents could understand and speak it a little bit, but my parents don't really speak it. I wish I knew Italian. I don't know why in high school I was taking Spanish classes all those years. I should have been taking Italian.

We grew up practicing a lot of the traditional Italian cultural habits. We cooked the seven fishes on Christmas Eve and that sort of stuff. My mother's got a ton of recipes from her grandmother. On the weekend she'd make big-time meals. In the part of New Jersey I was from, it was kind of traditional for Italian families to do that on Sundays. We're proud of our Italian heritage and come from an area of the country where there are a lot of Italian Americans. Not a lot of guys in baseball from other parts of the country are around a lot of Italians, so it's funny to see their reaction to some of the stuff.

I was five or six years old, whatever that age is when you start playing T-ball. I had an older brother and a younger brother, and we all played baseball, basketball, and football when we were kids. That was the kind of family we were in. It was a sports family. We all loved baseball, especially because of the lineage we had. It was kind of in our blood a little bit because of my grandfather playing. It kind of grew from there. My parents were extremely supportive of all the things my brothers and I wanted to do, but especially athletics. They made all that possible for us and it's only because of their sacrifices, taking me to practices and games that I'm able to live out my dream to play in the big leagues. I've got them to thank for everything.

I played Legion ball, I played for my high school, Seton Hall Prep, and on some travel teams. I made some trips along the East Coast, played a couple of tournaments in Florida and North Carolina. Honestly, I was playing as much baseball as I could possibly play. I pitched, obviously, and played shortstop. It really didn't matter what position I was playing; I just loved playing. Our senior year, it was just a blast. We won the state championship and were ranked number one nationally. It was just an awesome season for us. That was definitely my favorite childhood team.

I never thought that it would be my decision to play professionally. I don't know if that's a good or bad thing, but I always felt that I'm going to love playing, work hard at it, and see where it takes me. That's really as far as I let myself go when I was a kid. And even now that I'm playing at the major-league level, you can't deny the fact that it's really hard to get here. Statistically, it's pretty rare to make it to this level. I guess I was always realistic with myself in understanding that I might be good at the sport, but it takes more than being good to get to this level. You never know what's going to happen and where life is going to take you. I just enjoyed playing and that allowed me to be really passionate about it. That gave me the will to work hard at it and put a lot of focus into it. I think if I had put pressure on myself as a kid to get a college scholarship or make it to the big league level, I might have maybe burned out playing, or whatever happens during those years that makes you sick of training. That never really happened for me. I loved everything about it. In high school when I was sixteen, seventeen years old, you'd see a couple of scouts here and there. Then obviously in my junior and senior years a lot of them started showing up. They were at pretty much every game I pitched.

I played a full season in High-A ball in the Florida State League. I was fortunate to be in the right place at the right time. There was an opening in the Tigers rotation in spring training and some of the other guys that were lined up for that spot were battling different things and not performing. I was lucky enough to have a manager in Jim Leyland that was willing to take risks and willing to stick his neck out for a twenty-year-old kid and give him the opportunity to play at the big-league level. I just happened to be in that situation. I think if I was in any other organization they wouldn't even consider the possibility of a twenty-year-old kid coming out of high school to make the big-league team. It's one of those things where even if you look ready you usually get sent down for a little bit more seasoning.

It's important to build that foundation at the minor league level, but I got lucky and was able to start my big-league career off at a young age and start learning quickly. The one thing that Leyland said to me and the entire team that I'll never forget was that when he looks into the eyes of twenty-five guys in the room at the end of spring training, he wants them to know that he took the best twenty-five guys. There weren't any contractual or political things going on. He was putting the best club out there. I loved that and I respected that so much. That was why I was able to make the team. That was the philosophy he went by, and he felt I was one of the best twenty-five guys.

I can't say I was able to process at age twenty the fact that I was playing with and against the greatest ballplayers in the world. I definitely had wide eyes and was doing the best I could to take everything in, but I had made it to the big leagues very quickly. I didn't take the hard, long road that other guys had taken. I'm not going to say I took it for granted. I was very, very grateful for the opportunity. But at the same time, if you're not experiencing anything else and you find yourself in the big leagues, it's hard to really understand the magnitude of that sport. At the time I was just watching the veteran guys and learning how they did things, and trying to establish myself. I didn't really let anything else come into my head, which is a good thing and a bad thing. Sometimes you have blinders on and you can lose sight of some of the things that make you good and how you got to that spot in the first place. It's a great spot to be in as a twenty-year-old, but it also presents some challenges you've got to be ready to handle.

I remember the first pitch, first hit, first home run, first strikeout from my first game. What stands out to me was getting a couple of outs and realizing this is the same game I've been playing my whole life, and in that same game realizing that it's the same game with the best players in the world. I had a real good game going, then I threw a curveball to Adam Lind. He swung and missed and I thought, *Okay, I'm just going to throw him another one.* I threw another one about four or five inches higher than the first curve and he hit it out to dead center for a two-run homer, and I was out of the game. I went from having a five-plus-inning outing with one run, to five-plus innings with four runs. It was kind of all those things you're wondering about before you get to perform in that type of a spot all coming out in one game. It was a dose of reality in both aspects: the reality that I am good enough that my stuff plays at this level because I was able to get through five innings with pretty solid pitching, but also understanding that the more those hitters see you and the more your stuff is exposed to them, the tougher it is. Mistakes are very fine lines at this level, and it went from being a great outing to an outing in which we lost the game. You're in control of everything one second, and in the next second you get knocked back down.

I really started to struggle badly my second year, 2010. I just didn't have a complete repertoire. I developed a really good sinker in the minor leagues and I had a good changeup, but I didn't have much of a breaking ball. I really didn't have a whole lot of feel for pitching. I knew how to throw strikes and I knew the simple objectives, but as far as controlling and managing a game, all the things that make good starting pitchers at this level, I had no idea. That all caught up with me in my second year. I got sent down to Triple A for a month and started to revamp some things.

The first four years of my career were, I don't want to say all rocky, but definitely difficult after a lot of success my rookie year. The next three years, I started trying to search for who I was as a pitcher and kind of lost my way a little bit trying to figure out how am I going to be successful at this level for an extended period of time. What I was doing was only working for short periods of time. After one full season, all of a sudden the league has caught up to me and all the things that were working the first year aren't working. At the big-league level I went through that whole process that guys go through at the minor league level in polishing their pitches and their mental game. I don't know if it took me longer at the big-league level than maybe it would've taken me at the minor-league level, but it certainly was difficult because you had the pressure of being on a winning team and trying to make the World Series. But I'm also trying to figure out how the hell to get guys out on a consistent basis. It was good, though. It gave me a strong head as far as how to handle some of those struggles and the adversity you face on the field at the major-league level.

You're never a finished product. I didn't realize that I was working towards something that I'm always going to be working towards. I was under the mind-set that I'm going to work toward something and I'm going to be this guy forever, and it's not like that. You've got to find yourself every day at this level. It doesn't carry over from day to day. You've got to put the time in and that was something I just learned through experience, realizing what it took to be a consistent performer.

Finally, my last couple of years in Detroit I started to get back on track and was making some really good progress. I felt really good about what I was doing. I leaned on the pitching coach in Detroit, Jeff Jones, a lot during those last couple of years. He helped me stay on track when maybe mechanically or mentally I'd waver a little bit or start to drift. Then I get to Boston and all the things I started to get under control and do well in Detroit, I lost the feel for that. It resulted in a really difficult first season for me in Boston. Again, I got knocked back down and almost went through almost the same thing I went through my first couple of years and got back into this identity crisis a little bit. My sinker wasn't sinking as well as it had been in Detroit. I was throwing more four-seamers, and the four-seamer was a good pitch but I didn't really know how to use it. I got off track and had to fight hard to get back on track and reidentify myself and reestablish how I was going to pitch, how I was going to attack hitters, and what weapons I was going to use at what times. You know, manage games like a good major-league pitcher does.

I went through those struggles in Boston in 2015 and put a lot of pressure on myself, which didn't help. All of us, as humans, we have the final say on our own expectations. I was demanding a lot of myself, and it became toxic. It was something that I couldn't perform with because I was suffocating myself with every bad pitch I threw, every bad inning, every bad outing I had. It was kind of snowballing on me and I wasn't able to shake that stuff off. I was in a new place and I wanted to put my best foot forward and show everybody I was going to be a quality pitcher for this organization and help us win. I just didn't go about it the right way.

I ended up going on the DL for the first time in my career. That's when I kind of settled down and just had this kind of big sigh, like, *Stop putting pressure on yourself and just enjoy the game, enjoy the whole process of what I've got to go through to get back to where I want to get back to and being successful.* After I came back from the DL, I started throwing the ball like myself again and it just took off from there.

My success in 2016 really started that first year when I came back from the DL. Just having a bit of a clear mind and getting back to basic strike one, working down in the zone, timely elevated pitches, mixing my breaking balls in. All that stuff sounds really simple when you talk about it now, but when you're on the mound and the game is going a thousand miles an hour, you lose sight of it really quickly, especially when you're in a new environment. Getting back to all that, I just came in with that mind-set in 2016; work on my fastball command, that's what's going to get me through the season. I worked hard on executing my sinker down in the zone and my four-seamer up in the zone. I got my ass kicked in spring training, but I stuck with the plan and it ended up paying dividends for me.

I got more confident as the season went along. I was making adjustments very quickly in games, from pitch to pitch basically. I was able to identify what I was doing wrong and get back on track and execute the next pitch. The ability to do that allowed me to slow everything down. That was the key; the game was moving at a much slower pace for me. I was still working quickly, but it was clear in my head what I wanted to do with hitters and how I was going to do it. I was able to get into a zone where I could focus on that, and I ended up getting better as the season went on. I can't really explain it other than that I just got into that groove and was able to maintain it. I just built momentum as the season went on and was able to put up the numbers that I did.

Rick Porcello
Boston Red Sox.

A couple of moments stand out in my big-league career. The first was being told by Jim Leyland that I made the big-league team at age twenty; that was one of my biggest thrills and the start of my journey at this level. Our ballclub getting to the World Series in 2012 was another huge thrill for me. And last year, winning the Cy Young and being able to share that with my family and teammates and bringing that trophy back to this organization was just about my biggest accomplishment at this level.

2010–

Anthony Rizzo

*A*t the relatively young age of twenty-seven, Anthony Rizzo was acknowledged as the leader of the Chicago Cubs team that won the 2016 World Series, ending 108 years of frustration for the franchise and its fans. His leadership role was confirmed symbolically at the 2017 home opener at Wrigley Field when, standing in the center-field bleachers, he was the first to hoist the World Series flag, followed by his teammates. He then emerged from the grandstand and carried the World Series trophy across the field.

That the 6-foot-3, 240-pound left-handed first baseman would play such a big role in the Cubs' long-awaited triumph was hardly predictable when the Fort Lauderdale, Florida, native was chosen by the Red Sox out of high school in the sixth round of the 2007 amateur draft. He was traded twice before he was twenty-two. Not exactly the normal trajectory of a can't-miss prospect. To make matters worse, in 2008 he was diagnosed with Hodgkin's lymphoma and underwent six months of chemotherapy. In 2012, the Anthony Rizzo Family Foundation was established to raise money for cancer research and to provide support to children and their families battling the disease.

A tireless worker, Rizzo broke into the majors in 2011 with the San Diego Padres, who then traded him to the Cubs in the offseason. In 2013, he became the starting first baseman and was selected to the All-Star team three consecutive years beginning in 2014. He finished fourth in the MVP vote in both 2015 and 2016 and won the Gold Glove and Silver Slugger Awards in 2016. In 2013, Rizzo also played in the World Baseball Classic, hitting third for Team Italy, which advanced to the second round for the first time.

* * *

I'm Italian American with ancestors from Italy. My dad's side is from Ciminna, Sicily. I'm not sure where my mom's side is from, but I'm pretty sure they're from Sicily as well. I grew up doing most Italian American things, like Sunday dinners. I grew up in Florida, so I'm Italian, but I grew up as a normal American. My parents, John and Laurie, raised my brother and I. They were from New Jersey and moved down to Florida before my brother was born. They gave us everything we needed, spoiled us. They worked endless hours so we could go on the travel tournaments and do things like that. We're very close and I owe everything to them. My dad works for ADT, the security company. My mom used to be a bartender, but she stopped working a few years ago.

I never met my dad's mom, but I knew his dad, who passed away when I was younger. My mom's mom and dad, named Rapisardi, passed away when I was sixteen or seventeen. They were a big part of my life too. They were always over to the house and hung out with us. We went over to their place all the time. They helped raise us.

We went to Ciminna in 2014 for Christmas, my mom and dad, my brother and his wife. We went all over and it was a good time. We met family and matched up family trees. I think there were a lot of relatives there, but it was hard with the language barrier. Sicily is great; it's definitely different. Where we were, in the mountains, it was just a really old town. It was really cool. Simple living. We also went to Palermo, a big city with a lot going on.

My brother John kind of set the bar for me my whole life. He's two years older, so he set the standard for me. He's very competitive and I'm very competitive. He just kind of taught me the ropes. He was a football player, and I also played football in high school, so it was all good.

Growing up I played every sport, but I liked baseball the most and I just stuck with it. I started thinking about playing professionally when people started telling me I was good enough in high school. Every kid thinks you're going to become a professional, but when scouts began coming to the house it became more of a reality. I didn't watch baseball as much as I played it. I was always outside playing. I just like the game in general. No matter what race or color they are, I just like watching good baseball.

The process of getting to the majors was long, but it was a good experience. You grow up. When you're eighteen to twenty-one, that's an important part of your life. I learned a lot, but it was fun. There are memories I'll never forget. I always knew that I would make it to the big leagues. I think that if you're in this sport and you don't think you're going to make it, why are you playing? I always thought I was going to be here and was just determined to get here. Winning the World Series is definitely my biggest thrill so far. It was a long time coming for a great city. This offseason was a whirlwind. A lot of opportunities, a lot of fun. It was exciting.

I thought it was really cool to be able to play for Team Italy in the World Baseball Classic. My ancestors are from there, and I wasn't good enough to play for the USA. I never got to play in a tournament of that scale ever in my life, so I thought it was really neat to get to play with a lot of guys from Italy and our manager, Marco Mazzieri. It was a lot of fun. I remember talking to Mike Piazza about it, but I don't really remember who approached me. We got an

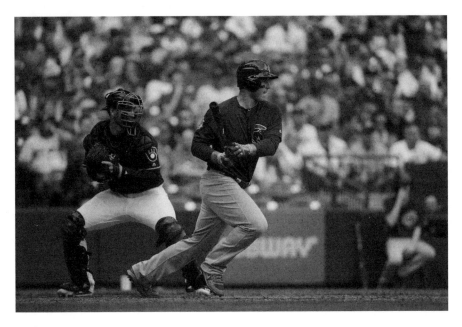

Anthony Rizzo
Photo by Scott Paulus.

e-mail from Marco, maybe. It was a good experience. We had a good team and we advanced to the second round. It was during spring training and we had a lot of fun with it.

Being diagnosed with cancer was not a fun part of my life. I overcame that and was able to build a very strong foundation out of it, and now we're giving back to a lot of families that are also going through it. We turned a negative into a positive, which is a great life lesson no matter what it is. You take the bad and you try to make a good of it, and that's what we do with our foundation. I go to the hospitals to visit children, and we give a lot of money to families to help them pay bills. We're involved in a lot of different ways.

Baseball is really all I know. I've been playing professionally for ten years now. I've had a lot of opportunities and have been fortunate enough to play, and I've pretty much stayed healthy other than the cancer hiccup. It's been fun. It teaches you a lot about yourself, a lot about life, and you get to play a game for a living. My goals are more team-oriented, making sure all the guys are clicking on the right cylinders, what gets guys going when we're down, and just being a good teammate, picking everyone else up. Bringing that energy, good things will happen. You just go out and do it by example. That's what I try to do every day; play hard and set the right tone.

APPENDIX

Interviewees inducted into the National Italian American Sports Hall of Fame

Frank Crosetti

Phil Cavarretta

Dom DiMaggio

Phil Rizzuto

Yogi Berra

Johnny Antonelli

Tommy Lasorda

Joey Amalfitano

Ken (and Bob) Aspromonte

Joe Torre

Ron Santo

Jim Fregosi

Tony La Russa

Rico Petrocelli

Sal Bando

Bobby Valentine

Steve Palermo

Dave Righetti

Larry Lucchino

Mike Scioscia

Ned Colletti

Craig Biggio

Mike Piazza

Jerry Colangelo

Barry Zito